FIELD & STREAM

TOTAL OUTDOORSMAN MANUAL

FIELD & STREAM

THE BEST OF THE TOTAL OUTDOORSMAN

T. EDWARD NICKENS
AND THE EDITORS OF *FIELD & STREAM*

WITH SPECIAL CONTRIBUTIONS BY
PHIL BOURJAILY, KIRK DEETER, ANTHONY LICATA,
KEITH McCAFFERTY, JOHN MERWIN,
AND DAVID E. PETZAL

CONTENTS

HUNTING

SURVIVAL

Foreword

In Scotland, there's an outdoor challenge called the Macnab. The rules: kill a stag, bag a brace of grouse, and land a salmon–all in one day. For those who don't hunt the Highlands, I've heard sportsmen assign less specific guidelines to the feat: kill a big-game animal, shoot a bird, and catch a fish–still, all in one day. Even then, it's a tall order. Conditions have to be perfect and the place has to be covered in critters. A little luck wouldn't hurt, either. Everything has to click. And, for me, one day last fall, everything did.

I was in Manitoba, Canada, with a group of hunters. This was actually my second trip of the year to the same lodge. In the spring, I'd traveled there to hunt black bears but failed to fill my tag. Since my tag would still be good in the fall, I was encouraged to come back and try again. As if that wasn't reason enough to return, in the fall I could also hunt waterfowl. Geese in the morning, bears in the evening—sign me up.

We had three days to hunt, and while the goose hunting was tremendous, the bear hunting remained as slow as it had been in the spring. I saw one small bruin on the first night, but never had a shot. The second night came and went without one bear. Our last goose hunt, on day three was the best one—not because the shoot itself was particularly good, though it was great, but because afterward we cooked breakfast in the field. We set up camp stoves and fixed goose-sausage, egg, and cheese sandwiches (which I dubbed the McHonker). It was a fun end to a fantastic few days of waterfowling. After breakfast, we all went back to the lodge and decided to fish for a couple of hours. The bite was slow, but I managed to land one hammer-handle pike.

I was happy to have caught the fish, but thought little of it until, just as I was about to leave for my final bear hunt, a friend said to me, "You're two-thirds of the way to a Macnab."

"What's that?" I asked.

"You shot a bird this morning," he said, "and just caught a fish this afternoon. Kill a bear tonight, and you've got a Macnab."

I wouldn't let my hopes get too high. Counting my spring hunt, I'd already put in nearly 80 hours in the treestand and had only seen three bears. I expected to eat my tag. But then, a couple of hours into my final sit, a big boar ambled into the bait. I had to wait about 20 minutes before he gave me a clear shot, which was for the best because it gave me time to calm my racing heart and gather myself before I peered into the scope and held the crosshairs on the left shoulder. The rifle cracked. The bear dropped.

Back at the lodge, after some congratulatory handshakes and Canadian-whiskey cheers, my friend congratulated me on the Macnab, which I'd forgotten all about. "Oh, yeah," I said. "Thanks!"

I don't share that story to boast or brag. To be perfectly honest, I care even less about the Macnab now as I did then. I value the time I spend outdoors too much to turn it into challenges or competitions. On that day in Manitoba, I had loads of fun hunting and fishing with friends, and I made a good, clean shot on the bear; for me, that's all that matters. The reason I share that story is because I do think there is one quality of the Macnab challenge that connects this book: A Macnab is a Total Outdoorsman quest. To succeed, you have to spend a lot of time in the outdoors and you need to utilize a variety of hunting and fishing skills.

Field & Stream's idea behind the Total Outdoorsman is simple: The more outdoor skills you acquire, the more time you can spend in the outdoors—which can only lead to more fun. And there's no one more qualified to teach you those skills than our resident Total Outdoorsman, Eddie Nickens. He hunts, fishes, camps, paddles, cooks, and, when necessary, survives. He's also a hell of a storyteller. But don't take my word for it. The proof is in the pages that follow—in the hundreds of skills, gear tips, and projects you're about to learn. By the time you get to the end, you'll be ready for any challenge the wild throws your way.

—Colin Kearns,
Editor-in-Chief, Field & Stream

Introduction

I found it on a ridge top where heavy rains the day before had scoured the top layer of earth in the muddy field furrows. I was headed for a deer stand and barely looking at the ground, but some primordial corner of my brain recognized the angles and edges. It was a stone point, perched on a tiny pedestal of red-clay dirt, a gift left by the ancients and unwrapped by time. Knapped perhaps 5,000 years ago, the lance point was made before the development of the bow and arrow. Its white-quartz edges were still sharp. I could lash the point to a straight sapling and kill a deer with it even today.

Whoever made that stone point—whoever hunted with it—would have had much in common with you and me. He appreciated good sporting tools—and not just for the sake of having stuff—but because having the right stuff would have helped him move quietly in the wild and stay fed and survive when things turned rough. He would have known enough about the woods to hunt this ridge above the river, stalking in the morning hours as the warming air carried his scent away. He wouldn't have approached hunting and fishing with half-hearted enthusiasm. He would have been obsessed about getting it right.

Just like I am. Just like you are.

Which is why you're holding this book.

This is a very carefully selected compilation of skills from two very successful *Field & Stream* books: *The Total Outdoorsman Manual* and its follow-up title, *The Total Outdoorsman: Skills & Tools*. This is the best of more than 700 entries from those books. Based on the planet's best outdoor magazine, this is the best how-to guide *Field & Stream* has ever produced.

These tips come from first-hand experience in every corner of North America. I've hunted and fished from Labrador to Alaska, from Mexico to northern Canada. I've met some of the continent's finest guides, and spent untold days and nights figuring it out on my own. And we've distilled all those expert angles, pro tips, hard lessons,

wrenched ankles, briar-lashed legs, and sweat-soaked shirts into the book you hold in your hands.

I'm sure that whoever knapped that white-quartz spear point would scratch his head at our GPS units, smartphones, $800 flyrods, and spinning wing decoys. He would have drooled over my knives, though, and he would have marveled at the modern riflescope.

And I think he would appreciate this book. It's all about doing the things we love—fishing, hunting, camping, and making our way in the woods—at the highest level.

Because the better we are with a rod, gun, or paddle, the farther, deeper, and wilder we can go.

—*T. Edward Nickens,*
Editor-at-Large, *Field & Stream*

Getting Out There

It was one of my most challenging days ever. On day 5 of a week-long paddling and fishing trip down Ontario's remote Palisade and Allanwater rivers, my buddy Scott Wood and I had to put in some monstrous mileage. We broke camp at dawn and paddled 22 miles, with a 3-mile lake crossing and mucky overgrown portages. We were still on the go at 11 p.m., with no food for eight hours and daylight fading fast, yet we had our largest rapid to run. At the base of Black Beaver Rapids, we dragged the boat to shore as an orange moon rose through spectral fire-blackened forest, too exhausted to cook supper. We stamped down a rough bivvy 10 feet from the water, running tent guylines to blueberry shrubs, and collapsed in the sleeping bags as northern lights arced overhead, wholly unappreciated.

We had a few more days on the river, and I spent the few fitful minutes before sleep triple-checking the map and wondering if it was worth all the hassle.

In the morning we limped out of the tents to find the blueberry plains sheathed in frost, a world glittery and serene. We caught a breakfast walleye, cleaned it on the bottom of an overturned canoe, fried it hot and fast and washed the fish down with pure, cold water from the river and handfuls of blueberries. And just like that—I was ready to do it all again.

For a lot of good reasons, a lot of folks can't conceive of taking a camping trip that doesn't involve a fishing rod. Or a hunting trip that doesn't end with a campfire and a cozy tent or backwoods cabin. If you're camping, you sack out mere steps from the pool where last night's white-fly hatch—and smallmouth bass—roiled the water. In the morning, you can lay out a cast while the coffee perks.

But you have to get up and go. You can't whine about how much trouble it is to pack up the gear. You can't blame anyone else if the tent leaks. That's why honing skills at old-fashioned campcraft matters. I once shot a pair of wood ducks while standing on the edge of a sandbar campsite in my pajamas, not 15 feet from my frost-covered sleeping bag. You can't do that if you wake up at home.

1 SLEEP UNDER THE STARS

Growing up we slept under the stars, sans tent or tarp, to prove how tough we were, but now I sleep in the Big Scary Open because I get a huge kick out of nodding off to shooting stars and waking to the first rays of the sun. And it's super cool to sleep with frost sheathing your sleeping bag. If you're squeamish about dozing off without the protection of a nylon cocoon, try it my way: Spread out a space blanket first, then a super-comfy sleeping pad. Having a spread of ground cloth between you and the bare ground is a mental comfort, and it also means you can spread your arms and thrash around a bit without actually wallowing in the dirt. I wear a toboggan to hold in extra body heat and keep a flashlight tucked in a boot near my head so I can find it quickly. If it makes you feel better, the other boot can hold a knife, handgun, pepper spray, or ninja death stars.

2 PITCH CAMP LIKE A WOLF

Wild animals know how to pick the right spot to sleep. You'll know it, if you know what to look for. The perfect campsite is a blend of the haves and the have-nots. It should have a view that makes you want to leap from the tent and high-five the rising sun. Good water within 100 yards. It should be sheltered from the worst winds but not so cloistered that the skeeters like it, too. Give bonus points for rocks and logs that double as chairs. Double reward miles for a pair of trees that will anchor a tarp. The ground should not be squishy.

The wolf and the dog turn in circles before choosing a bed, possibly to scan for danger, and so should you, at least, metaphorically. Study overhead trees for "widow makers"—the dead branches that could fall during the night and crush or skewer the hapless camper. Pace off the ground that will be under the tent, clear it of rocks and roots, fill the divots with duff. Sleep with your head uphill and your heart filled with gratitude for the call of the cricket and the shuffling sounds of unseen feet beyond the firelight.

3 MAKE GUYLINES SHINE

In 30 minutes you can replace all your old tent guylines with reflective cord, and never again trip over them while stumbling around during a middle-of-the-night pee, during which you stub your right big toe so badly that the nail splits and the toe swells and you can't wear wading boots for two days. Listen to me.

4 STRENGTHEN A TENT WITH PICKET STAKES

This supercharged guyout plan kicks in when the wind cranks up to 25 mph. Picket stakes boost the holding power of tent stakes, so use them on the guylines attached to the side of the tent that faces the wind.

STEP 1 Drive the first stake into the ground at the desired location, and attach it to the tent guyline. To make a picket-stake line, tie an overhand loop in one end of a 16-inch length of parachute cord. Attach the p-cord to the first stake by threading the running end through the overhand loop and cinching it tight against the stake.

STEP 2 Drive a second stake—this will be the picket stake—into the ground 8 to 12 inches from the first stake so that it's in a straight line with the guyline. Wrap the running end of the p-cord around the picket stake twice, then tie it off with two half hitches.

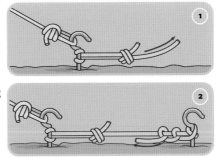

5 USE GARBAGE BAGS AS SAND SPIKES

It's always been a challenge to anchor a tent or tarp on beaches, river sandbars, and other places where tent stakes won't hold. The solution: bag it. Fill garbage bags or empty stuff sacks with sand, tie a knot in the opening, then tie the tent's stake loops and rain fly guylines to them. For high winds, burying the bags will provide a rock-solid stake point. And stuffing sand bags along the inside tent edge will help batten down the hatches.

6 FIX A TIRED TENT POLE

It ranks among the most humiliating of outdoor snafus: When you pull the tent poles from the stuff sack, where they have been lovingly stored since portable CD players were all the rage, the pole sections fall to your feet like pick-up-sticks, the shock cord holding them together slack and limp.

It's always best to replace old shock cord as it starts to lose its elasticity, not when it is gone forever. In most cases, elastic bungee cord is threaded through the pole sections and held in place with a stopper knot that jams against a washer or some other stop inside each terminal pole section. A few tent models require a kit if the shock cord goes south, but most can be handled with nothing more than new bungee.

First, remember to keep the pole sections in their original order throughout this process. Access the cord by prying off a pole tip. Remove the old cord.

Tie an overhand knot in one end of the new cord. Thread the cord through the poles one section at a time, joining the sections together as you make progress. If the bungee bunches up while being pushed, cut a straight length of coat hanger wire, attach to the end of the bungee, and feed the wire through the poles. When finished, pull the bungee cord fairly tight, but leave some slack. Tie another stopper knot, but don't cut off the excess yet. You may need to experiment with the cord length to get the tension right. You want enough to hold the poles together, but not so much that the cord is stretched too tightly when you decouple the sections.

7 SLEEP LIKE A LOG IN SWELTERING SUMMER HEAT

It's a cruel twist, but for years my summer camping trips made for blissful daytime memories and miserable nights. There were sweltering tents. Happy campers singing 'round the fire so late the coyotes even howled for them to shut up. And then the endless snoring. Many mornings I greeted a gorgeous dawn sleep-deprived and grouchy.

Then I figured out the system for the best summer night's sleep ever. I bugged out of the communal snuggle-up-to-the-campfire scene and went solo with a sweet one-man tent. While everyone else fought with snoring tentmates and fitful sleep close to the festivities, I tucked my selfish little shelter into some leafy nook half a football field away. Nite-nite, suckers.

Here's my setup. I like tents with a body made almost entirely of mesh to hold summer bugs at bay but let summer breezes right in. Since I'm a big tosser and turner, I like a sleeping bag with an integrated sleeping pad. They're so sturdy even a sumo wrestler could not push me off the pad. And because it breathes so well, I like my bag to be lightly filled with lightweight down—even in summer—and I prefer a pad that blows up to a comfy $3\frac{1}{2}$ inches thick.

Add a pair of soft earplugs and a half dose of melatonin, and I'm good till morning's light.

8 TAB A TENT

Make tent line tighteners with soda can pull tabs. Thread the cord through the tab, loop it around the tent stake, and tie it back to the tab. Slide to make adjustments.

9 HANG GEAR INSIDE A WALL TENT

If your wall tent has an interior frame, you can hang many items with inexpensive shower-curtain hooks. Place the hooks over the horizontal poles, and hang pots and pans.

10

SLEEP TIGHT WITH A POOL NOODLE

I'm not afraid to admit it: Sleeping on a camp's top bunk without a rail makes me a little nervous. I'm a thrasher in the sack, and the thought of plummeting off the side of the bed keeps me up at night. The answer to this sleepy-time conundrum: a pool noodle. Wedge a pool noodle under a fitted sheet on the edge of the bed closest to the abyss. Now when you roll over, that pool noodle is just enough to keep you from going over the side, knocking your noggin at the bottom of your fall.

11

ROLL OUT THE HOME TURF

A piece of indoor-outdoor carpeting makes a fine front porch for any tent. It keeps the dirt out and doubles as a changing-room floor if you have a large tent vestibule.

12 MAKE RAINY DAYS FLY

Sleeping pads make perfect game boards, and there's no better way to pass time during a downpour than with a rousing brain-smash of chess. Or a spirited tic-tac-toe challenge, if you'd rather. Come up with a friendly competition—the winner, for example, gets first crack at the best trout hole on the creek.

At home, use a warm wet rag to clean the pad of dirt, sweat, grime, and smashed-in candy bars. While the pad is drying, pull out your favorite board games, a ruler or protractor (remember those?), and a quiver of permanent markers.

Sketching out a chess and checkers board is as easy as drawing squares and coloring between the lines. Backgammon is a bit more complicated, but no big deal. And there's always tic-tac-toe. If you have kids, a boiled down board of Chutes and Ladders isn't that difficult to draw. And you could go hardcore and sketch out Monopoly if you like. The game pieces for these games aren't terribly heavy or bulky, and for checkers and backgammon, pebbles or trout flies will suffice. Die-hard chess fans should snip out cardboard cutouts and store in a pack pocket for a rainy day.

13 BUILD A FIRE FOR MAXIMUM COOKING COALS

The perfect call, the perfect shot, your bull quarters are hanging like clean laundry, and it's time to eat. Don't blow it by rushing the fire. Building the perfect grilling fire takes about 45 minutes, but the results definitely make it worth the effort. Follow the steps below to be sure of success.

STEP 1 Look for woody debris in the form of dead lower limbs on standing lodgepole and whitebark pine trees. When choosing limbs to break off, look for those with plenty of brown needles still attached. Once you have enough, pile them up in the fire pit. The needles will serve as tinder, the twigs as kindling, and the branches are the beginning fuel to get your fire going.

STEP 2 You'll need 4 to 6 inches of glowing coals, so pile on the pine. Forgo the tepee-style fire for a crisscross log cabin setup that allows more air to circulate around larger pieces of wood. Burn pieces that are 4 to 6 inches in diameter and short enough so that each chunk of wood burns in its entirety at the same rate.

STEP 3 As the last of the pine flames die down to coals, it's time to pile on dead aspen limbs. These should be about 20 inches long and 3 to 4 inches in diameter. Once they burn down to coals, and no flames are visible, slap on the steaks. The aspen smoke turns a good elk steak into a meal to remember.

14 BUTCHER A WET LOG

Forget searching for tinder fungus and belly-button lint to start your fire. With a hatchet, you can render fire-starting scrap from a wet log.

STEP 1 Find a solid log no more than 10 inches in diameter. A coniferous wood like pine or cedar works best due to its flammable resin. Cut a 12-inch section from the log.

STEP 2 Split the log into quarters. Lay one quarter on the ground, bark side down. Score the edge with two 1-inch-deep cuts, 4 inches apart (a). Shave thin 4-inch-long dry wood curls and splinters (b). Pound these curls with the back of the hatchet to break up the wood fibers and then rub some of these between your palms to separate the fibers further. This is your tinder; you'll need two handfuls.

STEP 3 Split pencil-size pieces from the wedge corners of a remaining quarter. Break these into 6-inch pieces for kindling.

STEP 4 Continue to split the quarters, utilizing the innermost and driest pieces. Use these as small and large pieces of fuel.

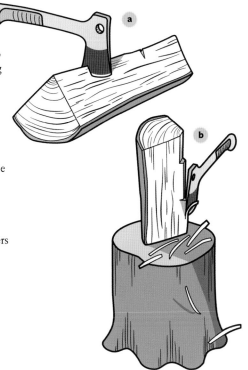

15 RECOVER A STUCK VEHICLE

Two difficult tasks await: summoning the courage to ask for help and getting your rig out of the soup without trashing the frame or maiming a bystander. You're on your own for getting help, but here's the step-by-step to follow once you do.

STEP 1 Clear the area around the wheels and differentials and then shovel out a trench in front of the wheels in the direction you need to move.

STEP 2 Shove floor mats, sticks, or sand under the wheels to give your vehicle traction.

STEP 3 Attach the tow strap to tow hooks, holes in the frame, or receiver hitches of your vehicle—and then to the other vehicle. Avoid attaching the strap to axles or anything else that moves. Don't use a trailer hitch ball as a recovery point. Share the tow load by using two tow points if possible.

STEP 4 Put both vehicles in four-wheel drive low, slowly pull out the slack in the strap, and bump up the RPMs in each vehicle. Pull in as straight a line as possible. If this doesn't work, have the tow vehicle back up a few feet and get a rolling start at 3 mph.

16 DIG A DAKOTA FIRE HOLE

Native Americans used a Dakota fire hole to hide cooking fires from their enemies. These small pits also excel in windy conditions and consume less wood while burning hotter than open fires. Plus, the layout provides a great platform for cooking. Here's how to channel your inner Sioux.

The fire hole works by sucking fresh air into the combustion chamber. Hot air rises from the hole, drawing air through the air vent and into the base of the fire. The cycle is self-sustaining, and digging the air vent on the upwind side of the fire hole helps capture the breeze like the air scoop on the Bandit's Trans Am.

Dig the fire chamber first. Excavate a pit 1 foot in diameter and 1 foot deep. Now widen the base of the chamber a few inches so it has a jug-like shape. This lets you burn slightly larger pieces of wood.

Dig the air tunnel next. Start about a foot away from the edge of the fire hole, on the upwind side, and carve out a mole-like tunnel 5 or 6 inches in diameter, angling down to the base of the fire chamber.

That's it. Top the fire hole with a grate or green saplings to hold a pot over the flames. When you break camp, refill the holes and leave no trace.

17 BURN YOUR GEAR INTO A HOT INFERNO

Marshmallows make awesome firestarters. What other odds and ends will burn long enough to catch a fire? Cheetos and greasy potato chips, for sure. Hand sanitizer. Plastic fishing baits. First aid bandages. Duct tape.

18 HANG A POT OVER A FIRE THREE WAYS

Forked sticks were the original duct tape—they could be used to make snares, make repairs, and hold down a buddy as you sawed off a gangrenous leg. (Maybe that last is a bit of a stretch.) But they do play a big role in one of the most basic of all outdoor skills: getting a pot boiling.

Technique A allows you to raise or lower the pot by adjusting the placement of the log.

Technique B is used on ground too hard to drive in a stick.

Technique C is downright futuristic: Unhook the stick from the short forked stick and you can swing the pot away from the fire.

19 MAKE A SUMMER FIRE

The log cabin council fire is a great summer blaze: It puts out plenty of light with less heat than other campfire lays, and burns a long time with smaller pieces of fuel so you don't break a sweat hauling Yule logs back to camp. It's a bit of a pyro mash up. The outside is a log cabin fire built of slow-burning green wood, inside of which burns a teepee fire that throws out tall flames to light your way.

SHELL CONSTRUCTION First, build the outer shell of a log cabin fire. Start with two 6-inch-diameter logs about 24 inches long, and build a log cabin fire of 2 logs for each of 4 "stories," using smaller logs as you go up. Choose whole green logs or branches of a slow-burning wood that won't throw a lot of sparks, such as white oak, ash, birch, or ironwood. Keep these structural logs whole. Split wood burns more quickly, and you want this to burn very slowly. The log-cabin walls will hold the sticks of the teepee fire upright, and that's the next step.

STOKE THE FURNACE Inside the log cabin structure, build a teepee fire of dry sticks, branches, and split woods. Break some of these pieces into lengths 6 inches taller than the log cabin structure. When burning, they'll produce tall flames that give out plenty of light.

TURN ON THE LIGHT Inside the teepee, lay your tinder bundle and light it. Now use wood as a mood-setting dimmer switch: Feed the teepee fire from the top as the flames consume the wood. If the log cabin walls start to burn too quickly, dose with water to knock back the flames.

20 OPEN A BREW WITH A BLADE

With practice, you can open a beer bottle by slicing off the neck with a single blow from a cleaver, but there's an easier and much safer method. Hold the neck of the bottle tightly, with the top of your hand just under the bottom of the cap. Place the back of your knife blade across the top of the third knuckle of your index finger and wedge it under the edge of the cap. Pry up.

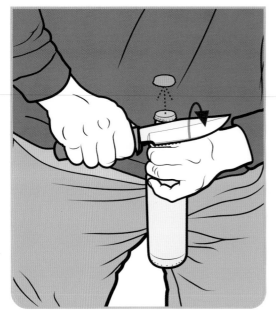

21 BUILD FOUR COOKING FIRES

In the same way that the proper ingredients make a recipe work, the right fire makes the cooking come together. The best backcountry camp cooks match the blaze to the dish. Here's how.

TEPEE FIRE If you need a steady, hot source of heat for a reflector oven or for roasting meat on a skewer, build a tepee fire of standing lengths of wood. Tall flames will produce the high-level heat required for even cooking. Keep plenty of small and medium-size pieces of wood ready to add to the fire for temperature regulation.

PINWHEEL FIRE To fry fish, you'll want a relatively small-diameter blaze closer to the ground, and one with precise temperature control. A pinwheel fire does the trick, with 1- to 2-inch-diameter sticks of firewood laid out in a starburst pattern. Build it inside a ring of rocks or logs to hold the frying pan and feed the fire with dry wood to keep the oil roiling.

LOG CABIN FIRE The log cabin fire is made of crosshatched logs. This arrangement provides lots of air circulation and plenty of wood surface for an even blaze. The result is a quick supply of cooking coals for a Dutch oven or foil-wrapped game.

KEYHOLE FIRE Multitask with a keyhole fire. Build a rock firepit in the shape of a keyhole. In the round part, build a tepee fire, whose tall flames provide both heat and light. In the narrow end, build a log cabin fire between the rock supports. The tepee will provide a constant source of coals once the log cabin fire burns down.

22 WHITTLE A WHISTLE OUT OF A STICK

Cut and peel the bark from a finger-length section of any stick with a soft pith, such as elder. Next, use a thin twig to bore out this pith, leaving a hollow cylinder (a). Cut a notch near one end (b). Whittle a smaller piece of wood that will fit snugly into the notch end and then slice a little off the top of that plug to allow for the passage of air (c). Fit the plug into the cylinder, trimming the end to shape (d). Place your finger in the other end and blow into the mouthpiece to force the air over the notch in the top of the whistle. When you get a clear whistle, the plug is well fitted. Permanently plug the end with a short piece of wood (e).

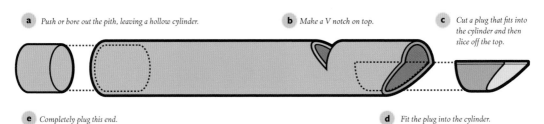

a Push or bore out the pith, leaving a hollow cylinder.

b Make a V notch on top.

c Cut a plug that fits into the cylinder and then slice off the top.

e Completely plug this end.

d Fit the plug into the cylinder.

23 CREATE SHELTER WITH A TARP

If you have two utility tarps with grommeted edges, you can create the Taj Mahal of shelters, complete with a handy campfire vent hole.

STEP 1 Look for four trees in a rectangle and a fifth located between two of the others on the short side.

STEP 2 Tie a tarp between the four trees. The back edge should be about 3 feet off the ground, with the forward edge as high as you can reach. Call this the lower tarp.

STEP 3 Now tie the upper tarp in place. Be sure that you position it so that it slides under the forward edge of the lower tarp by a couple of feet. Once it's in place, tie the side grommets together so that you create an open flap in the middle of the two tarps.

STEP 4 Tie a guyline from the middle of the back edge of the lower tarp to the fifth tree, cinching it tight. You now have a smoke vent.

STEP 5 Build a fire with a stacked-log back wall, and smoke will rise to the tarp roof and exit through the hole that you've created.

24 PACK A COMPLETE CAMP KITCHEN

The best way to make sure you always have what you need in the camp kitchen is to put together a complete set of cooking gear, pack it in an old cooler or plastic tote, and stow it in the basement or garage. The worst thing you can do: raid the camp kitchen just because you can't find the home kitchen spatula. Here's what you need to cook for a family or small group.

STOVE
(1) 2- or 3-burner camp stove

COOKWARE
(2) Pot set
(3) No. 10 Dutch oven
(4) Large fry pan
(5) Dutch oven lid lifter
(6) Measuring/mixing cup
(7) Pot grabber
(8) Coffee pot or French press and extra mugs

UTENSILS
(9) Opinel Knife No. 8
(10) Opinel Knife No. 10
(11) Mixing and serving spoons
(12) Spatula
(13) Metal tongs
(14) Stackable plates/cups set

CLEAN-UP
(15) Camp sink
(16) Biodegradable soap
(17) Quick-dry towels
(18) Pot scrubbers
(19) Trash bags

MISCELLANEOUS
(20) Strike-anywhere matches
(21) Charcoal chimney
(22) Bottle opener
(23) Corkscrew
(24) Spices, assorted
(25) Can opener
(26) Military can opener for backup
(27) Collapsible water container
(28) Plastic tablecloth and clips
(29) Aluminum foil
(30) Fire gloves
(31) Flexible cutting boards
(32) Thermacell

25 DIVVY UP KP

Assigning kitchen duty is no fun at home, and it's a drag at a hunting or fishing camp, too. There are plenty of solutions, and here are two that work.

HAVE A LOTTERY Each night of the season or trip has a number, and whatever number you draw, you're responsible for the evening meal, from preparation to clean-up. Have it catered, if you want to. Just don't ask for help.

USE THE BUDDY SYSTEM Assign 2-person teams for Kitchen Patrol: one to cook, one to clean. That way, no one misses out on the entire evening's festivities.

26 ACCESSORIZE DUTCH OVEN COOKING

Dutch oven cooking is a camp staple. Here are six items that will make it easier to channel your inner iron chef.

TONGS Useful for placing coals on top of an oven lid and turning food items during the cooking process.

LID LIFTER Cowboys call it a "gonch hook"—a lid lifter raises the lid while preventing it from tipping and dumping coals into your casserole.

SMALL WHISK BROOM Use to brush coals from a lid.

CHIMNEY STARTER FOR CHARCOAL Gets coals roaring fast, and prevents the need for lighter fluid.

HEAVY LEATHER GLOVES OR FIRE GLOVES Great for handling hot pots and lids.

PLASTIC PUTTY KNIFE Good for scraping away burned bits of food without scratching the oven finish.

28 CLEAN POTS WITH A SIX-PACK RING

If you forget to pack a pot scrubber to clean your dishes, remove the plastic rings from a few six-packs of canned beverages, stack and fold them as shown, and bundle them tightly together with a zip tie. It's very effective at scraping off food residue baked onto pans. Just make sure to dispose of the plastic rings properly at home.

29 DICE IT UP

I always pack a couple of flexible cutting boards on camping trips. They weigh next to nothing, stuff anywhere, and makes slicing and dicing— and cleaning fish—a snap.

27 SPICE UP A CAMP KITCHEN

Empty Tic-Tac boxes make the best camp spice bottles in the world. Mark the contents with a permanent marker. They're small enough that you can carry an entire spice rack in a very small package.

poll

head

cheek   *blade*   *edge*

30 SHARPEN A HATCHET OR AXE IN THE FIELD

Assuming that you're savvy enough to have a file and whetstone in the toolbox, here's how to give your axe an edge.

STEP 1 Drive a peg into the ground. Place a wrist-thick stick 4 inches from the peg.

STEP 2 Place the poll of the axe against the peg, resting the cheek of the axe head on the stick so that the bit is very slightly raised. Rasp the file perpendicular to the edge and inward from the cutting edge to prevent burrs. Flip the axe and repeat on the other side.

STEP 3 Finish with a whetstone. Use a circular motion that pushes the stone into the blade. Flip the axe and repeat.

31 PEE IN A TENT

Nothing says "expert" like answering nature's call inside your tent. (Sorry, ladies. You're on your own here.) Here's the drill.

STEP 1 Roll over on your stomach. Place your pee bottle near the head of your sleeping bag. Sit up on your knees.

STEP 2 Shimmy the sleeping bag down to your knees. Lift one knee at a time and shove the bag below each knee. Your bag should be out of harm's way.

STEP 3 Do your thing. Afterward, thread the cap back on the bottle and store the bottle in a boot so it remains upright. Better safe than soggy.

32 HANG FOOD FROM A TREE

STEP 1 Tie one end of a 40-foot length of parachute cord to the drawcord of a small stuff sack. Tie a loop in the other end of the cord and clip a small carabiner to it. Fill the sack with rocks and throw it over a branch that's at least 15 feet off the ground (a). Dump the rocks from the sack.

STEP 2 Clip the carabiner to the drawcord of your food storage bag, as shown (b). Run the sack end of the cord through the carabiner, and then pull on this end to snug the food bag against the branch.

STEP 3 Find a sturdy twig and, reaching as high as possible, tie a clove hitch around the twig. Stand on a rock for additional height if possible. Slowly release the rock-sack end of the rope (c). The twig will catch on the carabiner to keep the food bag hanging (d).

STEP 4 When you need to retrieve your food, pull the rope down, remove the twig, and lower the bag.

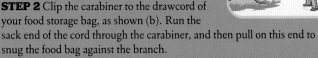

33 COOK FISH LIKE AN IRON . . . ER, TINFOIL CHEF

Store-bought reflector ovens work wonders, but they're a little tricky to fit into a fishing vest. All it really takes to turn this morning's fresh catch into a memorable shore meal is a pocketknife and some heavy-duty aluminum foil. Reflector oven cooking is fast because you don't wait for glowing coals. It's easy because you can dress up a trout with whatever herb or spice is at hand. It's tasty because your fish is hot and smoky. And best of all, cleanup is as simple as wadding up the foil.

STEP 1 Cut yourself two branched sticks about 20 inches below the Y. Drive them into the ground at the edge of the fire ring, 18 inches apart. Wrap a 22-inch-long stick with heavy-duty aluminum foil, place it in the forks of the Y-sticks, and unroll foil at a 45-degree angle away from the fire to the ground. Anchor the foil with another stick and unroll a shelf of foil toward the fire. Tear off the foil. Place four dry rocks on the bottom of the shelf. These will hold any baking rack or pan.

STEP 2 To create the oven sides, wrap one of the upright Y-sticks with foil. Unroll the foil around the back of the oven. Tear off the foil. Repeat on the other side. Pinch the two pieces of foil together.

STEP 3 Build a hot fire with flames reaching at least to the top of the foil. You want a tall fire to reflect heat downward from the upper wall of foil. To broil fish, line a baking pan (or simply use the bottom shelf as the baking pan) with onion slices. Add the fillets, seasoned with lemon juice, salt, and pepper. An easy way to punch it up is to slather the fillet with store-bought chipotle sauce. Top with a few more onion slices. Flip once and cook until the fish flakes with a fork.

34 ROAST THE PERFECT MARSHMALLOW

When you're roasting marshmallows, how often do you settle for a burned wad of ashy black marshmallow goo? Thought so. Achieving the perfect balance of golden smokiness and creamy gooliciosity (that's a real word—you don't have to look it up) is no small feat, so let's get serious.

ONLY JET-PUFFED OR CAMPFIRE BRANDS WILL DO

Many brands burn way too quickly. And only a chump uses a coat hanger as a skewer. Cut a straight roasting stick. No forked branches; no funky twigs. Keep it plain, straight, and simple. Hold the marshmallow level over embers, not flames. It's fine to have flames off to one side, but they shouldn't be directly under your precious glob of sugary wonderfulness. Rotate the marshmallow slowly, or go for a quarter turn at a time. (Here's where the straight stick comes into play: You don't have to change positions when you rotate it.)

WATCH FOR THE TELLTALE SAG
As the marshmallow turns a tawny golden color, it will sag on the roasting skewer. When a vertical slit appears where the stick and marshmallow meet, you know the insides are approaching that desired state of gooliciosity. It is time.

FIELD & STREAM CRAZY-GOOD GRUB

35 PERFECT THE DRUGSTORE WRAP

Many a campfire meal has been ruined with a fire-blackened version of this Boy Scout staple. It doesn't have to be that way. Start by learning the "drugstore wrap." Tear off a piece of heavy-duty aluminum foil approximately three times the size of your pile of food. Place it shiny side up on a flat surface. Put the food in the center of the foil (a). Bring up two opposite sides to form a tent, and roll over tightly three times (b). Press tightly along the fold to seal the seam. Seal the other two ends with three tight folds (c). Now add a second layer of foil, with looser folds. This layer protects the inner layer from punctures and keeps it clean so you can use it as a plate once opened.

What to put in a foil pouch? How about a Deer Hunter's Hobo Supper?

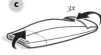

INGREDIENTS

10 oz. venison backstrap, cut into pieces
1 medium onion, quartered
1 potato, diced
½ red pepper, cut into 1-inch squares

20-oz. can pineapple chunks, drained
1 tbsp. pineapple juice
1 tbsp. soy sauce
Dash each coriander, ginger, cumin

Pile the venison, onion, potato, red pepper, pineapple chunks, pineapple juice, soy sauce, and spices onto the foil.

Fold the foil as shown at right and cook the pouches over hot coals for about 25 minutes. Unwrap, let cool, and enjoy.

36 TURN A CANOE INTO A CAMPSITE (ALMOST)

Sure, a canoe hauls mountains of gear, puts you in the fish, and floats out the biggest bucks with ease. But don't turn your back on this ancient craft once you get to shore. With a few tricks, that boat can make camp life a lot easier—and it could save your life.

CAMP TABLE AND KITCHEN COUNTER
Properly stabilized, a canoe makes a fine table for cooking and food preparation. Turn the boat upside down on level ground. Wedge rocks or logs under the bow and stern to prevent the canoe from tipping and wobbling. Now you have a rock-steady flat surface ready for a camp stove, wash bucket, and lantern. You can even fillet fish directly on the boat hull and let tomorrow's miles wash away the slime and guts.

WINDBREAK FOR FIRE Canoe campsites are often exposed on sandbars, gravel flats, islands, and windy shorelines. Turn a boat on one edge and prop it up with a pair of sticks to blunt fire-sucking winds.

EMERGENCY SHELTER A canoe can do double duty as a lifesaving shelter when the weather goes south. Turn the canoe upside down and prop one end on a low, sturdy tree branch, a boulder, or—in a pinch—a mound of gear. The high end of the canoe should be pointing away from the wind. Drape a tarp or emergency space blanket over the hull and stake down the edges. Crawl inside and wait out the weather.

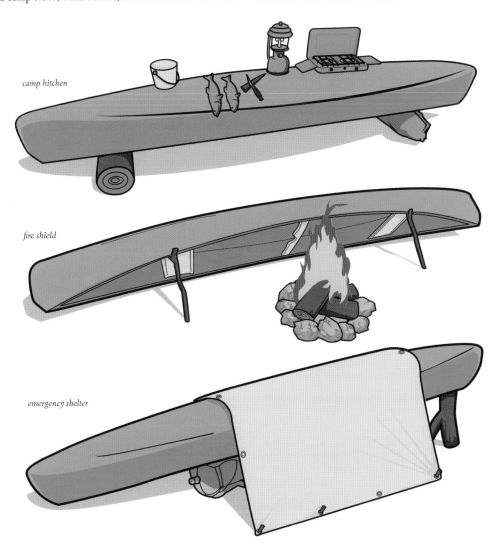

camp kitchen

fire shield

emergency shelter

37 MAKE A CAMP COFFEE CUP

Durn. You left your coffee mug at home again. But there's a tall can of beans in the camp cupboard and a hammer and tin snips in the shed. Get to it.

STEP 1 Remove the top of the can. Empty and wash the can.

STEP 2 Make a cut around the can's circumference (a) about 2 inches down; leave a vertical strip of can 1 inch wide.

STEP 3 Tap small folds over the sharp edges. Tamp them down smooth so you won't slice your lips.

STEP 4 Bend the strip down into a handle (b). Smirk at your buddies while you sip.

38 PUT UP A CAMP GUN RACK

Your guns are unloaded in camp—of course—but that still doesn't mean you want them leaning precariously against trees and walls. You can create an outdoor gun rack in 10 minutes with a sharp knife and two 5-foot lengths of rope.

STEP 1 Find or trim a downed branch about 6 to 7 feet long. It should have numerous smaller branches to serve as barrel stops; cut these to 2-inch lengths.

STEP 2 Select two trees free from branches to head height, about 5 feet apart.

STEP 3 Lash the support branch to the upright trees about 36 inches from the ground.

STEP 4 Institute a rule that all guns in camp must be placed in the camp gun rack. Violations are punishable by dish-washing and firewood-gathering duties.

FIELD & STREAM CRAZY-GOOD GRUB

tight ring of coals   Dutch oven

6 to 8 coals

39 MAKE A DUTCH OVEN CHICKEN QUESADILLA PIE

Making a one-pot meal in a Dutch oven is a campfire staple: It frees up the cook to sip whiskey and trade stories while pretending to be hard at work. This chicken quesadilla pie serves 10 to 12, and it's as easy as falling off the log you're sitting on while claiming to cook.

INGREDIENTS

5 lb. chicken breasts, cut into stir-fry–size chunks
2 medium sweet yellow onions, chopped
2 green peppers, chopped
1 large yellow squash, cubed
One 19-oz. can enchilada sauce
25 small corn tortillas
2 lb. shredded cheddar or jack cheese

One 16-oz. can corn kernels
One 16-oz. can black beans
3 boxes cornbread mix
3 eggs
1 cup milk

STEP 1 Sauté chicken, onions, green peppers, and squash until chicken is cooked through.

STEP 2 In a 14-inch Dutch oven, layer enchilada sauce, tortillas, cheese, canned ingredients, and cooked chicken-and-vegetables mixture.

STEP 3 Mix cornbread with eggs and milk according to box instructions and spread over the top.

STEP 4 Bake for 1 hour using 6 to 8 coals on the bottom and a tight ring of coals around the top.

40 LIGHTEN YOUR PACK

2 TO 3 POUNDS Replace your leather wafflestompers with a pair of midcut boots with synthetic uppers.

¼ POUND Ditch the flashlight for a lightweight headlamp. Some models offer both a long-burning LED for doing your camp chores and a high-intensity beam for nighttime navigation.

3 POUNDS Trade your tent for a tarp shelter. You can find some that weigh less than 2 pounds.

1 POUND Leave the hatchet at home. Carry a wire saw.

2 POUNDS Cook with an ingenious wood-burning portable stove instead of a gas burner and avoid having to carry fuel.

1 TO 2 POUNDS Pack only two sets of clothes: one for around camp, the other for hunting or fishing.

1 POUND Repack commercial food items in reclosable plastic bags and lightweight water bottles.

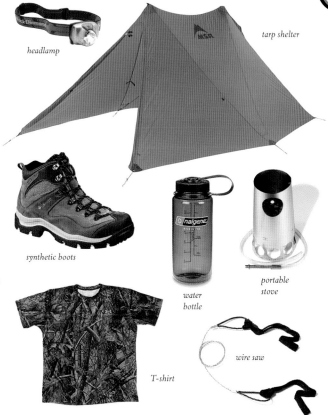

headlamp

tarp shelter

synthetic boots

water bottle

portable stove

T-shirt

wire saw

41 CUT THE CHEESE

Use a 12-inch section of one of the inner strands of parachute cord to slice cheese and salami when you leave your knife at home.

42 TIE A CANOE TO YOUR RACKS

To tie down a canoe correctly, follow the rule of twos: two tie-downs across the boat, two bow anchors, and two stern anchors.

STEP 1 Place the boat on the canoe racks upside down and centered fore and aft. Tightly cinch the boat to the racks, using one cam-buckle strap per rack or ³/₈-inch climbing rope finished off with a trucker's hitch. Do not crisscross these tie-downs. It's critical to snug the tie-down straps or ropes directly against the gunwales where they cross under the racks.

STEP 2 Run two independent bow anchors by tying two ropes to the bow, and the end of each rope to a bumper or bumper hook. Repeat for stern anchors. Do not use the same rope or strap to create one long V-shaped anchor. Otherwise, if one end comes loose, everything comes loose. Pad these lines wherever they run across a bumper edge.

STEP 3 Test the rig by grabbing the bow and shifting hard left, right, up, and down. You should be able to rock the entire car or truck without shifting the canoe. Do the same for the stern. Repeat after 10 minutes on the road and tighten the rig if needed.

43 CUT PARACHUTE CORD WITH FRICTION

No knife? No problem. Tie the piece of parachute cord to be cut to two stout points—trees, truck bumpers, whatever. Leave plenty of slack. Take another few feet of cord (or the end of the line you're cutting if it's long enough) and place the middle of it over the piece of parachute cord to be cut. Grasp each end of this second piece firmly, and saw back and forth. Friction will melt the parachute cord right where you want it cut.

44 TIE A BUTTERFLY LOOP

Tie this loop in the running part of a line and use it to hang gear, as a ladder step, or make a canoe bridle to tow a canoe behind a boat.

STEP 1 Hang a rope from your hand and coil it twice to form three coils (a). Move the right coil to the left, over the middle coil (b). The center coil now becomes the right coil.

STEP 2 Move this coil to the left over the top of the other two coils (c).

STEP 3 Take the coil you just moved to the left and pass it back to the right, under the remaining coils, to form a loop (d).

STEP 4 Pinch this loop against your palm, using your thumb to hold it. Slide your hand to the right, pulling this loop (e). Tighten the knot by pulling both ends of the rope (f).

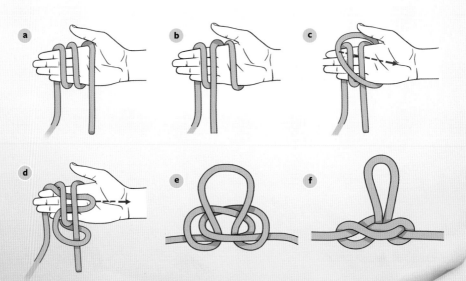

45 PACK LUNCH IN A WATER BOTTLE

Breakfast is simple. Dinner is meat. Lunch? It's always a problem. You don't want to take the time to cook. You don't want to pull out half your gear to prepare a meal. And you don't want yet another bagel and salami. Here's the solution: At home, grab a wide-mouth water bottle. Loosely roll up a few tortillas and place them inside, letting them unroll so they lie against the sides. Add a vacuum-packed foil pouch of tuna or chicken. Toss in a hunk of cheese and a small spice bottle filled with black beans. Presto! All the makings of a backcountry wrap, in a bombproof container.

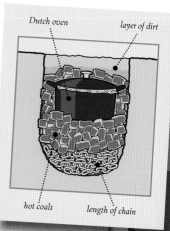

Dutch oven   layer of dirt

hot coals   length of chain

FIELD & STREAM CRAZY-GOOD GRUB

46 DIG A BEAN HOLE

Digging a bean hole is a storied tradition in the North Woods, but there's no reason you can't do it anywhere. The wood smoke and molasses flavors in this bean dish can't be duplicated any other way.

INGREDIENTS

10 cups dried Great Northern or yellow-eyed beans
1 lb salt pork, cut into 2-inch strips
2 large onions, diced
2½ cups molasses
4 tsp. dry hot mustard
2 tsp. black pepper
½ cup butter

STEP 1 Dig a hole that's twice as deep as and one foot in diameter larger than the Dutch oven you're planning to use. Next, toss a few rocks or a length of chain into the bottom of the hole. Fill the hole with hardwood and then burn the wood down until the hole is three-quarters full of hot coals.

STEP 2 Over your open fire (or on a camp stove), precook the beans by slow-boiling them for about 30 minutes. Drain and set aside.

STEP 3 Place the salt pork in the Dutch oven, layer onions on top, and pour in the beans, molasses, mustard, and black pepper. Slice the butter and place on top. Add enough boiling water to cover the beans by ½ to 1 inch. Cover the pot with aluminum foil and then the lid.

STEP 4 Shovel out about a third of the coals and put the bean pot in the hole. Replace the coals around the sides and on top of the oven; fill the rest of the hole with dirt. Cooking time varies, but give it a good 8 hours.

47 DIG A BOOTY HOLE

So it's not exactly what you're thinking. For a more comfortable night in your sleeping bag, dig a "hip hollow" or "booty hole" before pitching the tent. Dig or tamp down a slight depression in the ground—a couple inches is plenty—where your pelvis will rest once you lie down. If you sleep on your back, the hole relieves painful pressure points at the small of your back. If you're a side sleeper, your hip will nestle into the hole, keeping your spine aligned for a more restful snooze.

48 WIELD A FIELD WRENCH

Can't get a rusty bolt loose? Wrap parachute cord tightly around the nut counterclockwise, leaving a tag end long enough to grasp firmly and pull.

49 TIE A KNUTE HITCH

Simplicity itself, the Knute hitch is perfect for tying a lanyard to the holes in knife handles and other essential tools.

STEP 1 Start by tying an overhand stopper knot in one end of the cord. Thread a loop through the lanyard hole, and push the stopper knot up through it.

STEP 2 Snug it tight, and you are done.

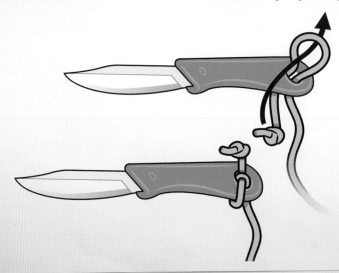

50 PACK FOR CAMPING IN 5 MINUTES

Plan your fun: Designate three large plastic storage bins and two large laundry bags for camping gear. Store the tent in one laundry bag and the sleeping bags in the other. In one bin, store air mattresses, pumps, pillows, and tarps. In another, pack up stoves, pots and pans, lanterns, hatchets, rope, saws, and other camp tools. Keep the third bin stocked with items that you'll need for camp and kitchen: a small bag of favorite spices, toilet paper, paper towels, camp soap, spare rope, the first aid kit, and the like. Resist the temptation to raid the bins when you're at home and down to your last paper towel. That way, when you're heading out for camp, all you have to do is load the bins and bags, and your work is half done. And once at camp the empty bins serve as great dirty laundry hampers and dry storage for firewood until it's time to pack up and head home.

51 KEEP YOUR COOLER COLD TWICE AS LONG

Cut a piece of cardboard or minicell foam to fit inside the top of each of your coolers. These disposable gaskets will seal in the cold and make ice last much longer, especially in partially filled coolers. In a pinch, layers of newspaper work like a charm, too.

52 FIX ANY TEAR, RIP, OR FRAY

Seam sealers are the best glues you've never heard of. Sure, the stuff waterproofs tent and tarp seams, but a urethane-based sealer also provides a flexible, waterproof, wear-resistant film that can save many a garment. Check out these uses.

WATERPROOF SYNTHETIC GUNSTOCKS Run a bed of seam sealer around butt pads and the threads of connecting screws. This will prevent water from leaking into hollow stocks.

REPAIR RAINCOAT RIPS Close the tear, using tape on the inside of the coat. Brush seam sealer on the outside, covering 1/8 inch on each side of the rip. Let it cure according to manufacturer's directions and then repeat the sealing step on the inside.

KEEP ROPES FROM FRAYING Use seam sealer to permanently whip-finish the ends of ropes and cords.

FIELD & STREAM CRAZY-GOOD GRUB

53 MAKE A TWO-STEP BACKPACKER'S MEAL

End of the trail, end of the day—the last thing you want to do is channel some television chef over a hot fire. This backpacking meal requires nothing but a single pot, a handful of lightweight ingredients, and minimum cleanup. If you and your buddy take turns digging a spoon into the mix, you can skip plates altogether.

INGREDIENTS
One 6-oz. package of instant stuffing mix
3 tbsp. olive oil
12 sun-dried tomatoes
Two 3.5-oz. tins smoked oysters
One 8-oz. can water chestnuts

STEP 1 To a 2-quart pot, add the stuffing's required amount of water, plus 3 tablespoons.

STEP 2 Follow box directions for stuffing with these exceptions: (1) Replace butter with olive oil. (2) Toss in the sun-dried tomatoes and simmer for five minutes before adding stuffing mix. (3) After stuffing is ready, stir in oysters and water chestnuts. Mix thoroughly.

54 PORTAGE CANOE AND GEAR

I thought I knew how to pack for a canoe trip—then I went paddling with a few Canadian friends. They made me look like some pioneer hawking fry pans in the backcountry.

Start with a monstrous portage pack, such as the indomitable Boundary Pack. Loaded like a standard backpack, there's still room for tackle bags and vests, daypacks, maps, and all the other crap that winds up strewn from bow to stern. Unless we plan to use our paddles as makeshift hiking staffs, we lash them, along with fishing rods, to the underside of the canoe seats.

Next, it's Canadian clean-and-jerk time. One paddler shimmies into the lightest portage pack and single-mans the canoe on his shoulders. The other paddler double-packs, with the heaviest pack on his back, and front-carries a lighter one by threading arms backwards through the shoulder harness. To be honest, with such a load, I sometimes peter out halfway down the trail. But there's a substantial psychic reward in at least humping the bulk of the gear partway in one giant effort.

55 CARRY A BACKPACKING BOAT ANCHOR

If you portage a canoe much or haul one into distant fishing holes, you know how much precious room a heavy folding anchor takes up in a pack. Solution: a basketball net. Tie off the bottom with a short piece of rope. When you need it, fill it with a few rocks, and tie off the other end with an anchor line.

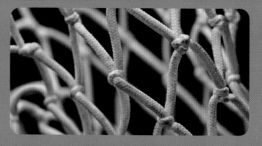

56 DRY BOOTS WITH A HOT ROCK

You almost made it across the creek—but now your feet are soaked, your boots are sloshing, and you're headed for misery, if not frostbite. There are no quick fixes to drowned boots, so don't hold off. As soon as you're in camp, strip off socks and shoes and get to work. Propping boots in front of the fire is one solution, but it's hard on rubber, hell on leather, and leaves a boot's inner workings still moist enough to soak your last dry pair of socks. Here's how to dry them from the inside out.

STEP 1 Remove the insoles and set them aside. Pack boots with absorbent material: paper towels or newspaper if you have them, dry leaves and grasses if you don't. Remove the materials and repeat until you've gotten as much moisture out as possible.

STEP 2 Heat rocks in boiling water or near the fire, then carefully place in spare socks or a bandana. Test the stones for 10 seconds to make sure they don't scorch the material, then fill up the boot. Or pour boiling water into water bottles or smaller spice bottles. Tuck the smaller bottles into the boot foot, and stand a full-sized water bottle in the shank.

STEP 3 While your boots are cooking, work on the insoles. Press them between spare clothing, paper towels or dried grasses, and squeeze hard to express water. Toss them in the bottom of your sleeping bag for the final overnight finish.

STEP 4 If you can't resist the temptation to prop boots and insoles by the fire, go easy. Fire-baked leather will crack and synthetic material can melt. Insoles can harden in the heat without much of a visual warning. If you can't press your hand to the warmed boot and leave it there, move it back from the fire.

57 KEEP GEAR DRY

There are lots of reasons to store camp foods in vacuum bags. Cuts of meat and poultry lie more or less flat, so they take up less room in a cooler. Vacuum bags don't permit food smells to permeate. And vacuum bags are watertight, so it's no big deal if your sealed-tight cheese goes swimming in the cooler slop.

But don't stop with the cold cuts. Use vacuum bags to keep these items dry, handy, and safely stored in duffels and day packs.

- Strike-anywhere matches
- Spare ammunition
- Change of thermal underwear and socks
- Maps
- Batteries
- Hunting and fishing licenses
- Toilet paper
- Trail snacks
- Items you don't want to rattle while hunting on the move (spare game calls, compasses, survival items)

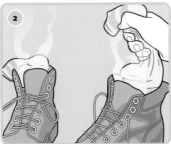

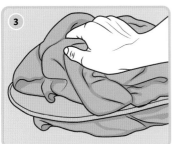

58 DRAW A POCKETKNIFE LIKE A GUNSLINGER

Folding knives are hugely popular, but there are choices when it comes to how to carry a clip-mounted knife and how to draw it quickly and ready for action.

DEPLOY THE KNIFE TIP DOWN Many prefer a tip-down carry for safety reasons. If the blade were to open slightly in your pocket, a tip-down carry will help prevent an accident slicing of your fingertips. Assisted opening knives should be carried tip-down. To deploy, reach into your pocket with your thumb on the inside of the knife, two fingers on the outside at the clip position, and draw. As the knife comes out of your pocket, grasp the pivot point between thumb and forefinger, and use the middle finger to catch the edge of the pocket clip and rotate the handle slightly into your palm, keeping your thumb on the opening stud or hole. You're ready to open the knife.

DEPLOY THE KNIFE TIP UP The tip-up position allows for very rapid deployment of flipper knives. To deploy from tip-up, reach into the pocket and slide your thumb down the handle almost to the pivot point, with other fingers on the clip side of the handle.

One slick modification for tip-up knives, such as many Spyderco knives with opening holes, is to use a zip tie to create a quick opening feature. Insert a small zip tie through the opening hole and cinch down tightly so that the protruding side of the zip tie is on the same side of the knife as the clip. Cut the tails off flush. (You might need two small zip ties to prevent each from wiggling around.) Now as you pull the knife from your pocket, pull back slightly so the zip ties catch on the back corner of the pocket seam, pulling the knife open. Practice the move and it can be impressively instantaneous.

59 SWITCH UP A POCKET CLIP

Many folding knives come with pocket clips that can be placed on either side of the handle, either tip-up or tip-down. Where and how you carry a knife is personal preference, but keeping a clip tightly screwed in place is critical.

Many clips are attached with the 6-sided star screws called Torx screws. Designed to prevent cam-out, Torx screws can be screwed down very tightly, but you'll have to have the proper size of Torx bit for the job. Add a tiny drop of blue Loctite, which is a medium strength threadlocker that will prevent clip screws from loosening.

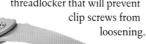

60 REMEMBER FOUR KNIFE NEVERS

Keep these tips in mind, and your favorite blade will last as long as you do—or even longer.

NEVER store a knife in a leather sheath; it can cause rusting or discoloration.

NEVER use water to clean a horn handle. Horn absorbs moisture and can splinter.

NEVER use hot water to clean a wood handle. If the wood is cracked or dried, rub it with olive oil.

NEVER touch the blade or metal parts after oiling. This can leave behind salt and acids, which can cause oxidation.

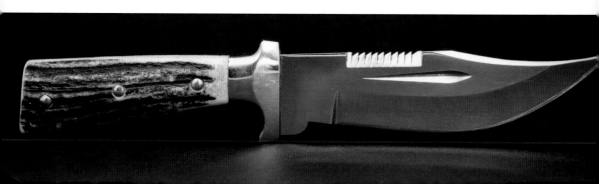

61 CHOOSE A KID'S FIRST KNIFE

How old is old enough for a knife? Some will consider it heresy, but I used a rotary tool to grind the blade on a Swiss Army knife down to butter-knife dull, and let my 5-year-olds putter around camp with it at will. That sparked plenty of early conversations about knife safety and has paid off now that they are teenagers.

General-purpose folders will whittle a stick, clean a panfish, and help take the hide off a deer. While shopping, look for features that make certain designs safer for smaller hands, and don't drop a pile of cash on a kid's knife.

For ages 10 and younger, look for a locking main blade. Some newer models of Swiss Army knives have been updated with locks, and they still have all the cool stuff—tweezers, toothpick, screwdrivers —with an ergonomic handle for an even surer grip.

For kids 11 to 13, blades shorter than 3 inches are still stout enough to cut through a squirrel. Look for jimping at the base of the blade spine to help provide control, and find a knife with a fat handle that will fit smaller hands well. I like indentations deep enough to serve as a finger guard.

For those 14 and older, flipper opening mechanisms create a nifty blade guard when the knife is open. Older kids will also appreciate a backup locking mechanism for an added measure of safety.

62 CHOOSE THE RIGHT KNIFE

No other tool is called upon to perform as many tasks, in as many ways, under as many conditions, as the knife. It can take a life and save one. Cut cord, open the belly of an elk, help spark a fire, and skin a fish. A good knife is a tool, an icon, a symbol of its bearer's take on what it takes to live well in the woods. And the know-how to use a sharp blade never goes out of style.

SPINE The back of the blade, most often unsharpened and unground. A thick spine gives a knife strength.

JIMPING Corrugated grooves in the blade spine, choil, or handle for increased grip and a no-slip feel.

THUMB RAMP An elevated hump on the spine of the blade near the handle. It provides increased control of the knife and reduced forearm fatigue during periods of extended use.

CHOIL The unsharpened edge of the blade between the end of the handle and the beginning of the edge bevel. Many knives have a finger indent at the choil to aid in choking up on the blade.

BELLY The curved arc as the sharpened edge nears the blade tip. A knife with a lot of belly will have a sagging, swooping profile, perfect for the sweeping cuts needed to skin big game.

RICASSO The shank of the blade between the handle and the beginning of the sharpened edge. The ricasso often carries the maker's identifying mark, or "tang stamp."

THUMB HOLE OR STUD A hole in the spine or a stud that protrudes from the blade of a folding knife near the handle and allows the user to open the knife one-handed.

GRIND The finished shape of the blade when viewed in cross section. There are two basic grinds. Hollow-grind blades have a concave shape and are easily sharpened, but tend to hang up in deep cuts. Flat-grind blades taper evenly from the spine to the cutting edge and hold an edge well.

FIXED BLADE KNIVES are inherently strong due to the tang, the extension of the blade that carries into the knife handle. Also called sheath knives, fixed blades are easy to clean and quick to put into action. They have no moving parts to break or gunk up with hair, blood, or grit. And the sleek lines of a fixed blade knife speak to the essence of outdoors competence—simple elegance and deadly efficiency.

FOLDING BLADE KNIVES can be smaller and easier to carry than fixed blade models. Larger folding blades with pocket clips and strong locking mechanisms are hugely popular. Many are designed to be opened with one hand through the use of a thumb stud or blade hole, and some are built with assisted-opening devices that propel the blade into a fixed position after the user opens it partway.

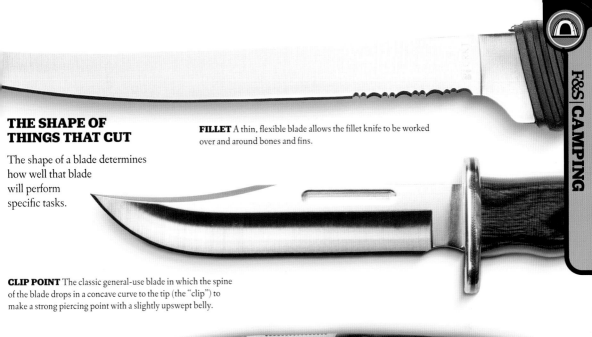

THE SHAPE OF THINGS THAT CUT

The shape of a blade determines how well that blade will perform specific tasks.

FILLET A thin, flexible blade allows the fillet knife to be worked over and around bones and fins.

CLIP POINT The classic general-use blade in which the spine of the blade drops in a concave curve to the tip (the "clip") to make a strong piercing point with a slightly upswept belly.

DROP POINT A downward convex curve along the blade spine forms a lowered point, which keeps the tip from cutting into an animal's organs during field dressing.

SKINNER The full curving knife belly is perfect for long, sweeping motions, such as skinning big game.

CAPER A short, pointed blade with a slightly downturned tip is easy to control in tight spots, such as removing the cape from an animal's head.

RECURVE The slight S-shaped belly forces the material being cut into the sharp edge. Recurves can be designed into most blade profiles.

63 KNOW YOUR AXES & HATCHETS

At the turn of the 19th century, more than 200 different axe-head patterns were being manufactured in America. In 1925, long after the crosscut saw had largely replaced the axe as an industrial grade tree-feller, True Temper Kelly still offered no less than 28 axe head patterns. The choices are more limited today, but being able to swing an axe—or deftly work a hatchet—remains a core skill of the American outdoorsman. Here's what you need to know to match the edged tool for the woodsy job.

ⓐ FELLING AXE The classic American axe design, the felling axe evolved into dozens of regional variations such as the Dayton and Jersey axe. The thin, sharp bits excel at tasks that require cross-grain cutting, such as felling trees and removing limbs, but they are not the best choice for splitting wood.

ⓑ BROADAX Designed to shape squared-off corners for timbers and railroad ties, or rounded poles for masts, the broadax was a fundamental tool in American history.

ⓒ HUDSON'S BAY With a smaller handle and head, the Hudson's Bay design was favored by fur traders traveling long distances by canoe. Hefty enough to work through medium-size logs, it's light enough for limbing. Choking up on the slightly elongated beard increases control when shaping wood.

ⓓ PULASKI Mostly used by firefighters and trail construction crews, the Pulaski boasts a traditional cutting bit on one side and a grubbing adze on the other.

ⓔ SPLITTING MAUL The wedge-shaped head splits wood apart along the grain. A poor choice for anything else, splitting mauls are unsurpassed for chopping log rounds into fireplace-ready fuel. Small splitting hatchets bridge the gap between mauls and standard bits and excel around the campsite.

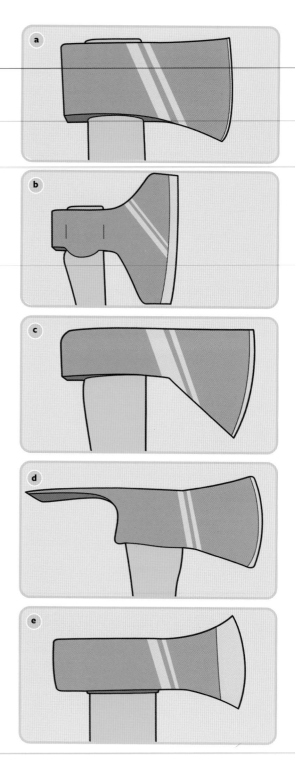

64 NAME THOSE PARTS

EYE The hole in the head where the handle is fitted.

HEAD The shape of an axe or hatchet head defines its primary use: cutting or splitting.

BIT General term for the cutting portion of the axe or hatchet head.

TOE Upper corner of the bit.

POLL An extended poll helps balance the tool, but only hardened polls are designed for hammering. Hammer with an unhardened poll and you risk mushrooming the head.

CHEEK Lies between the bit and the poll.

HEEL Lower corner of the bit.

LUG OR LIP Metal protrusion gives more wood to metal contact and helps secure head to handle.

BEARD A downward extension of the bit, common on tools designed for shaping wood, such as carpenter's axes and broadaxes. The beard allows the user to choke up the handle to control shaving.

BELLY The long midsection of the handle, or haft.

THROAT The sweep of handle towards the grip.

KNOB OR SWELL KNOB Prevents handle from slipping from sweaty hands.

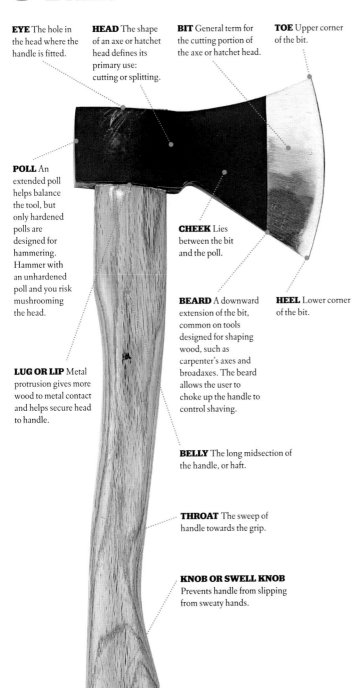

65 CHOOSE YOUR WEAPON

BIT BY BIT The bit profile is the most important aspect of performance. A thin cutting profile works well when limbing felled trees or cutting campfire wood. A more wedge-shaped profile excels in splitting log rounds.

CONSIDER THE CURVE

A pronounced curve in the bit lessens bit-to-wood contact, allowing for deeper cuts. A flat bit cuts more evenly, but not as deeply.

GET A HANDLE ON IT

Proponents of curved handles consider them more efficient and easier on the hands. Straight-handle fans point out the strength inherent in wood grain running the length of the handle. Both camps claim greater accuracy. The best choice is the one that feels best in your hands.

SINGLE OR DOUBLE?

A double-bit axe can serve double duty. One blade is sharpened to a narrow felling edge for taking down trees. The other is ground to a more blunt edge for working through knots and cutting trees on the ground. The single-bit axe or hatchet has other advantages. The poll can be hardened for hammering, but even an unhardened poll can be pounded with a wood baton to boost the cutting power of hatchet-sized bits.

66 BUCK A LOG WITH AN AXE

You round a trail corner and groan: A fallen tree blocks the path. Your buddy's default response is to stomp to the back of the truck, pull out the chain saw, check the tension, futz around for fuel, find ear plugs, and look for safety glasses. By the time he walks back to the log, you have bucked the tree into pieces with little more than an axe and attitude. Smirking follows.

Bucking a log this way is not a beginner skill. It's best to have experience with an axe and to wear protective clothing. Stand on top of the log and chop a V-notch into the side, between your feet, using a six-stroke count: Make three swings angling in from the right—the first one high on the log, then low, and then in the middle. Next, repeat with swings angling in from the left—high, low, and middle. On that sixth and final stroke, flick your wrist slightly outward—an inch will do—the instant the bit bites wood. This will help toss the chips out of the notch and prevent the axe from sticking.

Cut halfway through one side of the log, then turn around and chop another V-notch through the other side. Plan the Vs so the tips of the two notches are slightly offset. This prevents the final stroke from over-traveling and sending the axe bit between your legs and the handle into your nuts at warp factor 9.

67 SPLIT CAMP WOOD WITH A TIRE

Old tires piled up in the garage? Don't think of them as eyesores. Those are handy wood-splitting devices that can save you time and trips to the chiropractor. Stack spare tires on top or around a chopping block, and those worn-out Goodyears hold wood rounds in place while you work axe magic. You can load the tire with multiple smaller pieces to split, or one large round to work into quarters. The wood stays inside the tire, so you can split smaller and smaller pieces without having to bend over and pick them up each time the axe falls. When the wood splits cleanly, the tire helps keep your axe from biting deeply into the block. Miss the round entirely—hey, it happens—and the tire catches the errant edge and guards your legs against a horrific gash.

There are a couple of variations, depending on the size of your chopping block. Just remember to drill holes or cut drainage slits into the lower sidewalls of the tires so they won't collect rainwater for breeding mosquitoes.

For larger chopping blocks (A), use a single tire. To hold the tire in place, use a heavy knife to create tabs along the sidewall on the side of the tire facing the ground. Cut through the rim bead and a couple of inches into the sidewall, depending on the diameter of your block. Slide the tire onto the top of the block, tabs facing the ground, leaving plenty of tire above the block surface to hold up the wood rounds. Nail these tabs into the side of the chopping block.

Use a smaller block (B) that will fit completely inside spare tires, and stack four tires with the block in the middle. The top tire needs to extend above the chopping block surface. Tie the tires together with parachute cord. This arrangement provides stability to smaller splitting blocks.

68 HAUL FIREWOOD WITH A WEB STRAP

To make a handy wood hauler, take a broken 1-inch ratchet strap, cut off the end with the hook, and tie a loop at that end. Lay the strap on the ground and pile sticks on it, then pull the male end through the female end and throw the bundle over your shoulder. You can carry twice as much wood in half the time.

69 ROLL A PAPER LOG

You can make a lightweight, compact fire log using just an old newspaper, water, and string. Take your paper and roll it into a tight cylinder and tie it with string. Next, soak it in water. After a couple of days of drying, the brittle paper will catch a flame quick, and the "log" will keep its form for a longer burn.

70 SHARPEN A MACHETE

For lane clearing, you'll want a 25- to 35-degree angle on a machete blade. Anything finer will roll and chip with heavy chopping. Clamp the blade in a vise, edge up, tip pointed toward you. Use a 12-inch bastard mill file, and wear heavy leather work gloves. Push the file into the blade at the proper angle: two 15-degree bevels create a 30-degree blade angle. With a correct angle on one side, turn the machete around and repeat. Finish the edge with a sharpening puck, which you'll carry into the field for touch-ups.

71 FINISH A BLADE WITH A LEATHER STROP

Using a leather strop to hone a blade to a whisker-shaving edge isn't just for small-town barbers. This final stage in the sharpening process removes the tiny burrs, nicks, and microscopic rolled edges left by even the finest-grit stones. To polish a knife edge with a leather strop, the knife must be quite keen in the first place. Then it's a simple matter of taking the edge to atom-splitting sharpness.

You can use a leather belt, but better results come from a bench strop, which is honing leather mounted to a block of wood. Charge the strop with a thin film of honing compound made from either chromium oxide or diamond paste. Chromium oxide is a favorite of many, but if the blade is made of the newer, harder stainless steels, diamond paste may be required.

Lay the knife on the leather nearly flat. Draw the edge backwards along the leather strop. The leather will conform to the profile of the knife edge. Start with very light pressure and increase if needed. Start with a dozen strokes to each side of the blade.

Once the knife, is shaving-sharp, wipe the blade clean with a few drops of honing oil.

72 SHARPEN AN AXE

Before you begin, place your beat-up axe in a vise, with the head facing up. No vice? Use a stout C-clamp to secure it to the edge of a workbench with the edge just hanging over the table. Since you always push the file into the edge, never pulling it toward you, you'll need heavy gloves.

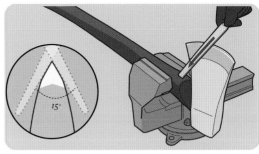

RESTORE THE PROFILE Hold the file and work it into the edge, maintaining the file at about 15 degrees. You want to work back into the axe head about 2 to 3 inches at the middle point of the bit, forming a clam-shaped effect on the cheek. When you can feel a burr on the backside of the blade, repeat the whole process on the other side.

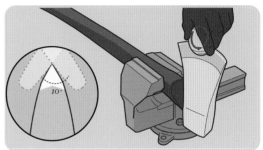

SHARPEN IT Put a primary bevel into the first bevel by filing again, this time at a 10-degree angle on both sides. Hone with a whetstone, coarse side, then the fine, moving a honing puck in small, circular motions.

73 GIVE YOUR KNIFE A SPA TREATMENT

Fixed-blades need only a quick wipe down with a damp cloth after each use and a light application of honing oil on the blade.

Folders and multitools collect blood and dirt at pivot points and locking mechanisms. If the tool has a plastic handle, immerse it in boiling water for one minute, then put it in a pot of warm water (so that quick cooling doesn't crack the handle). Scrub nooks and crannies with a toothbrush, working pivot points back and forth, then air-dry the knife before oiling. Use compressed air to blast out gunk.

Wipe away surface rust with an oily cloth or 0000 steel wool. Carbon blades naturally discolor with use. Bring them back to near original luster by rubbing with a cork dipped in cold wood ashes.

74

SHARPEN USING A SHARPIE

When sharpening a knife (or axe or hatchet), it can be difficult to know for certain that you are maintaining the proper angle, and sharpening the exact edge and not the "shoulder" of the bevel. One way to tell is to "paint" the edge with a Sharpie or other marker. Look closely after each few strokes. If the ink is removed at the very edge of the knife, then you are sharpening the edge. If the ink comes off on the shoulder, leaving color on the edge, your angle is to shallow. If all the ink is being removed, you're re-profiling the edge to match the original angle. It's a great way to monitor your progress.

75 TEST GEAR IN THE STORE

What can 5 minutes of serious study tell you about the gear you're about to buy? Plenty, if you take advantage of these in-store gear tests. Just ignore the stares of other shoppers, and think twice about buying from a store that won't let you put its products through these paces.

SLEEPING BAG Take off your shoes, spread the bag on a cot or the store floor, and climb in. Sit up in the bag and try to touch your toes. If it binds you, opt for a longer size. Next, lie back down. Zip the bag open and closed three times from the inside, and three times from the outside. If the zipper hangs up on the zipper tape or draft tube, keep looking.

BOOTS Shop in the late afternoon when your feet will have swollen up as much as they're going to over the course of a day. Be sure to wear the sock combination you prefer in the field. Put them on, and then lean forward slightly. Slide your index finger between your heel and the inside of the boot. There shouldn't be much more than a half-inch gap. Next, kick the wall. If your toes rub or bump the front of the boot, tie the laces a bit tighter, and try again. Still bumping? Keep shopping.

DAYPACK Load the proposed pack with a volume similar to a typical day's worth of hunting or fishing gear, stuff one more spare vest inside, and sling it on. Raise your arms overhead to make sure the sternum strap doesn't cut across your throat. Hip belts should ride on the hips, not above the navel. Rock your shoulders back and forth—if loose webbing flies around, you can be sure it will catch on branches.

FLASHLIGHT First make sure you can manipulate all settings while wearing gloves. Headlamps, in particular, tend to have small switches. Next, tape a piece of unlined white paper to the wall of the store's changing room or bathroom, and turn off the light (if possible). Look for a bright central spot beam with enough spill—light around the edges—to illuminate the sides of a trail. Dark spots and circles show on the paper? Grab a different light.

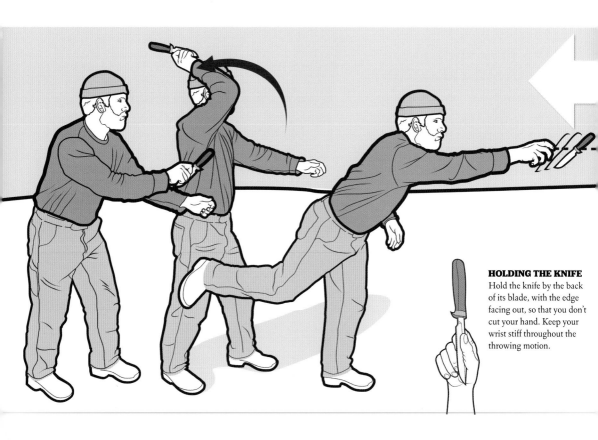

HOLDING THE KNIFE
Hold the knife by the back of its blade, with the edge facing out, so that you don't cut your hand. Keep your wrist stiff throughout the throwing motion.

76 SPLIT LOGS THE SMART WAY

Splitting firewood doesn't require the strength of an ogre. But whale away without a plan, and you will generate more body heat than campfire BTUs.

FORGET THE AXE Use a 6- to 8-pound maul, erring on the light side—velocity matters more than mass. Dulling the edge slightly prevents it from sticking in the wood. Set up a chopping block. Get a hard surface under the log. Otherwise the ground will absorb the blow.

THINK BEFORE YOU STRIKE Look for splits in the log that extend from the center outward, or other cracks in the end grain. Exploit these weaknesses first. Otherwise, aim your first blows toward the barked edge of the round. It's easier to extract the blade with a rocking motion if it's on the edge. Use your next blows to walk the split across the round.

AIM LOW Strike as if the first 3 or 4 inches of wood don't exist. Visualize the maul moving all the way through the wood. Make every swing count.

FIND THE DISTANCE WHERE THE KNIFE STICKS IN THE TARGET

77 THROW A KNIFE

Throwing a knife isn't difficult once you learn how to gauge the speed of rotation. Special throwing knives are unsharpened and have metal handles, but with practice—and caution—you can throw a hunting knife. Three tips: Keep your wrist stiff, use the same speed and motion for each throw, and step toward or away from the target until you find the distance where the rotation turns the knife point-first. Experts can accurately gauge up to seven rotations, but start with one and a half. This will result in a point-first direction with about a 4-yard throw.

78 SIPHON GAS THE SAFE WAY

This method relies on physics to work. You need 6 feet of clear tube, a clean container for the gas, and possibly something to stand on.

STEP 1 Run the hose into the gas tank until the end of it is submerged. Blow gently into the hose and listen for gurgling noises to know you've found the liquid.

STEP 2 Form a loop in the tubing with the bottom touching the ground and the end rising to a level higher than the gas in the tank. Here's where something to stand on helps.

STEP 3 As you gently suck on the hose, watch the gas move to the bottom of the loop and start to rise. Stop sucking at this point; the gas should now come to the level of gas in the tank on its own.

STEP 4 Stick the tube's free end into a container and then slowly lower it to the ground. When you have enough, raise the container to a level higher than the gas tank. Remove the hose from the container and straighten it so excess gas reenters the tank.

FIELD & STREAM-APPROVED KNOT

79 TWIST UP A CONSTRICTOR KNOT

Easy to tie and extremely reliable, the constrictor knot is one of the most useful knots on earth. It exerts a ratchetlike grip on any curved surface, such as a post, rail, tree, or human appendage. You can use it to close the mouths of food bags and gear bags large and small; make a whipping in string around the end of a larger rope, preventing the latter from fraying; secure a rod tube to a backpack; and fashion a string leash for your eyeglasses. Tie it around the snout of a bear after placing a hardwood stick through the jaws behind the fangs, and, with a noose over the nose and around the ends of the stick, you can tote the critter without ruffling its fur. To hang camp tools, file a rough groove in each tool's handle, tie a constrictor hitch around it, and then knot together the ends of the cord. The constrictor's virtues are, alas, also its only vice: It is not easily untied. Then again, it won't come undone accidentally, either.

STEP 1 Make a simple loop, crossing the working end of the rope over the other.

STEP 2 Circle the working end behind the item you're tying up then pass it under the standing end and under your "X."

STEP 3 Pull both ends to constrict.

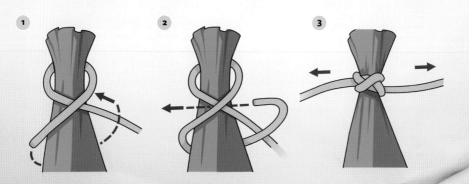

80

CLEAR A DOWNED TREE WITH A CHAIN SAW

Before attempting to buck a fallen tree, take time to figure out the binding pressures. Next, clear out any saplings or branches that the downed tree has fallen on; these can spring up forcefully when pressure is released. Stand on the uphill side of the tree and come prepared with a few plastic wedges to keep the chain-saw bar from binding.

TREE FLAT ON THE GROUND Cut from the top. Don't let the chain touch the ground, which dulls the blade and can send shrapnel flying. Cut partway through the log, then either roll it to continue or lever it up from the bottom and shim it with a piece of wood.

TREE SUPPORTED AT ONE END Make an initial cut from the bottom up, about one-third of the log's diameter. Finish with a second cut from the top down to meet the first.

TREE SUPPORTED AT BOTH ENDS Make the first cut from the top down. Watch for binding, use wedges if need be. Then cut from the bottom up.

81 MAKE WATERPROOF MATCHES

To make your own waterproof matches, use clear nail polish instead of paraffin wax. Nail polish is more durable and won't gunk up the match striker.

STEP 1 Fill a soft-drink bottle cap with nail polish (a).

STEP 2 Dip each match head into the polish (b) and then lay the match on the tabletop with its head extending off the edge (c). Repeat.

STEP 3 Once the polish has dried, hold each match by the head and dip the entire remaining wooden portion of the match into the nail polish bottle (d).

STEP 4 Place matches on wax paper to dry.

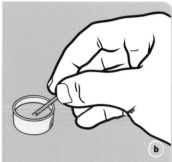

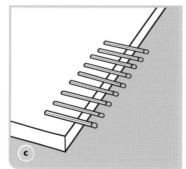

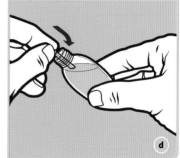

82 BREAK WIND LIKE A COMMANDO

The occasional bout of morning thunder is as much a part of deer camp as five-card stud. Foster a universally appreciated rip with a combination of nuance and nerve.

AMBUSH Approach your pals with detached nonchalance and let fly with a drive-by toot. Go easy on the volume and vacate the premises promptly.

CAMO JOB Get the wind moving. Ruffle papers, stand by a fan. Light a cigar.

BLAME GAME Don't draw attention to yourself. Try a slight turn of the head and a softly muttered oath, followed by a rhetorical "Someone need a little private time?"

JUST THE TWO OF US If you're stuck in a car or tent with just one pal, name it and claim it, buddy. Be loud. Be proud.

83 RE-WATERPROOF YOUR RAIN SHELL

Rain should roll off your shell in beads. If it doesn't, you need to restore the fabric's DWR, or durable water repellent, finish. Otherwise the outer fabric will "wet out" and prevent sweat vapor from passing through.

Wash with a mild powder detergent like Dreft, or a specialized outerwear formula such as Nikwax Tech Wash, and dry on medium setting. If water beads up, you're done. If not, iron the garment with a warm iron. Heat redistributes the DWR coating throughout the fabric. Still wetting through? Apply a new coating of spray-on DWR. Brands to consider: Nikwax and Granger's. Cabela's sells a cleaning kit with both detergent and DWR packaged together.

84 TRY BEFORE YOU BUY

What can 5 minutes of serious study tell you about the gear you're about to buy? Plenty. Just ignore the stares of other shoppers, and think twice about buying from a store that won't let you put their products through the ringer.

ⓐ SLEEPING BAG Roll the bag out on the floor, and climb in. Sit up and try to touch your toes. If you bind, opt for a longer size. Next, lie back down. Zip the bag open and closed three times from the inside, and three times from the outside. If the zipper hangs up, keep looking.

ⓑ BOOTS Shop in the late afternoon, when your feet are swollen. Wear the sock combination you prefer in the field. Lean forward and slide your index finger between heel and boot. There shouldn't be more than a $1/2$-inch gap. Next, kick the wall. If your toes hit the front of the boot, keep shopping.

ⓒ FLY ROD Wiggling a rod won't tell you much, so walk into the store with a reel loaded with your favorite line, with leader attached, and a few flies with the hook points snipped off. Ask if you can try a few casts in the parking lot, on a nearby lawn, or off the loading dock out back. They'll let you.

ⓓ BACKPACK Load it with a volume similar to a typical day's worth of hunting gear, stuff one more spare vest inside, and sling it on. Raise your arms overhead to make sure the sternum strap doesn't cut across your throat. The hip belt should ride on the hips, not above the navel. Test zippers for binding.

85 PACK A POOP TUBE

"Pack it in, pack it out." That's the leave-no-trace mantra of many wilderness areas, and it's not just talking about candy bar wrappers. Packing out your own poop is actually required in some backcountry regions, and it's not as gross as you think. The elegant solution, devised by big-wall climbers who spend days aloft, is called the Poop Tube.

STEP 1 Cut a length of 4-inch-diameter PVC pipe to size. For a three-day trip, 6 to 10 inches should suffice. Better too long than too short. This is irrefutable.

STEP 2 Glue a solid cap to one end of the tube, and a threaded fitting to the other. Attach a tether of parachute cord to the tube and a screw cap.

STEP 3 When duty calls, bring along a plastic grocery bag. Reach behind your back, grab one handle of the bag in each hand, pull the handles toward your hips, and get 'er done.

STEP 4 Tie the bag, then deposit into the Poop Tube.

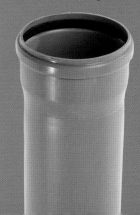

"If people concentrated on the really important things in life, there'd be no shortage of fishing poles."

—Doug Larson

The Allure of the Lure

The Ozark Puffball was born on a picnic table in Missouri, where photographer Colby Lysne and I sat drinking beer and licking our wounds after going nearly fishless at one of the premier trout parks in the country. All morning long, stocker trout had snubbed our dough baits, following them through slow riffles, eyeing them warily in the pools, but simply refusing to eat. We were stumped. We needed some kind of hack, some trigger to turn the trout's ho-hum interest into a committed bite. That's when we started mixing PowerBait with a powdered scent we found in a local bait shop. Enter the Puffball.

To work the Puffball's magic, I'd cast it down and across the stream current and watch the drift until a trout eyeballed the mutant wad but refused to eat. That's when I'd snap the rod tip, sending a pulse of energy down the line, which twitched the Puffball with just enough energy to release a brown stain of atomized bait stink into the stream. Like squid ink, sort of. Intrigued by the smelly fog, the fish would then spot the bright orange PowerBait emerging from the mist. Imagine waking up from a dream about Thanksgiving dinner to find a ham biscuit on your pillow. The wiliest trout couldn't resist.

That's what I love about fishing. You can follow every rule and catch fish, or break every rule just the right way and catch just as many. Every day is different. Every hour can change everything. Every species—every single fish—requires a specific set of actions and decisions designed to entice a fish to eat.

It shouldn't be all that complicated. Sometimes it isn't. But on a lot of days, it takes everything you've got—gear and smarts—to get a fish to open its mouth.

And then the real fun begins.

86 HAVE A MIDDAY QUICKIE

Most family therapists agree that an occasional midday quickie results in greater concentration on work tasks and overall happier relationships. But pulling off a successful lunch-break mini-fishing trip requires a bit of logistical foreplay and the proper tools. Here's the drill.

PLAN IN ADVANCE In addition to your rod and tackle, stash a few specific items in the backseat. Hip boots will pull up and over your chinos, keeping mud off your work pants. Waterless hand sanitizer is great for a quick cleanup behind the wheel during the frantic drive back to the office. A small pump bottle of spray fabric freshener will knock the fish-slime funk from your French cuffs, but a clean dress shirt could come in handy, as well.

BE EFFICIENT Know where you're headed as soon as your butt hits the car seat. A 20-minute drive to a bass pond still gives you 50 minutes of fishing time during a 90-minute lunch break, which you should be able to pull off every now and then. Figure on high-percentage casts: frothy buzzbaits that get a bass's attention, or weedless worms that won't hang up in brush.

STAY SUBTLE Keep your itinerary on the down low. Bosses that look the other way at a three-pint lunch might go ballistic if they knew you'd punched out for the perch pond.

87 MASTER THE PALOMAR KNOT

The Palomar is crazy strong and a cinch to tie in the dark. Thread a 6-inch loop of line through the hook eye (1), and tie a loose overhand knot so the hook dangles down from the middle (2). Slip the loop formed by this overhand knot over the hook (3). Moisten loops and pull both the tag and standing ends together, making sure that the finished knot rests against the hook eye.

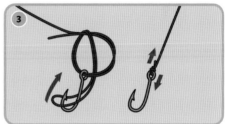

88 BE A 21ST-CENTURY ANGLER

When buying a fishing vest, I would caution you against buying one with too many pockets. I've seen some anglers wearing one of the modern vests that have so many pockets that I'm afraid if they fell down, they would be unable to get up without assistance. The more pockets you have, the more you are tempted to fill them up. Soon you have enough fly boxes and other equipment slung on your upper body that you could open a fly shop right on the stream. In addition, at the end of the day, carrying all that stuff, most of which you did not need, will add to your fatigue.

CATCH KILLER BROWNS

Just about every trout stream has them—huge, predatory brown trout that fishermen rarely see and hardly ever catch. Few fishermen are as dialed in to the nuances of catching large brown trout as Michigan guide Ray Schmidt. For 45 years, Schmidt has been chasing browns in the waters where the species was initially introduced to the United States. Schmidt's biggest Michigan brown is a 26-inch, taken on a streamer at night next to a logjam. Schmidt says that most anglers have no clue what really lurks below the surface of their favorite trout stream. At the right time—usually night—that gentle, meandering river can radically transform into a veritable "killing field" for predatory browns. "These large browns sometimes go on the hunt for food, traveling a mile or two each night in search of prey," says Schmidt. "This is a predator that eats mice, baby ducks, and other creatures in, on, or around the water." In other words, if you want to catch large, you have to fish large, and usually in low-light conditions.

Summer is a particularly opportune time to fish for big nighttime browns. The warm water increases trout metabolism, meaning they must eat more. And these big predators will go on the hunt when the waters cool down at night.

1 SHUN THE RIFFLE

Sure, riffles typically hold trout—rainbows. When you're stalking big browns, you want to avoid the water where smaller fish will seize the opportunity to take your bait or fly. If you're looking for a trophy brown, they're distractions.

2 SCOUT AND LISTEN

Some of your most productive time may be spent on a high bank. Learn to recognize the sound that a brown trout makes as it gulps something from the surface. And watch for subtle disturbances in current lines.

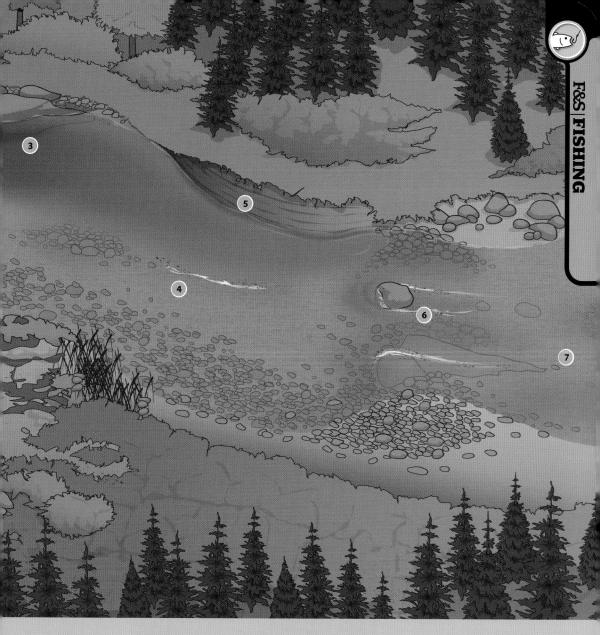

3 FIND THE LION'S DEN

Large brown trout thrive in river runs with three ingredients: depth, cover, and slow and steady current. Find the spot in the river where currents and obstructions have scoured a deep hole.

4 FOLLOW THE BUBBLES

Look for seams where fast currents meet slow or where deep water meets shallow currents. Cast into the bubble line created on the surface. Memorize these locations and fish them at night.

5 CASE THE BANK

Big browns will often lurk in the shadows of undercut banks, where they are protected from their predators but can easily dart out and inhale a baitfish or a grasshopper. Fish tight to the bank to catch them.

6 TARGET THE CUSHION

Large browns frequently ride the hydraulics in front of a large rock or tree stump in the river. You want to cast both in front of that rock or stump and into the deep scour behind it.

7 FISH MARGINAL WATER

The biggest browns are hardy fish that can thrive in waters often overlooked by most trout anglers. Don't hesitate to fish downstream from the "prime" section of your favorite trout river.

90 WIN THE TOUGHEST FISH FIGHT

Occasionally, when it all comes together, a true behemoth will suck in your lure. What you do next is the difference between glory and another "almost" story.

KNOW YOUR KNOT WILL HOLD Most big fish are lost due to failed knots. Wet each knot with saliva before cinching it tight, and make sure you seat it properly. If you are less than 100 percent confident in the knot you just tied, take the time to retie it. Every time.

CLEAR THE COVER Bruiser fish will quickly burrow into weeds or head for a snag, so establish authority as soon as you set the hook. Resist the temptation to hoot, holler, and point. Put pressure on immediately and keep your rod tip up. Don't force the action but steer the fish into the clear.

TURN AND BURN Once the fish is in open water, let it wear down. As the fish moves, bend the rod away from the direction in which it's swimming and lower the rod to tighten the angle. Don't winch it; you simply want to turn the head and guide the fish in a different direction, burning energy all the way.

DON'T CHOKE The few seconds after your first boat-side glimpse of a bona fide monster are critical. If you can see him, he can see you. Prepare for a last-ditch escape maneuver. Be ready to jab the rod tip into the water if the fish dives under the boat. Don't grab the line. Stay focused on keeping the fish off-balance until he's in the boat. If you're using a net, make sure you lead the fish in headfirst.

91 TIE A CLOVE HITCH

The clove hitch is Boating 101—good for a temporary stay to dock or piling.

It's also the foundational knot for many pole-lashing techniques, which may be useful if you don't tie it correctly the first time, your boat drifts away, and you have to lash a long pole together to snag it back. —T.E.N.

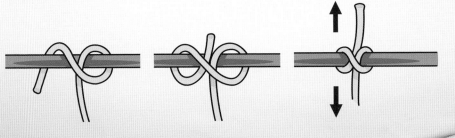

92 LAY YOUR HANDS ON A RIVER MONSTER

There are a number of ways to get your hands on a really big catfish. Noodling expert Gerald Moore places casket-shaped catfish boxes—with a hole the size of a football in one end—in chest-deep water.

On the other hand, some hand-grabbers seed their favorite waters with old water heaters modified for fish. After a few months, a three-person team returns to the box and takes the following steps.

STEP 1 The "checker" blocks the hole with his feet and checks for a fish with a 7-foot pole.

STEP 2 A "helper" stands on the box and helps to steady the checker. Meanwhile, the "grabber" goes underwater and sticks his right arm in the box, up to the elbow to grab the fish.

STEP 3 If the fish bites, he will get all four fingers in the pocket behind its teeth, with his thumb on the outside, then pull it out and wrap it with his left arm.

93 FLY CAST FROM A KAYAK

Casting from a kayak will test the skills of even the best fly angler. Here's how to modify your style for the confines of a sit-on-top.

MIND YOUR LINE The tall sides of a traditional stripping basket don't cut it when you're casting from a seated position, but you need something to keep your fly line from tangling. A cheap 9 x 11-inch baking pan works as a makeshift stripping basket.

OVERLINE YOUR ROD Using a line weight one step up from the weight of a fly rod will add distance and cut down on false casts.

CUSTOMIZE YOUR CAST Keep your back cast out of the water. To begin, hold your rod arm farther in front of your body than normal to move the power stroke forward of the stopping position on the back cast. Start with the rod tip low and with zero slack in the line, accelerate smoothly, and stop the back cast a bit higher than normal.

94 PLANT A CRAPPIE TREE

Crappies crave structure, and a PVC tree will attract slabs to the most barren lake bottom. The slick pipes keep hangups to a minimum, and the PVC will last.

THE TRUNK Drill a small hole through one end of a 4-inch-diameter PVC pipe. (The pipe length depends somewhat on the depth of its final destination. A 4- to 5-foot tree works well.) Next, drill three ¾-inch holes along each side of the pipe "trunk" at angles so the "branches" will angle upward and shed hooks easily. Insert a long nail into the small hole you drilled at the bottom of the trunk and anchor it in a 3-gallon flowerpot with concrete.

THE BRANCHES Cut six 3-foot lengths of ¾-inch PVC pipe for your branches. Drill a small hole through the end of two of these. Insert the PVC branches into the holes in the trunk, securing them with PVC glue.

To attract crappies, fill two empty 20-ounce water bottles—punched with small holes—with dry dog food and cap the bottles tightly. Tie these to the branches that have the small holes.

PVC may not register on many fish finders, so mark your tree's location on your GPS.

The right canoe is the one that can handle the conditions you'll most likely encounter and haul your stuff while allowing you to cast, plunge over a 3-foot ledge, or stay straight out on open water. Here's a guide to features to consider in a fishing canoe.

HULL MATERIAL Forget aluminum. For a tough, sturdy, maintenance-free craft, there are two choices: cheaper (and heavier and also more susceptible to sun damage) rotomolded polyethylene or the old proven Royalex laminate. If you want to get to where you want to be fast, and there are no rocks in the way, consider a fiberglass hull or a more modern composite such as those including Kevlar. These are the lightest canoes ever made—a 16-footer can tip the scales at less than 45 pounds—but they are expensive.

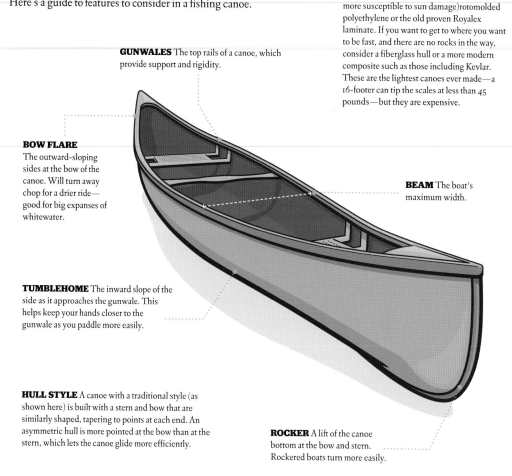

GUNWALES The top rails of a canoe, which provide support and rigidity.

BOW FLARE The outward-sloping sides at the bow of the canoe. Will turn away chop for a drier ride— good for big expanses of whitewater.

BEAM The boat's maximum width.

TUMBLEHOME The inward slope of the side as it approaches the gunwale. This helps keep your hands closer to the gunwale as you paddle more easily.

HULL STYLE A canoe with a traditional style (as shown here) is built with a stern and bow that are similarly shaped, tapering to points at each end. An asymmetric hull is more pointed at the bow than at the stern, which lets the canoe glide more efficiently.

ROCKER A lift of the canoe bottom at the bow and stern. Rockered boats turn more easily.

THE BOTTOM LINE If you're canoeing out in quiet waters, beamy, rockerless boats are stable enough so you can stand up and cast, and they swallow minnow buckets, tackleboxes, spare rods, and a couple of kids with ease. Crank up the paddling conditions, however, and you'll need more technical goodies. For big-lake fishing with wind and waves, a deeper bow and a more pronounced bow flare will turn away wind-blown chop. If getting to big fish requires finessing through Class III whitewater, you'll definitely want a boat with rocker and a good Royalex layup. No matter the water, a bit of tumblehome makes it easier to land fish over the side.

96 PULL OFF A CHEAP CANOE-CAMP TRIP

It's late spring and the dogwoods have bloomed. The first quail chicks are in the nest. Nothing could be finer. The water is warm enough for a quick dip, the nights still cool enough for a fire. Every element of the natural world is begging with you, pleading with you: Put a paddle in your hand, now.

You're not going to find an easier getaway. In a three-day canoe-camping trip, you might spend 75 bucks if you really try. There's a 90 percent chance that you'll find a canoe-camping river within 20 miles of your garage, and it's a good bet that the gear and food you need are in your gear closet and refrigerator right this very minute.

KEEP IT SIMPLE Grab twenty bucks for gas (maybe $25 tops), another $10 for live bait from the gas station. Pack half the clothes you think you should, because you'll only wear shorts. Bring two rods: a good spinning outfit and a 7-weight fly rod that's light enough to make panfishing fun and heavy enough to handle a middling-size river monster. You'll want simple lures that you can lose in heavy timber—in-line spinners are a good bet—and hooks and sinkers for live-bait rigs. River fish are willing, so pack half the food you think you'll need, and eat what you catch. (Don't scrimp on the frying pan, though. Bring the big one.) Pack a tarp and leave the tent. Stow an extra paddle. Drag live baits along the bottom of the deep scour holes you find on the outside of river bends, and fire those spinners at every blowdown, rock pile, and current seam you pass.

SET ASIDE $40 FOR GROCERIES Make a list on the fingers of one hand. Eggs, bacon, oil, fish batter, and beer. Grab a loaf of bread from the cupboard and rake all the leftover lunch meat into a cooler. Fill some jugs with water. Leave a note for your spouse and food for the dog. Cut the grass so the neighbors won't talk. Go now, right now, before the phone has a chance to ring.

Pared down to the basics, every moment on a river is seasoned with the memory of the moment just before, and the promise of the next river bend, and the next cast, the next shooting star that streaks across the sky and brings a grin to your face when you think of your best wish ever: next weekend, spent just like this.

Working a river from a canoe, especially one loaded with gear, requires different skills than shore fishing. These tactics will help you succeed.

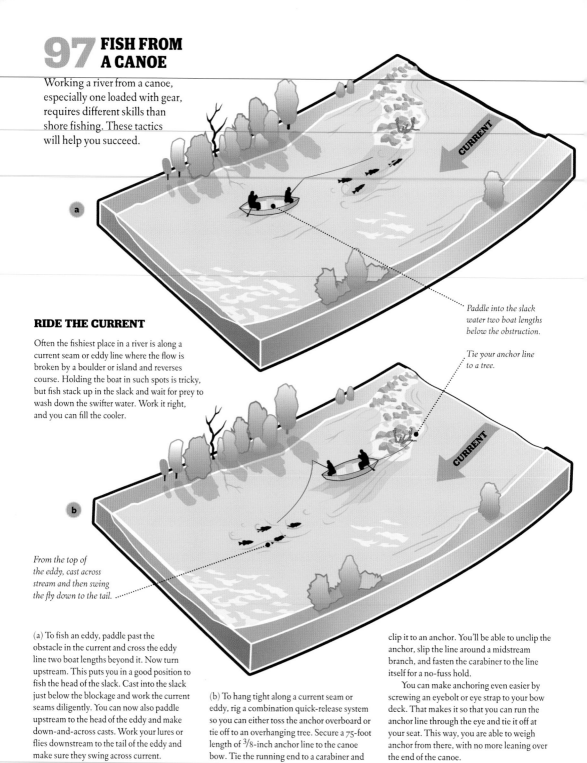

Paddle into the slack water two boat lengths below the obstruction.

Tie your anchor line to a tree.

RIDE THE CURRENT

Often the fishiest place in a river is along a current seam or eddy line where the flow is broken by a boulder or island and reverses course. Holding the boat in such spots is tricky, but fish stack up in the slack and wait for prey to wash down the swifter water. Work it right, and you can fill the cooler.

From the top of the eddy, cast across stream and then swing the fly down to the tail.

(a) To fish an eddy, paddle past the obstacle in the current and cross the eddy line two boat lengths beyond it. Now turn upstream. This puts you in a good position to fish the head of the slack. Cast into the slack just below the blockage and work the current seams diligently. You can now also paddle upstream to the head of the eddy and make down-and-across casts. Work your lures or flies downstream to the tail of the eddy and make sure they swing across current.

(b) To hang tight along a current seam or eddy, rig a combination quick-release system so you can either toss the anchor overboard or tie off to an overhanging tree. Secure a 75-foot length of 3/8-inch anchor line to the canoe bow. Tie the running end to a carabiner and clip it to an anchor. You'll be able to unclip the anchor, slip the line around a midstream branch, and fasten the carabiner to the line itself for a no-fuss hold.

You can make anchoring even easier by screwing an eyebolt or eye strap to your bow deck. That makes it so that you can run the anchor line through the eye and tie it off at your seat. This way, you are able to weigh anchor from there, with no more leaning over the end of the canoe.

DRIFT AND DREDGE

A drifting canoe is a superb platform from which to dredge deep water. You're covering fresh structure constantly and moving at the same speed as the river lets your lures—especially sinking flies—probe deeper down in the water column. Cast straight across the current for the deepest drifts, or slightly downstream so the lure swings across the current and then turns toward the boat. Fish often strike right when the lure changes direction.

To slow your drift, turn the canoe around and float backward. You and your buddy should take turns fishing because the stern paddler has to control the speed with occasional paddle strokes. This is a great way to fish long pools. Another option is to rig a "drag chain." Attach a length of heavy chain to your anchor rope—remove the anchor first, of course—and drag it behind the boat. Covering the chain with a bicycle-tire inner tube dampens the noise from any contact with the hull and bottom.

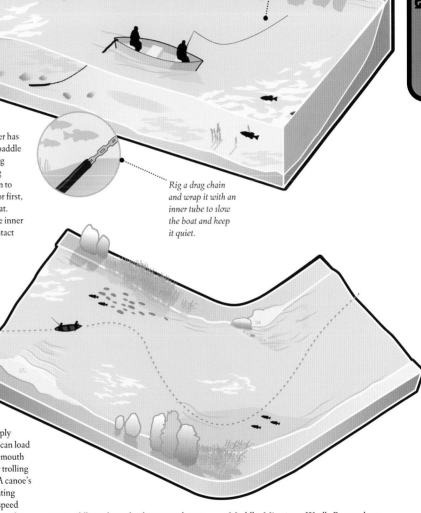

CURRENT

Cast just downstream, working the lure across the current.

Rig a drag chain and wrap it with an inner tube to slow the boat and keep it quiet.

Troll in zigzags, bringing lures past weedbeds and deep runs.

PADDLE TROLL

Why waste all that paddle power simply getting from point A to point B? You can load up on pike, lake trout, walleyes, largemouth and smallmouth bass, and panfish by trolling streamers and plugs behind canoes. A canoe's typical pace seems designed for imitating baitfish, and the inconsistent rate of speed keeps your lure moving up and down in the water column—a strike-inducing action.

To troll a floating or floater-diver plug, attach a few split shot to the line 2 feet ahead of the plug. Or work a shallow-running crankbait over beds of submerged vegetation. Run 100 to 150 feet of line behind the canoe and vary

your paddle strokes to lend a stop-and-start action to the plug.

Trolling streamers and wet flies for rainbow and brook trout is a classic lake tactic, but you can also effectively apply the same set of steps to rivers. Use an intermediate or sinking fly line to put a

Muddler Minnow or Woolly Bugger down deep. Trolling through long, apparently unproductive stretches will ensure that you leave no structure unfished. Paddle from bank to bank and back again to find where fish are holding. No, it's not really flyfishing. But the fish sure taste good even so.

98

TIE THIS FLY IF IT'S THE LAST THING YOU DO

The Clouser Minnow has joined the likes of Woolly Buggers and Muddlers as a global standard among fly patterns. Unlike the others, though, Clousers are easily made by novice fly-tying fishermen. The fly's jigging action works great for everything from crappies and brown trout to striped bass and redfish (Lefty Kreh has landed 86 different species on it). Vary the fly size and color to suit your quarry.

For this example, you'll need a medium-shank-length streamer hook, some nylon or polyester size 3/0 thread, some dumbbell-style eyes, natural white plus dyed chartreuse bucktail, and some Flashabou or similar material. Use clear nail polish as a fly-tying cement. Here's how to put it all together.

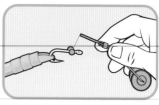

STEP 1 With the hook in a tying vise, secure the thread one-third of the shank length back from the hook eye. Tie dumbbell eyes securely on top of the shank with figure-eight thread wraps. Add a small dab of cement to the wraps.

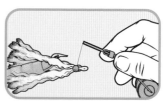

STEP 2 Tie in a sparse bunch of white bucktail behind the hook eye and in front of the eyes. Wind the thread to a position right behind the eyes. Pull the white bucktail firmly into the groove between the eyes, and tie it down again right behind the eyes.

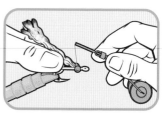

STEP 3 Turn the hook over in the vise so that the hook point is up. Add about six strands of Flashabou or a similar material.

STEP 4 Tie in a bunch of chartreuse bucktail, and build a neat conical head with thread wraps, finishing with two half hitches. Coat the finished fly head with nail polish (two coats).

99 PADDLE A CANOE INTO A GALE

The right way seems wrong: Trim the canoe slightly bow heavy to keep it heading into the wind. Kneel in the bottom of the boat and use short, quick strokes. Feather the paddle on your return stroke, turning the blade parallel to the water surface so it won't catch the wind. Keep the boat pointed into the waves and use every bit of windbreak possible—even distant land points can provide relief from wind and swell.

100 SET ANY ANCHOR, ANYTIME

Head upwind or upcurrent and then lower the anchor all the way to the bottom. Anchors grab best when they first lie down. Reverse the engine and slowly back away to a distance of 7 to 10 times the depth of the water.

fluke hooks for sandy coastal waters

mushrooms for lakes

river anchors for moving water

101 DRESS A FLY CORRECTLY

It's easy to destroy a fly's profile by smashing and grinding in floatant. Here's the lowdown on the correct way to make your fly float.

Grasp the hook point between your thumb and index finger. Place one drop of floatant directly on the top of the hackle fibers. Instead of applying the floatant to your fingers and then working it into the fly, use a finger on your other hand to flick the floatant into the fly materials.

102 STROKE LIKE A PRO

These four paddle strokes will get you there and back with efficient style,
whether you are headed to fish camp or trying to line up the perfect cast.

	J-STROKE	DRAW	PRY	LOW BRACE
WHY	To keep the canoe moving in a straight line.	To move the canoe toward the paddler.	To move the canoe away from the paddler.	To stabilize a tilting boat.
HOW	As the paddle approaches your seat, turn the thumb of your top hand away from your body. At the end of the stroke, point your thumb straight down, and pry the blade slightly.	Keeping your top hand as high as possible, extend the blade as far from the canoe as you can. Draw the blade through the water in a short, powerful, inward stroke.	Turn the blade parallel to the gunwale and slide it into the water so that the blade is under the canoe. Pry the paddle blade at an angle perpendicular to the boat.	Reach out with the paddle horizontal and perpendicular to the water, both hands below your chest. Smack the water and push down quickly and powerfully.

103 USE THE MIRACLE OF MINICELL FOAM

Everyone knows about the multiple and miraculous uses of duct tape. Fewer know about an equally useful material: minicell foam. Used by experienced canoers and kayakers to build pedestal seats and pad brace points for their knees and thighs, minicell foam is inexpensive, incredibly lightweight, absorbs little water, and glues well in both wet and dry applications. Available at specialty paddling shops, it comes in sheets from ¼ to 2 inches thick. I go through the stuff like water.

- Line boat rod tubes with a cylinder of foam to protect guides and graphite.

- Keep a square in your truck for a dry, cushy surface to stand on while changing into waders or hippers.

- Carry a square for a quiet, dry seat at the base of a tree.

- Cut out insulating boot insoles.

- Wrap vacuum bottles for better insulation.

- Make handy fly patches by wrapping boat rails with strips of foam, or glue small squares to boat sides or consoles.

- Pad boat seats.

- Cut a sheet of minicell the size and shape of a cooler, and place it on top of the cooler's contents before shutting the top. The "cooler gasket" will dramatically lengthen the life of the ice.

- Glue together a cylinder and bottom for an inexpensive, lightweight case for electronics you stash in a tackle bag.

104 WEAVE A CANOE SEAT WITH DUCT TAPE

I blew out the cane seat on my canoe 8 years ago and put together a duct-tape field fix that I figured would hold up till I got home . . . did I mention that was 8 years ago? The seat is still as comfortable as ever, drains rain and splash, and scores admiring looks from other duct-tape junkies. I know you can also do this with nylon webbing and a staple gun. But why would you?

STEP 1 Remove the old cane or nylon webbing. Nylon webbing is held in place with removable screws. Cane is most commonly held in a groove cut into the frame and pinned with a wood strip, much like a door screen. To remove cane, pry the strip out. Clean the seat frame with warm water and a mild detergent, and let dry.

STEP 2 Run a band of duct tape four layers thick vertically across each end of the seat frame. Take care to avoid wrinkles.

STEP 3 Wrap a four-layer-thick duct tape band horizontally around the bottom of the seat frame, leaving a half-inch gap between the tape and the frame edge. Next, alternate with vertical and horizontal bands until the seat frame is filled.

STEP 4 Maintenance is critical. Apply sunlight, butt sweat, and fish slime regularly.

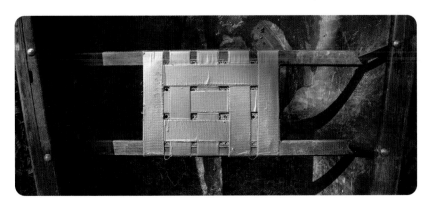

105 ROCK A BENT-SHAFT PADDLE

At first I felt a bit dorky using a bent-shaft canoe paddle, like I came off as some efficiency freak who analyzes mathematical power functions for fun. But a bendy lets me paddle farther, faster, and easier, and also saves my shoulders for tasks like pounding bass bugs into a summer breeze hour after hour. Now I won't paddle without a bent-shaft paddle, and I've shipped my favorite paddles to waters as distant as Alaska and Labrador.

There's no denying the oomph it puts in my stroke, especially in slack water. A bent-shaft paddle gives you a longer sweet spot at the peak place for energy transfer—right as you muscle the blade past your hip. And a bendy won't push as much water upward as you sweep it out of the river.

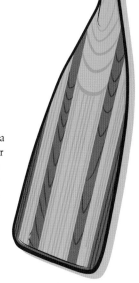

106 TOTE YOUR OWN BOAT (LIKE YOU HAVE A TITANIUM SPINE)

It doesn't take Herculean strength to hoist an 80-pound canoe onto your shoulders for a solo carry. The trick is to roll the canoe up your thighs first, then perform a bit of carefully timed clean and jerk to use momentum to lift the boat above your head. It's easy once you know how to do it—and incredibly impressive to perform in front of a crowd.

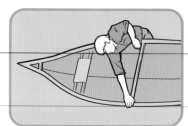

STEP 1 Face the canoe amidships and turn it so that it stands on the gunwale, the bottom resting against your knees. Bend your knees and roll the canoe up on your thighs, with your right hand grasping the far gunwale right at the center thwart and the left hand gripping the near gunwale. Stop and take a breath.

STEP 2 Rock slightly backward two or three times and, on the last rocking motion, push the canoe up and over your head, using both your thighs and your arms.

As your right elbow crosses your face, push with your left arm, straighten your bent legs, and lean back slightly to balance the weight.

STEP 3 When the outside gunwale rises above eye level, lower your head slightly and twist your body to the right. At the same time, push the outside gunwale upward. Now lower the canoe gently with the center thwart resting on the back of your neck. Move your hands slightly forward on the gunwales to fine-tune balance.

107 SHOOT A FLY

If it's hunting season, then it must be time to start thinking about fishing—especially if you like to tie your own flies or bucktail jigs. Many commonly (and not so commonly) hunted birds and animals can and will provide prime fly-tying materials, as long as you know what to clip, pluck, or cut, and how to store and maintain the stuff. To preserve hides, you simply need to salt the patch of fur you wish to keep. If you're saving bird feathers, store them in a zippered plastic bag or screw-top jar. To keep matched feathers from curling or getting smashed, tape the quills together, and you'll have a perfect pair for streamer tails.

The most common natural material for lures is the tail of a whitetail deer. Here's the 4-1-1 on preparation.

STEP 1 Before you convert a whitetail's white tail into jigs or streamers, there's some prep work you'll need to do. Start by skinning the tail. First, split the underside with a fillet knife to within a few inches of the tip. Then peel back the skin, wrap the tailbone with burlap, grasp it firmly, and pull the bone free. Continue the incision to the tip of the tail and scrape away all flesh and fat. Rub with salt or borax and freeze.

STEP 2 To dye the hairs, soak the tail overnight in water and dishwashing detergent, rinse, and dry completely. Mix a solution of sugar-free powdered drink mix (such as Kool-Aid™), water, and vinegar at a ratio of 2 ounces vinegar to 1 cup water. Pour this into a glass jar and submerge the tail. Place the jar in a larger pot of gently boiling water for 20 minutes to an hour or more. Check often for color. Remove the tail, blot, and tack to a piece of plywood to dry.

ANIMAL	FLY MATERIAL	FLY PATTERN
Elk	Bull body hair	*Elk Hair Caddis and parachute wings*
Whitetail deer	Bucktail, natural or dyed	*Body and wings for Clouser and Deceiver patterns; tails for bucktail jigs*
Rabbit	Fur strips	*Leech, Rabbit Candy patterns; guard hairs for white streamer throats*
Gray squirrel	Tail hairs	*Dry-fly tails and wings, crayfish legs*
Red squirrel	Red, black, and gray tail fur	*Collar on tarpon streamers*
Wild turkey	Secondary wing quills	*Wings for caddis, hopper, and Atlantic salmon patterns*
Wood duck	Barred body feathers	*Classic streamer patterns, tails on dry emergers*
Ringneck pheasant	Rooster tails	*Knotted grasshopper legs*
Sharptail grouse	Body feathers	*Pheasant Tail Nymph tails*
Ruffed grouse	Neck feathers	*Patterned body on tarpon flies*
Hungarian partridge	Neck and body feathers	*Hackles for wet flies*

108 BUMP BAITS OFF AN UNDERWATER CLIFF

Contour trolling is deadly. Walleyes herd baitfish against sharp dropoffs and walls and then cruise the breaks for targets. Approach these sharp breaks with your boat. As soon as the bottom starts coming up, turn away at a 30- to 45-degree angle. Your baits will still be swinging into the breaks as you turn, and they'll actually dig right into the wall, drag for a few seconds, and then drop out of the sand or rock and dart away. Wham! Many times that erratic action will trigger a bite you'd never get otherwise.

109 MISS A RAFT-EATING BOULDER

When you're dealing with long cumbersome oars and a craft that has all the maneuverability of a 14-foot-long wet pillow, oaring a raft doesn't come naturally. Here's how to manhandle these river monsters.

SETUP Sit just aft of center so the oars are centered in the middle of the raft for maximum pivot power. Adjust the length of the oars by starting with 4 inches of space between the handles.

COILED SPRING A proper oar stroke is part leg press, part upper-body row. Stay compact and don't overextend your body or arms. Reach too far with the oars and you lose control.

A GOOD DEFENSE A back-ferry stroke is the rafter's best move. [1] To skirt a rock or obstacle, use oars to swing the bow at a 45-degree angle to the obstacle and back-row. [2] Now fine-tune raft placement by pushing with one oar (a) and pulling on the other (b) to realign the boat, then slip by the rock in the current.

110 CAST WITHOUT DRAG

There's a step-by-step process to master the short, accurate slack-line cast. First, choose the target, be it a rising fish or a rock. Too many people skip this part, and the game is over. Account for current speed and drag and guesstimate the exact spot where you want the fly to land. Second, as you cast, carry 2 to 3 feet of extra slack in your line hand. When you carry through that final forward stroke, aim precisely at your target spot. As the fly reaches the target, release the slack line, and, when the line straightens out, check the rod tip abruptly. That will cause the line to recoil and drop in a series of S-curves that will defeat drag.

111 THROW A CAST NET

Despite its reputation, throwing a cast net requires neither voodoo nor the gyrations of a matador. These simple steps are the stripped-down basics, good for nets up to 6 feet wide, which should cover most freshwater needs.

STEP 1 Cinch the rope around your right wrist and coil all the rope in the palm of your right hand. Hold the top of the net with your right hand, with a few inches of gathered net sticking out from the bottom of your fist. Hold your right hand at waist height.

STEP 2 With your left hand, reach down and grab a lead weight; it should be the one that's hanging as close to directly below your right thumb as possible. Bring it up to your right hand and grasp it between your thumb and index finger. Pick up another weight that's an arm's length from the first. Hold this between your left thumb and index finger.

STEP 3 Next, point your feet toward the water; rotate your upper body to the right; and in one swift, smooth motion, swing your right arm out at a slightly upward angle. Release your right hand first and then your left. The net should open into a circular shape and drop.

112 SCALE FISH WITH BOTTLE CAPS

Do you drink beer from a bottle? Can you scrounge up a piece of wood about 6 inches long? Do you have two screws and a screwdriver? If so, you can assemble this handy-dandy fish scaler.

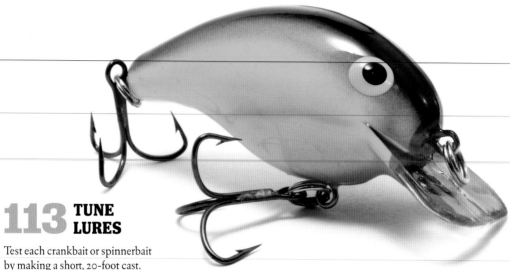

113 TUNE LURES

Test each crankbait or spinnerbait by making a short, 20-foot cast. Hold your rod tip straight up, and reel. A lure that runs more than 5 or 6 inches off to one side needs tuning. To tune a crankbait, replace bent split rings. Straighten out hook hangers with needle-nose pliers. If all appears fine, hold it so that the lip faces you and use light pressure to bend the line tie in the direction you want the lure to run.

Retest. Repeat until you're satisfied. For a spinnerbait, hold it with the line tie pointing at you. Look straight down the top wire; it should be situated directly over the hook and aligned with the shank. If not, bend it into place. If the spinnerbait rolls left or right during the retrieve, bend the top wire in the opposite direction.

114 TIE A BLOOD KNOT

Join the tippet to the leader with this classic flyfishing knot.

STEP 1 Cross the tag ends of the lines, and leave 6 to 8 inches overlapping. Hold where the lines cross, and wrap one tag end around the other standing line four to six times.

STEP 2 Repeat with the other line, and bring the tag ends through the gap between the wraps, making sure to go in opposite directions.

STEP 3 Pull the lines, moisten, and draw the knot tight.

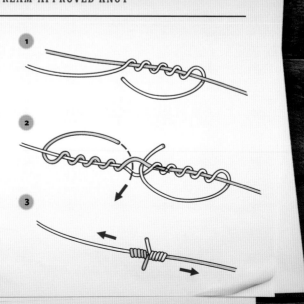

115 CATCH A CAT WITH PANTYHOSE

Dough balls are notoriously difficult to keep on a hook. Here's a way to solve this problem. Make dough balls by mixing bloody hamburger and flour, liver and dough, or hot water and cornmeal mixed with licorice and sugar. Toss one into the toe of a pantyhose leg and tie it off with a piece of dental floss snugged next to the dough ball. Now tie another piece of dental floss next to the first knot; snip the hose between the knots. Turn the remainder inside out. You'll have an encased hunk of catfish bait, and the pantyhose is ready for you to make some more.

116 STICK IT TO SHORT-STRIKING FISH

Steelhead regularly short-strike, one of the many reasons these fish drive anglers crazy. Teach nimble-lipped steelies a lesson with a trailer-hook streamer pattern, tied with bunny strips, Flashabou, and other materials. Easy to tie, it's a great fly for largemouth and striped bass, pike, and other fish with a big appetite. (Check local laws for multiple-hook regulations.)

STEP 1 Make a loop with approximately 5 inches of 20-pound Dacron backing. When the fly is completed, the tail materials should not extend past the trailer hook, so decide now how long the fly will be. Thread the loop through the eye of an octopus hook for drop-shot rigs, with an upturned eye.

STEP 2 Lay the two tag ends of the Dacron loop along opposite sides of the shank of the fly-pattern hook. Next, rotate the loop so the dropper hook point rides up. Apply drops of a super glue or epoxy to secure the loop to the hook shank. Wrap very tightly with thread.

STEP 3 Build up the body of the fly in whatever pattern you choose.

117 AVOID SINKING YOUR BOAT IN HEAVY WATER

Some lakes dish up big, nasty rollers day after day, but just about any lake can throw up bruising water in the right—or wrong—wind.

You don't want to pound through endless 4-footers in an 18-foot boat, so tack across the rollers as long as they're not breaking. As the roller approaches, run down the trough parallel to the crest, as far as you can or need to, and slide over the crest into the trough behind it. Then turn the bow straight into the swell and ride up and down the rough spots until you need a break. It's slower going, but it's better than getting beat up for miles.

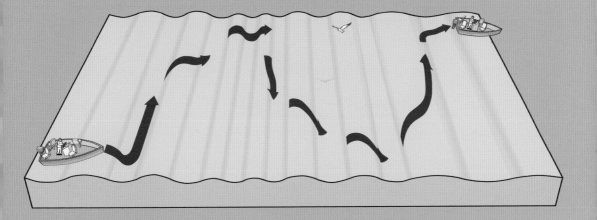

At the most basic level, a fishing reel is simply a device used to store, deploy, and retrieve fishing line. But in the hands of a skilled angler, a strong, well-designed reel is a tool used at every step in the quest to catch a fish. It helps vary the speed and action of the lure, lets a light-biting fish take the bait without a hint of your presence, halts the strongest drag-screaming run, and controls the line when the fish is just about in hand. Here are the three most common reel types. To know them is to love to put them to hard use.

REEL FOOT Slides into mounting slots of the rod's reel seat.

SPINNING REEL

Spinning reels have fixed spools that do not rotate—the line uncoils from the front of the spool, pulled by the weight of the lure. Since the cast lure doesn't need to have enough force to spin a rotating spool, spinning reels can utilize very light lures—ultralight spinning reels can handle lures as feathery as $\frac{1}{32}$ of an ounce—and backlash is rarely an issue. The downside to spinning reels: stopping a cast isn't a straightforward task. And spinning reels are notorious for twisting line. It's best to pump the rod up and reel on the way down to minimize twist.

BAIL Serves as a line pickup device to return the line evenly on the spool after the cast.

DRAG ADJUSTMENT KNOB The drag is a system of friction washers and discs. Front-mounted drags are typically stronger than rear-mounted drags.

SPOOL Holds the fishing line. A skirted spool covers the main reel shaft like a skirt to prevent line entanglement.

GEAR HOUSING Protects the internal gears that connect the handle to the spool.

ANTI-REVERSE LEVER Prevents the reel handle from turning as line is playing out.

HANDLE Activates the gears to retrieve line. Spinning reels come in a wide range of gear ratios, which is the number of spool revolutions to the number of gear handle revolutions. High-speed retrieve reels have gear ratios in the 4:1 class or higher. Lower gear ratios support more cranking power.

SPOOL Holds the fishing line.

STAR DRAG
Adjusts tension on a stacked series of washers and brake linings that make up the reel's internal drag.

LEVEL-WIND GUIDE
Attached to a worm gear, this device moves the line back and forth across the face of the spool evenly to prevent line from getting trapped under itself.

SPOOL TENSIONER Is a braking device to reduce spool overrun and resultant "bird's nest" line snarls.

POWERHUMP GRIP

BAITCASTING REEL

The spool on a baitcasting reel revolves on an axle as it pays out line. By applying thumb pressure to the revolving spool, an angler can slow and stop a cast with pinpoint precision. Baitcasting reels require skill and practice and are a favorite of bass anglers, many of whom insist the reels afford more sensitive contact with the line than spinning reels. Baitcasters get the nod from trolling fishermen, too, for the revolving spool makes it easy to pay out and take up line behind a boat and also reduces line twist.

HANDLE The latest upgrades offer ergonomic grips with grooves for better control.

FREESPOOL BUTTON Allows the spool to turn freely for the cast.

DRAG KNOB Adjusts drag tension. Some smaller reels have a spring-and-pawl drag, while reels for larger fish sport strong cork and composite disc braking systems.

FRAME Holds the spool. A weak frame will warp, causing friction as the spool revolves.

ARBOR The spindle around which the fly line is wrapped. Many modern reels have larger arbors that help recover line more quickly when a fish swims toward the angler.

FLY REEL

Flyfishing reels don't revolve during a cast, since fly anglers strip line from the reel and let it pay out during the back-and-forth motion called "false casting." In the past, fly reels have served largely as line-storage devices with simple mechanical drags. Advancing technology and an increase in interest in flyfishing for big, strong-fighting fish have led to strong drag systems that can stop fish as large as tarpon. Other recent developments include warp- and corrosion-resistant materials and finishes and larger arbors—the spindles around which the line is wrapped—that reduce line coils and help maintain consistent drag pressure.

SPOOL Many reels are fitted with removable spools. Having different fly lines ready on a number of spools allows an angler to switch tactics more quickly.

HANDLE Unlike spinning and baitcasting reels, rotating the handle of a fly reel typically turns the spool a single revolution.

119 MAKE A CUSTOM FLY ROD

Working just an hour or two a night, you can build a fly rod in less than a week, and fish with your handmade custom beauty for the rest of your life. Rod kits contain all the components and instructions, and you can use rod blanks that vary from basic to cutting-edge.

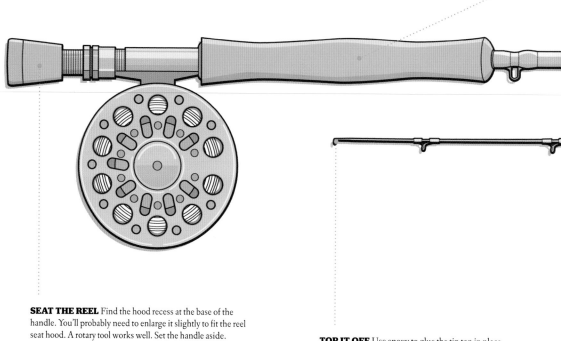

SEAT THE REEL Find the hood recess at the base of the handle. You'll probably need to enlarge it slightly to fit the reel seat hood. A rotary tool works well. Set the handle aside.

Use $1/2$-inch-wide masking tape to create two bushings under the place where you'll glue the reel seat, just thick enough so that the reel seat fits snugly over the bushings. Spread waterproof two-part epoxy over these bushings, then slowly slide the reel seat into place. As you slide the reel seat down, fill all gaps with epoxy. Attach the butt cap with epoxy.

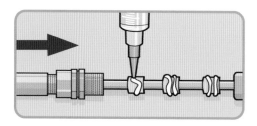

TOP IT OFF Use epoxy to glue the tip top in place.

HANDLE IT The rod channel needs to be custom fitted to your blank, so use a tapered rat-tail file to create a good fit. Go easy and check the fit frequently. You should have to use gentle pressure to fit the handle into place. Once you have it right, prepare the blank by gently sanding under the handle with 200-grit sandpaper. Spread more epoxy at the location of the handle, and slide the cork into place. If your kit has a winding check, glue it into place now.

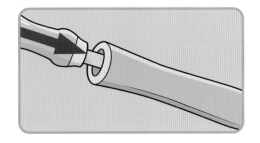

GET GUIDANCE Taper the end of each guide foot with a fine-metal file. Rod-building kits will come with a spacing chart. Hold guides in place with thin strips of masking tape. For a consistent width, mark up a business card with the desired width of the wrap, and use it as a template to mark the beginning and ending points of each guide wrap with a grease pencil.

Begin by wrapping the rod blank with a half-dozen tight wraps over the tag end of the thread. Snip off the tag and continue. As you spin the rod, angle the thread from the spool slightly so that each wrap is snug against the previous one. To finish a guide wrap, stop when the wrap is $1/8$ inch shorter than the planned finished length. Form a loop of monofilament with an overhand knot, pinch it so that the closed end is narrowed, and place this closed end on top of the wraps so that the pinched end sticks out just a bit. Wrap

over this loop to the end of your wrap marks and cut the winding thread with a 3-inch tail. Thread this through the exposed end of the loop, then pull back toward the wrap. This will pull the loop and the tag end under the wraps. Trim the excess with an X-Acto knife.

To hold the rod in place and provide thread tension while wrapping the guides, make a rod wrapper: Cut notches in a cardboard box to hold the rod blank horizontal. Run thread under a book and through a small hole punched through the box.

Last, wrap the female end of the ferrule with a $3/4$-inch wrap to give it added strength.

Apply rod finish to all the windings. To prevent the finish from running, support the rod in a horizontal position and rotate 90 degrees every minute for 15 minutes.

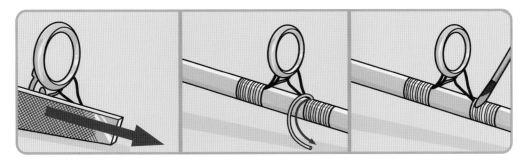

120 MASTER THE BIMINI TWIST

Tying the Bimini twist seems to be every angler's nightmare—at least among those who haven't tried it. Although it can look intimidating, it isn't all that difficult. After 30 minutes of practice, you should be able to tie this important knot easily. The Bimini creates a doubled line ending in a loop. The doubled line can then be tied directly to a lure, swivel, or hook. Often, a Bimini is tied in a light running line or leader, and the loop is then tied to a heavier shock leader. That's standard procedure in flyfishing for bigger fish like stripers, tarpon, marlin, and tuna.

STEP 1 Start by doubling about 3 feet of line. Hold the tag end and standing line together in your left hand. Put your right hand into the loop at the end. Rotate your right hand clockwise 20 times to make a series of spread-out twists in the doubled line.

STEP 2 While seated with your knees together, use your right hand to spread the end loop over both of your knees. Keep holding the tag end and standing line with your left hand so the twists don't unwind. Now grab the tag end with your right hand, still holding the standing line with your left.

STEP 3 Pull on the line with your hands upward and slightly apart. At the same time, spread your knees to put tension on the loop. This will make the twists pack closer together.

STEP 4 Now move your right hand (tag end of line) downward so the line is roughly perpendicular to the twists, and slightly relax the tension from your right hand. Maintain tension on the loop with your knees and on the standing line with your left hand. You'll feel the tag end start to wrap itself around the twists. Keep loosening tension with only your right hand as the tag end wraps downward, over the twists and to the beginning of the loop over your knees.

STEP 5 Anchor the resulting wraps by making a half hitch with the tag end wrapped around one side of the loop. Then make three half hitches around both loop strands, pulling the hitches up tightly against the base of the wraps. Trim the tag end, breathe a sigh of relief, and try it again.

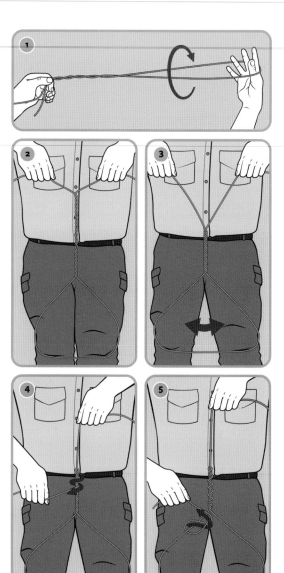

121 RIG A KILLER CANE POLE

The simplest pursuits—such as attempting to catch every panfish in the pond with a cane pole—still benefit from careful attention to detail. Here's how to rig cane the right way.

STEP 1 To keep line kinks to a minimum, use Dacron line and tip it with 2 feet of monofilament leader. You'll need a working line the length of the rod, plus 4 feet.

STEP 2 Tie the line off at the midpoint of the cane pole. Spiral-wrap the line to the tip, and tie it to the pole with a half hitch. If a cruising hawg bass crashes your crappie party and breaks the pole, you'll still be able to fight it to the finish.

STEP 3 Rig the line with a slip bobber that you can peg for varying depths, pinchback split shot, and a longshanked Aberdeen hook to make it easier to slip the point from a fish's mouth.

122 ORGANIZE HOOKS WITH SAFETY PINS

Tired of getting varying styles and sizes of hooks mixed up in your tacklebox? Use safety pins to keep them organized. Simply feed the pin's point through the eyes of the hooks and clip the pin shut. A load of hooks can fit onto one pin, and it's an easy way to keep the different kinds sorted.

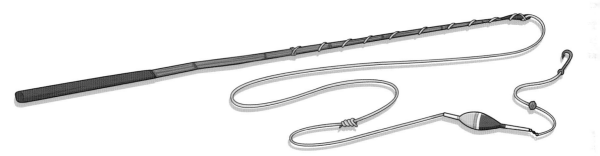

123 PATCH GRIP POTHOLES

Favorite rods get used hard and can develop nicks, dents, pits, and cracks in the cork handle that might lead to total breakdown if not patched. Smoothing out a grip is a snap. First, create a few tablespoons of cork dust by sanding an old grip or even wine cork with 60-grit sandpaper. Mix in carpenter's glue in about a 50-50 ratio, and stir to create a thick paste. Next, pick out any loose shreds and pieces of cork in the grip's damage zone, then pack in the cork paste. Use a bit of excess, as the paste will shrink while it dries. Once dry, shape and smooth with 220-grit sandpaper, and you're ready to go.

124

RUBBERIZE YOUR REEL HANDLE

You've probably walked by Plasti Dip in the hardware store a hundred times without giving it a second look, but the liquid rubber can provide great tackle applications. Use it to coat the end of your reel handle for added grip when burning spinnerbaits or aggressively twitching jerkbaits. Your fingers won't slip off from rain, sweat, or fish slime. You can also rubberize the front of your spinning reel's drag cap to allow easier adjustment. To increase the grip even more, pour the amount you need for coverage into a separate container and mix in some fine sand.

125

REPLACE DRAG WASHERS

If you've noticed your drag getting a little sticky lately, or want top-shelf drag from a mid-shelf reel, upgrade the reel's drag washers. Several companies, including Smooth Drag and Australia's Jack Erskine Precision Reel Engineering, machine custom drag washers for myriad reel models. Many aftermarket washers are carbon fiber, which is lighter, stronger, smoother, and more heat resistant than that used in most stock washer materials.

Reel companies such as Daiwa, Shimano, Penn, and Abu Garcia also offer drag upgrade kits for many models. Kits often include drag components from their high-end reels that will also fit on their less expensive models.

126 ROPE-TAPE YOUR GRIP

Having a good grip on your rod can make or break a fish fight, especially when you're fishing for big species like salmon or muskies. Even if the rod's handle is tucked under your arm, the less it slips and moves, the more control you maintain.

To increase that grip, try wrapping your handle hockey stick–style. Start with a spool of cloth stick tape; you'll find it at sporting-goods stores. Make a few wraps around the butt of the rod, unwind about a foot of tape, and spin the spool to create a thin tape rope. Wrap that rope in inch-wide spirals around the handle toward the reel. Next, wrap the tape flat down the handle toward the butt, covering the thin rope. Not only does this wrapping style boost your grip as you hold the rod, it's extra protection against the rod's slipping out of a holder on the troll.

127

CHANGE BEARINGS

Tournament distance casters need skill to send weights out hundreds of yards with a bait-casting reel—but gear factors in, too. Many of the casters replace the reel bearings with custom upgrades.

Even if you don't need to cast a lure up over the moon, extra distance is always useful.

Companies like Boca Bearing and Big Green Fish produce custom ceramic and ceramic-metal hybrid reel bearings for many models that won't corrode, are much lighter than stock metal bearings, and spin more freely than many factory bearings. Working on the guts of a round-profile baitcaster takes patience and focus (reading the manual helps), but new bearings can extend a reel's life and can get a muskie spinner, striper plug, or a big chunk of catfish bait into distant honey holes much more frequently. And that equals more fish.

128 STORE FISHING LINE

Since heat and sunlight are hard on fishing line, you need to be careful when storing spare monofilament and fluorocarbon line. Most manufacturers will tell you that storing line for up to a year is no problem, but there are some significant caveats. First, always use bulk spools for long-term storage. The larger diameter of bulk spools will cut down on the problem of line memory, in which the coiled line retains loops that will snarl your casts come springtime. Equally important to line stability is a relatively constant environment without large temperature fluctuations. A simple solution: Stack bulk spools in a couple of shoeboxes and jam them up on the highest shelf in the hall closet.

129 RIG AN ON-THE-STREAM FISH STRINGER

If you find yourself without a fish stringer, here's an easy way to keep your catch. Cut a 2- to 3-foot vine—muscadine, greenbrier, you name it. Strip off the leaves and sharpen one end. Now thread the sharp end through the fish's gills and mouth, and wrap the vine ends around themselves a half dozen times to form a hoop. Anchor it in the water with a stick driven into the mud.

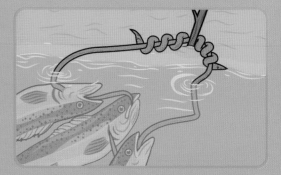

130 FEATHER A SPINNING REEL 50 FEET

An open-face spinning reel may not have a baitcaster's reputation for minute-of-angle accuracy, but you can still cast lures into tight spots from a decent distance with these popular rigs.

The secret is to feather the out-going line against the lip of the spool, much as you slow the revolution of a baitcasting spool with your thumb. It feels a little goofy at first, especially since you have to cast with both hands near the reel. But then you get used to the technique, and you start dropping lures into lily pad openings the size of a cheeseburger bun, and you'll remember that disentangling your spinnerbaits from low bushes felt a lot goofier. Here's the drill for right-handed casters.

WIND UP Start with the reel handle pointing up (a). This will ensure enough clearance so you can . . .

BAIL OUT Place your left hand under the handle and cup the spool in your palm (b). Open the bail with your left thumb or the fingers of your right hand. With your left hand, reach around the bottom of the spool, and extend your left index finger so you can . . .

HOLD THE LINE Trap the outgoing line against the spool rim with the tip of your left index finger. Now comes the goofy part: Make a standard cast, while keeping the outgoing line pressed against the spool rim (c). Your left hand will travel with the spinning reel. Keep holding the lines with your left index finger so you can . . .

CONTROL THE CAST Release the line to send the lure toward the target. Use slight finger pressure against the spool lip to slow the line (d), then stop the at the precise moment so you can . . .

HOOK A BASS Drop it so close to bass cover that a fish will strike out of sheer admiration for your marksmanship.

131

CONVERT TO MANUAL SHIFT

Pro bass anglers rarely, if ever, trip the bail on their spinning reels by turning the handle. That's because closing the bail with the handle can spin a little slack line onto the spool, which can lead to twisting. The bail is also the part of a spinning reel that fails most often. To prevent knots and malfunction, unscrew the side plate that houses the internal bail gears and remove the spring. Some reels require the removal of small bail-tripping mechanisms as well, but on many models, ditching the spring will suffice. A manual bail forces you to close it by hand, letting you keep tension on the line by flipping it as soon as your bait or lure splashes down. Look online for free reel schematics that can help you remove the correct parts.

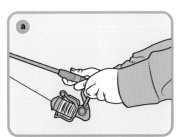

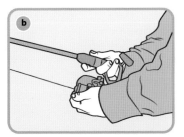

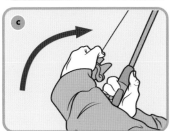

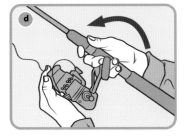

134

DAMPEN LINE TWIST

A big problem for spinning anglers, whether using live bait or lures, is dealing effectively with line twist. This can cause tangles or affect the action of a lure to the point where it won't attract fish. Here's how to keep the line running straight and true.

STEP 1 Close the bail with your hand, not the reel handle. When you turn the handle, the spool also turns slightly before the bail snaps shut, which causes the line to twist.

STEP 2 Set the drag properly. If the line slips too much while you're playing a big fish, you'll end up with line twist.

STEP 3 Let the rod fight the fish. Spooling line under tension creates line twist. When you have a big fish on the line, raise the rod. Reel in line only while lowering the rod (when the line is no longer under tension).

132 MARK FLY LINES

I had wads and wads of mystery fly lines until I started marking each new fly line with a permanent marker: eight tiny little hatch-marks at the end of the fly line for an 8-weight, seven hatch-marks for a 7-weight, etc. Simplified my life and saved money.

133 FLOAT A LINE WITH AN EARPLUG

For a cheap yet effective bobber for light-tackle fishing, use a foam earplug. Just thread the hook through and slide it to the desired position on the line. You can make it a slip bobber by inserting a length of plastic coffee stirrer.

135 FISH A GREASED LEADER

Before strike indicators, fly casters greased leaders to provide bobber action and fly suspension. It's still a great tactic. Fishing with a greased leader suspends pupae and midges at predetermined depths and makes it easier to track the path of a fly by keeping an eye on the floating leader. But there's a cost. A leader floating in the film is more visible to trout. Beware.

Use a thick silicone paste, and smear the goo on your thumb and forefinger. Pinch the leader butt with these fingers, and pull the leader through. Stop a few inches farther from the end of the tippet than the depth you want to suspend the fly.

136 SEE RED (OR NOT)

There are line companies that sell red line because it's supposed to disappear underwater, and lure companies selling red lures and hooks that they say make a lure look like a bleeding baitfish. Confused?

Fish can see color and lots of different hues as it turns out. You get a thumbs-up, then, on adding crimson hooks and those cutting-edge realistic colors to your tacklebox—as long as you're not fishing too deep. Here's why: Red is produced by some of the longest wavelengths in the visible spectrum, and these longer wavelengths are the first to be absorbed by water. That means that the color red nearly disappears in water below, say, 12 or 15 feet. Next to go are oranges, yellows, and greens.

Which is where those red lines are a factor. The deeper you go, the less distinguishable red objects will appear. If you want to fish with red line in shallower water, use a fluorocarbon leader.

137 PROTECT HAIR-THIN TROUT TIPPETS

The trout stream is transparent and the hatch consists of super small bugs, so you've tied on a hair-thin 7X tippet. You're landing plenty of small trout, but suddenly a 22-inch sips the fly. How do you keep it on and get it to the net?

"Nothing can be sudden," says Joe DeMalderis, a trophy trout hunter who guides from the upper Delaware River in New York to Patagonia in South America. "Everything has to be done easy, starting with the hookset. You want to gently lift to set. If you swing hard, it's already over. The whole key is managing your line and keeping pressure on without doing anything jarring. When the fish gets on the reel, loosen your drag and keep your hands off. If the fish wants to take line, let it go.

Whether you're wading or in a drift boat, chasing the fish is a must. When it's time to net, try to gently lead the fish into a bag that's already submerged. Don't take a sudden swipe, because if you hit the tippet, it'll break.

"If you panic, you don't have a chance. People are afraid of light tippets, but 7X is a lot stronger than you think. I tell clients to tie their 7X to a bush and slowly bend the rod. They'll bend it almost in half. But if you whip the rod fast, the tippet will snap. As soon as you try to stop the fish by choking off the line or changing directions too suddenly, it's over. It's a balancing act, and if you do one tiny thing wrong, you risk losing the trout. Most mistakes happen because the angler is panicked and does something too abruptly."

138 SET A SPOOL BRAKE

Calibrating a baitcasting reel is one of those skills it behooves the total outdoorsman to develop. Do it correctly and you'll head off those annoying bird's nests that result from an over-running spool. Follow the steps below if you're a right-handed angler. The adjustments will be opposite for southpaws. Recalibrate each time you change lures.

STEP 1 Hold the rod in your left hand at a 45-degree angle, with the lure attached to the line and about 4 inches of line out from the tip top.

STEP 2 The clutch knob should be on the handle side of the reel. Turn it clockwise a few turns to overtighten. Rest your left thumb on the reel spool.

STEP 3 Push the thumb bar with your right thumb. Remove your

left thumb from the spool. The lure shouldn't drop; if it does, tighten the clutch knob.

STEP 4 Slowly turn the clutch knob counterclockwise until the lure begins to descend from its own weight.

STEP 5 Give it a cast. If it feels like the brake is too tight for the distance you want, loosen the clutch knob. If the spool backlashes, tighten it slightly.

139

STRIP INTO A HAMPER

Collapsible laundry hampers make a fine stripping basket for fly anglers casting from an open boat. They collapse down to an easily storable disk shape, weigh little, and will keep fly line from blowing around the boat and catching on everything. To customize, cut a circle of plywood to match the bottom of the hamper and glue egg crate foam to the top of the plywood. The weight of the plywood keeps the hamper from turning over, while the egg crate foam will help keep the line from tangling as you double-haul towards the horizon.

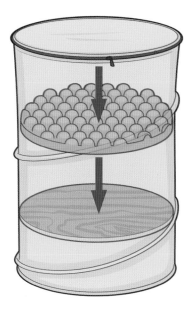

140

IMPROVE FLY LINE MEMORY

If you know you won't get a chance to flyfish for a while, keep your fly line from developing a curl memory by wrapping the first 50 feet around a large cylindrical object. Coffee cans work great, as do boat bumpers, large dog training dummies, and empty 2-liter bottles. Once your dark hiatus is over, your line will cast farther and lie straight on the water.

141 CARRY A TACKLE BOX AROUND YOUR NECK

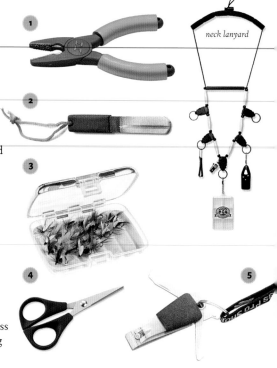

neck lanyard

Trout anglers figured this out ages ago: Why weigh yourself down when all you want to do is blitz a local creek? Bass busters can do the same. Turbocharge a flyfishing lanyard with the items listed below, and you can work your way around a pond unencumbered.

Start with a neck lanyard with at least five disconnects. If your lanyard comes preloaded with floatant holder, small nippers, or other trout-specific tools, remove them. Then load it up with the following essentials.

PLIERS Look for the lightest fishing pliers you can find. Some models even float (1).

FILE A short hook file. Yes, you need one (2).

SPINNERS AND JIGS Stuff a small fly box with a few spinners and jigs and whatever else you might need once you're on the pond (3).

SCISSORS Super braid scissors will cut heavy gel-spun and superbraid lines (4).

MULTITOOL Look for a small multitool that can do business as a mono clipper, a screwdriver, and a bird's-nest detangling aid (5).

142 FINE-TUNE A WACKY WORM FOR PENNIES

Rigging a wacky worm the traditional way—driving the hook through the middle—results in a lot of expensive baits flying off the hook or hanging up in brush. Here's how to solve two sticky wacky-worm problems at once.

SHOP IT Take your favorite wacky-worm baits to a hardware store and start shopping: You need black rubber O-ring washers like you'd use on a leaky kitchen sink, and they need to fit snugly on the body of your worm. While you're there, pick up a few small black panel nails or brads.

RIG IT Snip off the nail head with wire cutters and insert the long part of the nail into the head of the worm. Slip the O-ring down to the midpoint of the worm. Thread your hook through this O-ring, so that the hook point is in line with the worm.

FISH IT Cast into the salad with confidence. The rubber O-ring absorbs the force of the cast, preserving the bait. And the weight will make the worm fall slightly headfirst, carrying the hook with the point facing up. You'll snag less often—and catch more fish.

143 FISH UNFISHABLE WEEDS

Pulling hog bass from heavy slop requires the right gear. Long, stiff rods have the muscle to horse them out of weeds. Baitcasting reels have the winching authority. Braided superlines cut through heavy vegetation and have near-zero stretch, which makes hooksetting much easier.

Drop a weedless plastic frog right into the mess. Wiggle, skitter, pause, and pause it some more. Watch for a bulge of water behind the frog, created by a stalking bass waiting for open water, but be ready for an out-of-nowhere explosion. When the fish hits, hold off on the hookset for a count of two or three. Then stick it hard and keep your rod tip high. Try to get the fish's head up and pull it out of the very hole it made when it surfaced. Keep up the pressure to skitter the fish across the slop and turn back all attempts to head for the bottom.

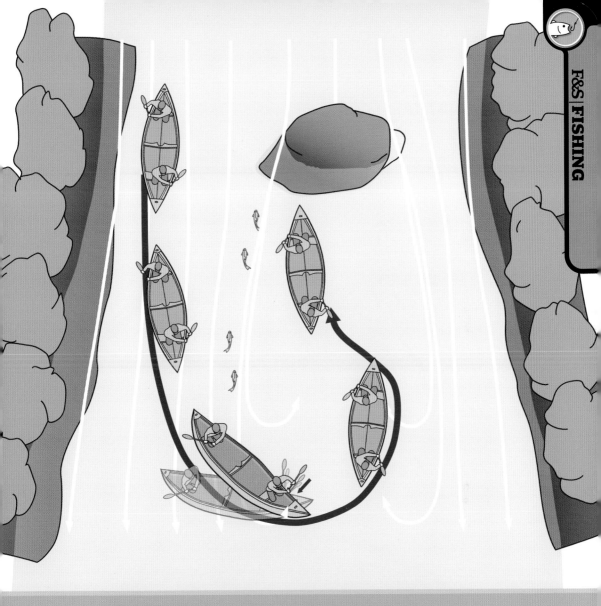

144 CROSS AN EDDY LINE FOR STACKED-UP FISH

It's a fact that strong eddy lines below rapids and boulders hold fish, but it's also true that it takes a good eddy turn to place a boat in casting position. Remember the word PAT: *power*, *angle*, and *tilt*.

POWER The canoe has to be moving forward in relation to the current speed. You need enough momentum to cross the eddy line.

ANGLE Position the canoe at a 45-degree angle to the eddy line. Aim high in the eddy—higher than you want to go because the current will carry you downstream. Maintain angle and speed until the center of the boat crosses the line; then the bow paddler should draw to turn the boat into the eddy.

TILT Two guys in a loaded boat sitting on the seats risk a quick flip as the eddy pushes on the hull. You have to lean and bank the boat into the turn; the stronger the eddy, the harder the lean.

145 CHOOSE THE RIGHT BASS LURE

Bass lures can be divided into five broad categories depending on the lure's design and how the angler manipulates the bait. Pack a tackle box with a few lures from each of these categories, and you'll catch bass in any weather, from any water.

SOFT PLASTIC Few baits have changed the fishing world as much as soft plastics. Introduced as a large worm imitation in 1951, the realistic, lifelike baits now come in a dizzying array of shapes—worms, salamanders, baitfish, crayfish, snakes, slugs, frogs, lizards, mice, and more. Fishing tactics for soft plastics are just as varied. Many are threaded on to a lead jig. Others are rigged with no weight on a weedless, wide-gap hook. And some of the most popular soft plastics are among the most pungent—many of these baits are manufactured with natural or artificial scents and oils that prompt bass to chow down. If you ever feel overwhelmed by soft-plastic selections, it's hard to go wrong with a purple or black worm slow-twitched across the bottom.

SURFACE LURE Otherwise known as topwater lures, these hard-bodied baits kick up a fuss. They gurgle, pop, jerk, waddle, and dart across the water surface and can draw explosive strikes from hungry bass. Surface lures with a cupped face are known as "poppers," and pop and spray water as the angler snaps the rod tip. Poppers can imitate anything from dying baitfish to frantic frogs. Thin, lightweight "pencil poppers" skitter like a minnow on its last legs—and few bass will turn down such an easy meal. One of the best retrieves for cigar-shaped surface lures is called "walking the dog," in which the lure glides back and forth with a zigzag action as the angler twitches the rod tip low to the water.

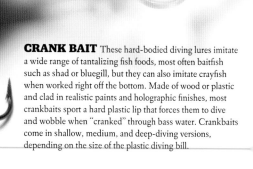

CRANK BAIT These hard-bodied diving lures imitate a wide range of tantalizing fish foods, most often baitfish such as shad or bluegill, but they can also imitate crayfish when worked right off the bottom. Made of wood or plastic and clad in realistic paints and holographic finishes, most crankbaits sport a hard plastic lip that forces them to dive and wobble when "cranked" through bass water. Crankbaits come in shallow, medium, and deep-diving versions, depending on the size of the plastic diving bill.

STICKBAIT Imitating everything from long, slender minnows to full-grown trout, stickbaits are most often fished with a twitching, stop-and-start motion that looks like prey species darting in and out of cover, or an injured and crippled baitfish struggling to stay alive. That herky-jerky death dance action spawns vicious strikes by feeding bass and can coax even the most close-mouthed largemouth to open wide. Many stickbaits come in a jointed version for even more emphatic action.

THE ONE LURE YOU NEED FOR ...

WALLEYE   *grub lure*

PIKE   *spoon lure*

SMALLMOUTH   *grub lure*

PANFISH   *mini-tube*

SPINNERBAIT Safety-pin style spinnerbaits look nothing like a natural food—but they catch bass like crazy. Built on a V-shaped wire frame, the baits have one or more revolving blades threaded to one wire shaft, while the other is tipped with a weighted hook dressed with an often garish skirt of brightly colored rubber or silicone. The spinning blades produce flash and vibration, while the wild, undulating rubber skirts—often glittering with metal flakes—give bass a temptation they often can't resist. Depending on the rate of retrieve, spinnerbaits can be skittered across the water's surface, helicoptered straight down through the water column, or bumped along the bottom. Many anglers consider spinners "search baits," because they allow you to cover lots of water fast and help you figure out where bass are holding in short order.

TROUT   *in-line spinner*

STRIPER   *stickbait*

146 SUPERCHARGE A LURE WITH A NAIL

With nothing more than a simple nail, you can make your softbait do all kinds of crazy moves. Here are a few.

ⓐ HANG YOUR HEAD Make a wacky-rigged worm or Senko even wackier by putting a small finishing nail into the head of the bait. The soft plastic will flail more erratically.

ⓑ MAKE A BACKDROP Push a nail into a soft-plastic shad's back just ahead of the tail and run a plain hook through the nose. The lure will drop back when you pause the retrieve.

ⓒ STICK IN THEIR CRAW Put a finishing nail into the tail of a soft-plastic crawfish and hook the bait through the head. The nail keeps bait and hook at a better fish-hooking angle.

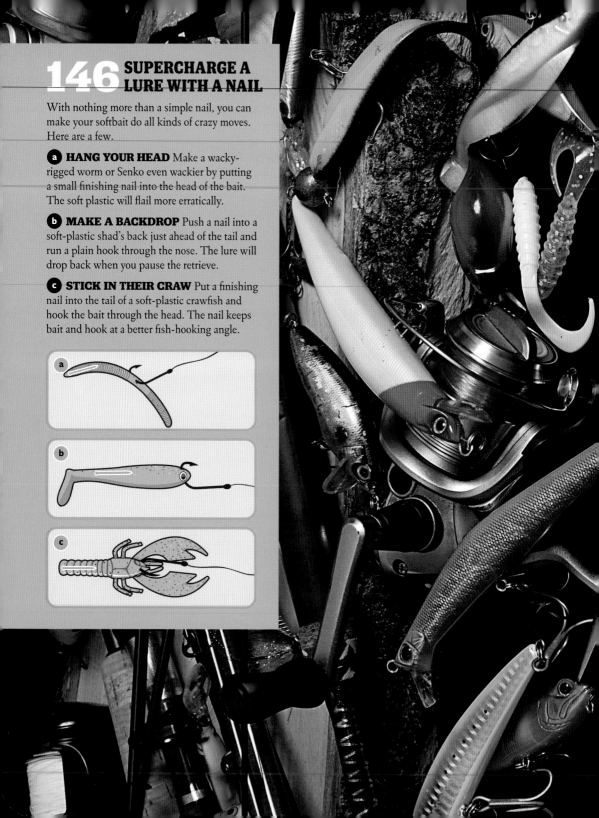

147 HACK YOUR PLASTICS

You don't have to fish with a standard lure. With a careful trim, your lures can take on new life.

a MAKE A MINISKIRT One solution to bass tapping at your spinnerbait without connecting is to add a trailer hook. That's fine for open water but can result in more snags around any structure. Instead, trim the skirt so it hangs evenly with the hook bend.

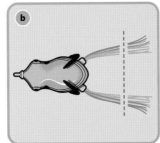

b SHAVE YOUR LEGS Sometimes bass grab the skirt legs of a hollow-body frog lure and miss the hook. Trimming legs back even ½ inch can reduce short strikes and actually give frogs a smoother side-to-side glide when "walking the dog."

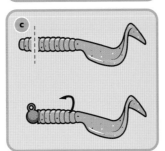

c TAKE A BACK SEAT How many times have you reeled up a curly-tailed grub with no tail? Solve this by cutting away a portion of the front so the hook sits just in front of the tail. Cut back a soft-plastic shad for the same hook placement.

148 MAKE A WOODEN DOWEL POPPER

Making custom diving lures is a challenge. Lips, weights, balance, and buoyancy all factor in to getting one to swim properly. But making a popper is cheap and easy. All you need is a wooden dowel, some screw-in eyelets, hooks, split rings, and some simple tools, like a drill and sandpaper.

Cut the dowel to your desired length, taper one end of the cut piece with the sandpaper, drill out the mouth with a large bit, and screw an eyelet into the tail, the belly, and the mouth. How you decorate the popper is up to you, but it will float and it will pop, and you need not be an engineer to get it right.

149 AVOID TREBLE

I recently spent half an hour un-trebling a trio of snarled plugs and—more than once—I've had to extract trebles from human flesh. And they can rip fish mouths to pieces. If you're fishing with kids, especially, replace treble hooks.

Most spinner hooks aren't attached with a split ring, so use side-cutting wire snips to remove the trebles. If the hook eye is particularly stout, clip it in two places to create a gap, and slip it off the body wire. Replace with open-eye hooks.

Before replacing trebles, evaluate the track of topwater and diving lures so you can compare their performance with single hooks. Most will do fine. For many largemouth baits, replace the hooks with some 1/0 or 2/0 ringed live-bait hooks. Remove the belly treble entirely, or just replace it with a ringed live-bait hook with its point facing forward. The point on your trailing hook should face up.

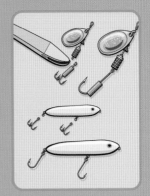

Nothing beats the heat like wet-wading a smallie stream. Here are all the lures you'll need for a great day on the water.

CABELA'S FISHERMAN SERIES WALKING DOG The scooped mouth on this 3½-inch walker throws a bit more water than a classic Spook.

ARBOGAST HULA POPPER When smallmouths get more dialed in to sipping bugs than chasing baitfish, break out a 1¾-inch black Hula Popper.

ZOOM FLUKE A Fluke shines when a subtle presentation is in order. Rig a pearl-white 4-inch bait on a weedless hook, cast upstream of the zone, and let it flutter down with the current like a dying baitfish.

JIGHEADS Whether for stuffing a tube or jigging a Fluke in a hole, a small assortment of plain round and tube jigheads is a must. Pack ¹⁄₁₆- through ¼-ounce weights.

STRIKE KING BITSY TUBE These 2¾-inch baits imitate everything from darters to crayfish to hellgrammites. Let them tumble over the bottom or jig them hard.

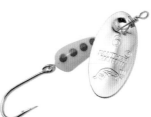

PANTHER MARTIN SPINNERS Panther Martins get down fast in strong current, and a single-hook model tipped with a grub kills on the swing.

MATZUO NANO POPPER This 2-inch bait is a go-to popper on smallmouth streams. It splashes down softly and can be worked subtly on light gear.

HOOKS Wide-gap worm hooks in size 2/0 come in handy for rigging baits weedless. Carry some size-4 finesse hooks for wacky-rigging soft plastics or in case you happen to find a live crayfish scurrying around the rocks.

RAPALA JOINTED ORIGINAL FLOATER Sometimes a joint can make all the difference in drawing strikes, especially in broken water where the current helps impart the action.

RAT-L-TRAP When you come across a deep hole and can't turn a fish in the middle of the column, a 'Trap ripped tight to the bottom often scores.

RAPALA X-RAP This stickbait on steroids is a hands-down favorite small-stream hard bait. It shines in faster water where a few forceful jerks make it slash violently.

RAPALA ORIGINAL FLOATER In slow stretches, where you want to work a stickbait with a little more finesse, it's tough to top an Original Floater.

YAMAMOTO SENKO Wacky-rig a 4-inch Senko and drift it, weightless, through seams and eddies with your rod held high and a finger on the line.

151 MAKE YOUR OWN IN-LINE SPINNERS

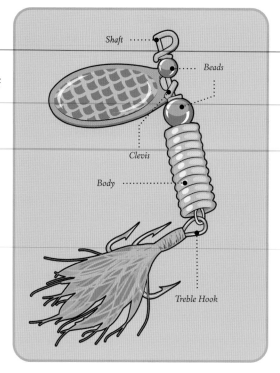

Shaft · · · · · ·

Beads

Clevis

Body · · · · · · · · ·

Treble Hook

Building a spinner takes all of two minutes, and the only tool you need is a pair of needle-nose pliers. You can buy kits at the big sporting goods shops that include a range of bodies, blades, and beads, or order parts individually for more customization. Here's how you can create your own inexhaustible supply of deadly fishing lures.

Before you begin assembling the spinner, add desired details to components, such as paint or flash tape to blades, and squirrel-tail hair or colored tubing to treble hooks.

STEP 1 Thread a treble hook onto an open-eye wire shaft.

STEP 2 Pinch the ends of the shaft together and slide a spinner body over the top. Solid brass bodies add heft for deeper-running lures and greater castability. Trim any excess wire and add beads.

STEP 3 Thread the blade onto the clevis, and slide the clevis onto the shaft. The blade's concave side should face the body.

STEP 4 Using your pliers, grasp the shaft firmly about ³⁄₁₆ to ½ inch above the clevis or terminal bead. Hold the pliers steady and slowly bend the shaft three-quarters of the way around the nose of the pliers and under the main shaft until you have formed a loop.

STEP 5 Wrap the tag end of this loop tightly around the shaft twice, as close to the pliers as possible. Trim the end with wire cutters.

152 WIDEN YOUR GATHERING GUIDE

Ask a custom rod builder about common requests they receive, and one will invariably be using a gathering guide wider than what is typically used on stock rods. The gathering guide—the guide closest to the reel on a spinning rod—allows line to peel off the reel smoothly during the cast and feed back on the spool evenly during the retrieve.

A wide gathering guide increases both casting accuracy and distance by giving the line more freedom of flow during the cast and will let you feather the line more effectively when you need to put a frog between two pads. During the retrieve, it can reduce kinking and memory by adding more tension to the line as it winds back onto the reel. You will also be able to use a reel with a wider spool on a lighter rod. That means you can increase your line capacity without the need to downsize line strength and lure weight. And you'll be able to use a lighter outfit for bigger fish.

153

MASTER THE WORLD'S FAIR KNOT

This easy knot was the winner of a Great Knot Search event sponsored by DuPont (Stren fishing line) at the 1982 World's Fair. Use it for tying on hooks, lures, or swivels with nylon monofilaments. It's almost like the Palomar knot because you place a doubled line around the hook's eye, but this knot does not require you to pass the hook or lure through a large loop of line.

STEP 1 Insert a doubled line loop about ¹/₂ inch through the hook eye.

STEP 2 Fold the loop back on itself as shown, keeping it in position by pinching with your left thumb and index finger at the hook eye.

STEP 3 Feed the tag end downward through the loop, under the doubled line in front of the hook eye, then go back up through the loop.

STEP 4 Next, run the line's tag end through the loop that was formed in the previous step.

STEP 5 Pull steadily and firmly on both the standing line and the tag end to tighten.

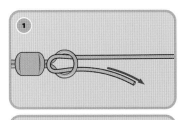
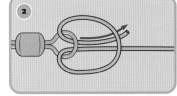
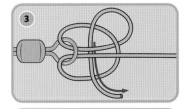
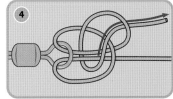
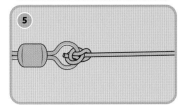

154

BUILD A PREDATOR RIG

Gather up all your tired, your lipless, your scarred and rusty Rapalas, the wretched refuse of your ancient tacklebox . . . And make from them a truly awesome predator rig.

Remove the hooks from a plug. Tie it to your line, and then tie a short stout dropper between the trailing eye and a big in-line spinner or spoon, such as a Dardevle. (If fishing for toothy predators like muskies, use wire.) Now you have a rig that looks like a fish that's chasing after a smaller fish, which can trigger a bite like nobody's business.

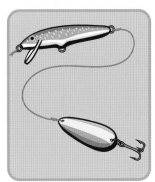
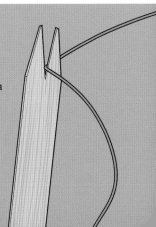

155 REMOVE HOOKS WITH A POPSICLE STICK

Traditional hook disgorgers, such as hemostats and needle-nose pliers, can tear up popper bodies and wings, damage hooks, and nick tippets and knots. The best hook removal tool for smallmouthed bream is a simple wooden Popsicle stick. Whittle one end of the stick to a width of ¹/₄ inch. Place the stick on a hard wooden surface, such as a picnic table. Use a knife blade to cut a V-notch into the narrowed end of the stick. Now just slide the V-notch down the line to the hook eye, and pop the popper free.

156

PIMP A RIDE FOR YOUR FLY

Dark, gnarly undercut banks often hold the biggest trout in the stream. But getting a fly under those banks, and getting it deep enough to prompt a strike from a monster trout, requires expert fly casting and a precise presentation. Or a leaf. Here's how to use fall foliage to float your fly into the perfect position.

STEP 1 Hook a weighted streamer or nymph fly, such as a Woolly Bugger, to the outer edge of a dry, buoyant tree leaf.

STEP 2 Carefully sneak upstream to a position above the undercut bank you're looking to target. Then strip off a few feet of line and ease the unconventional rig into the current.

STEP 3 Pay out line as the leaf drifts to the target area. As it approaches to within 2 to 3 feet of the hole, give the line a sharp snap back with your line hand to rip the fly from the leaf. Your weighted streamer will drop into the current, which will carry the fly under the bank and down to your target trout.

157 FOOL THE WARIEST TROUT IN THE RIVER

Large brown trout don't behave like small ones. Here's what sets them apart:

SMALL BROWN	VS	TROPHY BROWN
Juvenile brown trout eat frequently and typically focus on invertebrates like worms, aquatic nymphs, and smaller insects.	Forage	Large brown trout eat fewer, larger meals. They key on calorie-rich foods like baitfish, mice, leeches, and nightcrawlers.
Smaller brown trout are in tune with natural bait and fly presentations.	Attraction	Motion on a fly or lure often piques the interest of a large brown.
Smaller browns feed at various times, including midday.	Feeding Times	Large browns feed in low light, often in the dead of night.
Small browns cling to "ideal" trout habitat where insects are plentiful and easy to feed on. You will occasionally find these fish sharing the riffles with rainbow trout.	Location	Trophy browns travel to hunt for food, but they will defend the heart of the run. Large browns can survive and thrive in sections of the river with warmer water and fewer insects.
Small fish will forgive any casting faux pas. If you see a fish strike at your lure or fly and miss, and then come back, assume it's small. They are also sensitive to overhead shadows and motions but are forgiving of underwater vibrations.	Spookiness	You won't fool a monster brown trout if you make a bad cast. And if you rip that bad cast out of the run, that stretch is finished for the evening. Large browns will shut down entirely if they sense any of your movements.
Smaller brown trout are influenced by river currents as the battle ensues.	Fighting Ability	A hooked big brown isn't very affected by current and will head for cover.

158 HARVEST NATURE'S BAIT SHOP

If you have a shovel and a lawn, you've got all the worms you need. But that's not the only productive bait around. The creek you fish can supply its own—for free. (Just be sure to check bait-collection regulations in your area before heading out.)

IN-SEINELY CHEAP

You probably have most of what you need to make your own seine at home. First, get a 6x9-foot piece of nylon mesh from a fabric shop. Find two old broom handles and position one at each end of the net. Staple the mesh to the handles, leaving a few inches of net hanging past the tips at the bottom. Finally, attach some $\frac{1}{2}$-ounce fishing sinkers a foot apart across this bottom edge with zip ties. You're ready to drag.

Good bait shops carry some of these critters, but expect to pay a lot more for a dozen hellgrammites than you will for 12 shiners, or a pound of crayfish.

1 HELLGRAMMITES
Rare is the fish that won't devour one of these nasty aquatic larvae. Pick them off the bottom of submerged rocks by hand or stretch a seine across a fast-water section of the creek and flip rocks upstream. The current will then flush the bugs right into the net.

2 MINNOWS
Minnows are easier to catch off the main current. Approach from midstream with a seine and corral the school against the bank as the net closes. If the bait is thick and the water is fairly shallow, a quick swipe with a long-handled dip net will also work.

3 CRAYFISH
Choose a stretch of slow to moderate current; flip rocks and scoop the crayfish with a dip net. You can also stretch a seine across the creek and walk toward it from upstream while splashing and kicking rocks to spook crayfish down into the mesh.

4 SALAMANDERS
Often overlooked, this bait is like candy to bass and big trout. Look for them under larger rocks near the water's edge. The most productive rocks are dry on top but cool and moist underneath. Moss-covered rocks farther up the bank are prime spots, too.

5 GRUBS
Find some rotten wood near a creek bed. Peel away the bark to expose the soft, dead wood, or poke around in the dirt underneath, and you'll probably find some fat white grubs. Find a trout or crappie that won't eat them and you've done the impossible.

6 GRASSHOPPERS
The best way to catch all the hoppers you'll need is to walk through the tall grass that likely will be flanking almost any given stream. Use a butterfly net to skim across the tips of the blades and you'll have a dozen or more hoppers in a flash.

159 RIG A PORK RIND

Tipping your lure with a pork rind may feel a bit like pulling on a pair of old scratchy wool pants, but a little BBQ on a bass bait can transform a slow day on the water to epic status.

To attach a commercial pork-rind trailer, find the small slit on the front end of the chunk. Insert the hook through the fat side first, and out the skin side. That's it. Pork rinds dry out quickly and will lose their wiggle, so drop your bait into a small water bucket whenever you're motoring to a new spot. To make hook removal easy, snip a coffee straw into half-inch lengths, slide one over the hook tip and barb (a), and slip the pork off the hook.

NEW-SCHOOL TWIST Dial up a triple threat for a jig-and-pig by adding a glass rattle. Or add a strip of colored yarn (b) to a spoon tipped with a pork rind.

160 BAIL A BOAT WITH A JUG

Cut the bottom 2 inches off a 1-gallon plastic milk jug and you'll have the best boat bailer on the planet. The squared-off profile swallows a load of water in a single swipe, or turn it so that a corner of the jug fits into canoe ends or hard-to-reach bilges. The thin sides have the perfect amount of give to match the shape of boat hulls.

161 MASTER THE ARBOR KNOT

The best way to connect line to a reel is also the simplest. The arbor knot works with any type of reel and line (although superbraids require about 10 yards of mono added to the spool first to prevent slipping.)

STEP 1 Pass the line around the reel spool and back out again the same way the line entered. For example, on a baitcasting reel, pass the line through the levelwind eye, around the spool, and back through the levelwind eye.

STEP 2 Use the tag end to tie a simple overhand knot around the standing line. Tighten that knot.

STEP 3 Tie an overhand knot in the tag end, then tighten and trim. This will keep the first knot from slipping free.

STEP 4 Pull on the standing line until it tightens on the spool with the two knots binding securely against each other. Now you can spool the reel.

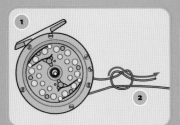

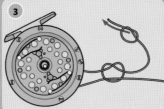

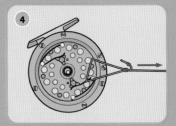

163

UPGRADE YOUR LIVE BAITS

Still globbing your worm on an Aberdeen hook? Seriously? Here are three smart bait-rig tweaks to help you catch more fish.

KEEP AN EYE OUT

Pinch one eye from large baitfish such as a shad or bluegill. The bait will struggle in the water, attracting predators.

GET A DYE JOB

Clean dirt from a dozen nightcrawlers and put them in a bowl. Add 1 tbsp. food coloring (green is great) and stir. Cover and refrigerate for at least three hours and as long as overnight.

PLAY SHELL GAMES

Add crushed eggshells to catfish dough. The fragments catch light, adding a bit of sparkle to dull dough baits.

162 FISH A CRICKET ANYWHERE, ANY TIME

Loads of fish go wild for crickets, and if you fish with a cricket bait, make sure you give it a little lively action to draw the fish's attention.

SWIPE THE PLASTIC A black Rebel Crickhopper crankbait is the best light-tackle cricket lure you'll find. But don't simply cast and retrieve. Let this lure sit on the surface, then give the rod a sharp, short sideswipe. The Crickhopper will duck under and wobble like a struggling cricket. Let it float back up and sit again for a few seconds. Repeat until a trout or crappie sucks it down.

LAY THE SMACKDOWN Big streamers are usually associated with nighttime flyfishing for trout, but

a black foam cricket can do equal damage. Foam is a loud fly material and makes a harder slap when it hits the water. Lay the fly down aggressively to enhance the pop. Then just let it drift through dark eddies or seams until you hear the louder pop of a striking brown trout.

GO ON A WEIGHT-LOSS PLAN Live crickets are often fished under a bobber with a split shot, but they don't live long. Instead, rig the bait on a bare dry-fly hook to reduce the weight and coat the first foot of your line with dry-fly floatant. The bobber will still give you casting distance, but the cricket will squirm on the surface, drawing up big bluegills for exciting strikes.

164 USE SALT TO KEEP EGGS ON A HOOK

Have you ever wondered how to keep from losing your fresh salmon-egg bait to a strong current? Simply empty your jar of eggs on a saucer and sprinkle lightly with

table salt. Return them to the jar and go fishing immediately. Your eggs will seem to have become "rubberized" and will stay on the hook.

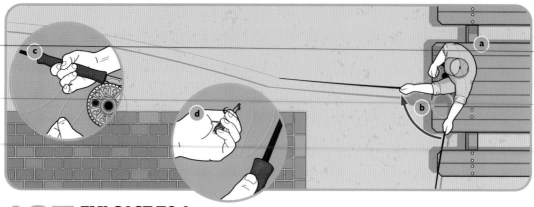

165 FLY-CAST TO A MOVING TARGET

Got that double-haul down pat? Then you'll need it for this challenge: Drop a fly in front of a moving gamefish, at 60 feet, with no more than two false-casts—all while you're standing up on the bow of a boat with your guide shouting, "Two o'clock! Now! Now!" Here's a backyard drill for the redfish marshes, the bonefish flats, and the stripers grounds.

STEP RIGHT UP Stand on a picnic table (a). It's about the size of the casting deck on a flats boat and will give you a sense of being out on the edge where the action happens.

DOUBLE STACK Strip 50 feet of shooting line from the reel and stack it in large loose coils in front of your left foot (b). If you shoot that line now, it will be pulled from the bottom of the stack, all but guaranteeing an

unrighteous tangle. You can avoid this problem, though: Grasp the line where it exits the reel in the crook of the pinky on your rod hand (c). Now, with your free hand, grab the fly line and pull all of it through your pinky, essentially re-stacking the line so it will shoot tangle-free.

FIRE WHEN READY Pull 10 to 12 feet of the stacked line through the rod tip. Hold the fly at the bend of the hook in your reel hand (d) and point your rod tip up. This is the ready position.

GET ON A ROLL Begin with an aggressive roll cast to load the rod, and let go of the fly as you snap the rod forward. Back-cast with a haul, then shoot the line with a forward cast with another haul. If you need some more distance, false cast one more time.

166 GET A FLY TO THE BOTTOM OF THINGS

There was a time when my buddies and I set out to catch every fish possible on a fly rod. When the fish is an amberjack, skulking in 60 feet of water, that presents a difficulty. To sink the flies, we tied a small dropper line of light trout tippet from the hook bend in a big nasty fly to a 3-ounce surf sinker. We marked wrecks with the bottomfinder, then we dropped our weighted fly rigs overboard. When the sinkers hit bottom, we hauled hard on the lines to snap the mono, freeing the flies to flitter seductively in front of bottom-dwelling predators. Now, that was a fight.

167

DO THE CHUCK 'N' DUCK

Adding on four big split shot ahead of a nymph can take the sexy out of fly casting in zero time flat. But when faced with a deep, dark hole that might just be a home for a massive brown trout or a big steelhead, there are times you have to suck it up and dredge. Getting that much lead out to the top of the pool without smacking yourself in the back of the noggin takes skill. Master the chuck-'n'-duck cast, and you'll score more fish and suffer fewer welts.

STEP 1 You have to avoid false casting, so start out by feeding line straight downstream with the rod tip held high to stop the weights from snagging on the bottom until you have enough length to reach the top of the hole you're trying to fish.

STEP 2 In one smooth motion, swing the rod up and over your downstream shoulder, getting the line swinging in an arc over the water behind you. Keep the line tight so that it stays straight and extended. If the line should collapse, get ready for a thump to the cranium.

STEP 3 When your line gets to the 1 o'clock position, get down, bow your head, and then bring the rod straight over your body, pointing the tip exactly where you want the rig to land.

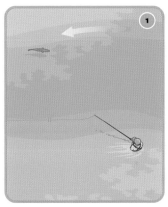

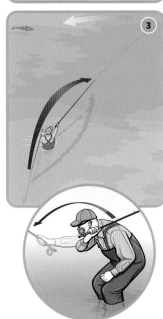

168

MAKE A SPIN-FLY MASH-UP OUTFIT

Putting a spinning reel on a fly rod might not seem to make much sense unless you understand all the intricacies of presenting various tiny jigs and spinners on small streams full of easily spooked trout. The whippy tip makes it possible to toss light lures farther and with more accuracy than a shorter spinning rod. Likewise, the rod length allows you to fish into tight seams and eddies without casting at all. When a trout strikes, the longer, softer rod will let you maneuver it around rocks and overhanging limbs more delicately. Some steelhead anglers customize such outfits further by fitting fly rods with large gathering guides and spinning-reel seats; for small streams, those tweaks aren't necessary. Ultralight or ice-fishing reels will fit the seats of most 3- to 5-weight fly rods. If you prefer a longer grip, tape your reel into place farther up on the rod's handle.

169 READ A TROUT'S TABLE MANNERS

When trying to figure out which fly to cast to a rising trout, most of us will take any help we can get. And in fact, there's help to be had right in front of you: A close look at how a trout is surfacing—its rise form—can speak volumes about what it's eating. Here's a guide to five common rise forms. It's not foolproof, but it will help you catch more fish.

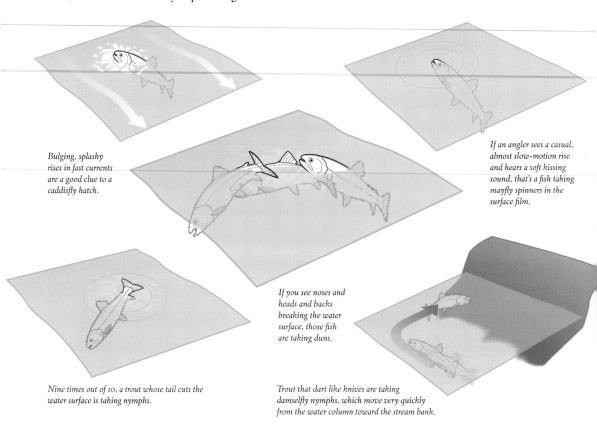

Bulging, splashy rises in fast currents are a good clue to a caddisfly hatch.

If an angler sees a casual, almost slow-motion rise and hears a soft kissing sound, that's a fish taking mayfly spinners in the surface film.

If you see noses and heads and backs breaking the water surface, those fish are taking duns.

Nine times out of 10, a trout whose tail cuts the water surface is taking nymphs.

Trout that dart like knives are taking damselfly nymphs, which move very quickly from the water column toward the stream bank.

170 MAKE A QUICK-SINKING FLY LINE

Fast-sinking fly lines are the bomb for catching shad surging up spring-swollen rivers, and they're deadly on striped bass, too. They're a cinch to build out of a few inexpensive materials and the leftover fly line that lies snarled on your workbench. For this, use LC-13, a lead-core line that weighs 13 grains per foot.

START SNIPPING (These are directions for a 9-wt line; experiment with lengths of lead-core for other line weights): Cut off the running line section of an old fly line. Cut a 28-foot section of LC-13. Cut a 6-inch length of 30-pound braided monofilament running line.

BRING ON THE KNOTS Attach backing to one end of the running line with a nail knot. Then insert the free tip of the running line into one end of the braided mono. Next, work the running line into the braided mono almost halfway by grasping the braided mono between thumb and forefinger of one hand and pushing toward it with the thumb and forefinger of the other hand, creating a bellows-like accordion.

FINISH Repeat above with one end of the LC-13. Tie a whip finish to the two ends of the braided mono sleeve and apply a few drops of pliable glue. Finally, tie in a loop—commercial or homemade with 40-pound mono—directly to the end of the sinking line. You're ready to dredge.

171

CRIPPLE A FLY FOR AN IRRESISTIBLE TREAT

Heavily fished trout often require triggers in your fly pattern to prompt a strike. Many fish will key on malformed or wingless duns or crippled flies—put a fly out there with beautiful tails or upright wings, and they won't even look at it. That means you need to go with a pattern of trailing shucks. And get creative. Cut the wings off flies. Trim them so they fall over on one side. Most anglers can't bring themselves to take scissors to a perfectly good fly, but not every fish is a perfectionist.

172 PULL OFF THE INVISIBLE CAST

You can perfect an arm-roll cast to deliver the fly upstream of the fish and to prevent false-casting over your target. Here's how it's done.

START Begin with the rod tip at the surface and pointing downstream. Load the rod with the tension of the line dragging on the water (1). Be sure to keep your forearm and wrist straight while you bring your arm up in a rolling motion (2).

FINISH Roll your arm down to the water, pointing the rod tip upstream (3). Allow the line to unroll in front while reaching out (4) before the rod tip stops at the water's surface.

173 STICK A FISH WITH A FLY FROM A MILE AWAY

Flyfishermen moving from freshwater trout to quarry such as river stripers, migrating shad, and most saltwater fish need to learn how to strip-strike. Raising the rod tip on armor-mouthed or deep-running fish won't set your hook. Nor will it do the trick when you're dredging striper holes with weighted lines or battling currents and tidal rips with long lengths of fly line. Here's what to do once you feel a fish on the line.

STEP 1 Keep the rod tip pointed at your fly at all times.

STEP 2 Release the pressure on the line with the same rod-hand finger you use to control stripping.

STEP 3 Strip line in with a hard, quick, jabbing motion with your rod—from a foot to your full reach, depending on how much of your line is in the water. If there's a lot of slack in your fly line—a deep belly from fishing weighted lines, or swooping curves caused by river or tidal rips—then strip-strike while lifting the tip of the rod in several short pumping motions. Or follow up a strip-strike with a so-called body strike by holding the fly line taut and rotating your body to sweep the rod to one side. You can also pull the fly line and rod in opposite directions. This is a a strip-strike offspring known as a scissors strike.

174 MASTER THE TUBE JIG

Stream-bred smallmouths are pigs for crayfish, and nothing imitates a craw like a tube jig.

SCENT CONTROL Jam a small piece of sponge soaked with scent into the tube.

DEPTH PERCEPTION In still water, use a $3/4$-ounce jighead for water less than 10 feet deep; $1/4$-ounce for water 10 to 20 feet deep; and $3/8$ for water deeper than 20 feet. Add weight in moving water.

CRAW CRAWL Let the jig fall to the bottom. Reel up the slack and count to 10. Bass will often strike right away. Start a series of rod-tip lifts. The jig should swim a foot off the bottom and then flutter down.

Nothing imitates crayfish like a crayfish-colored tube jig.

175

CAST LIKE A CHURCH STEEPLE

A steeple cast solves some of the roll cast's deficiencies. It's easier to use with weighted flies or lines, and you can change the direction of your cast midstroke.

But it's not easy. Practice first to prevent unholy language.

STEP 1 Start with the rod tip almost touching the water, and the rod hand rotated away from the body so the reel faces up. Begin with a sidearm backstroke, but rotate at the elbow and then raise the casting arm swiftly vertical. This is an outward and upward motion. With the rod tip directly overhead, the upper arm is at a right angle with your forearm, which is vertical.

STEP 2 Stop the rod abruptly at the 12 o'clock position. The line should be tight and straight overhead.

STEP 3 Make a brisk forward cast, stopping abruptly at the 2 or 3 o'clock position.

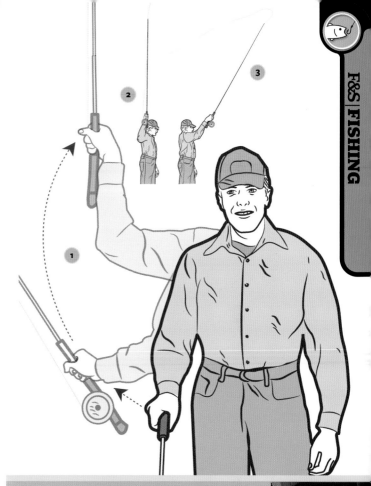

176 KILL A FISH HUMANELY

The American Veterinary Medical Association's guidelines on euthanasia propose "cranial concussion [stunning] followed by decapitation or pithing [severing or destroying the spinal cord]." It's just five seconds, and you're done— and a better person for it.

STUN The brain of most fish is located behind and slightly above the eye, at about a 10 o'clock position relative to the pupil. Strike there using a short, heavy baton or a rock.

PITH Insert a knife blade into the skull and twist. Or slice just behind the brain to completely sever the spinal cord.

177 WINTERIZE AN OUTBOARD ENGINE

Make sure your outboard motor starts with the first pull come spring.

STEP 1 Add fuel stabilizer to gas, following the manufacturer's directions. Run the motor for 5 to 10 minutes and then disengage the fuel line until the engine dies.

STEP 2 Remove spark plugs and spray fogging oil into each cylinder. Replace spark plugs. Crank the engine to spread the oil.

STEP 3 Change the lower-unit oil. This removes all water that might freeze and expand over the winter.

STEP 4 Pull the propeller off and grease the shaft splines. Replace the propeller.

STEP 5 Clear the lower-unit water inlets and speedometer pitot tube of any junk with a pipe cleaner.

Beads resembling eggs are the fly patterns of choice wherever trout, char, and steelhead follow spawning salmon. Unaltered beads will draw strikes right out of the package, but you can make them more effective by applying a realistic finish and softer texture, so the fish won't spit them out before you can set the hook.

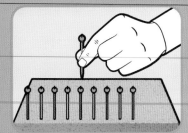

STEP 1 Stick one end of a toothpick through the hole in the bead to use as a handle. Paint the entire bead with fingernail polish (something sheer or clear). Stick the toothpick upright into a block of Styrofoam and let dry one hour.

STEP 2 Pour some soft epoxy into a bowl and roll the bead in it, coating all sides. Stick the toothpick back into the Styrofoam in a horizontal position. The epoxy will gather more heavily on the bottom side, so the bead will be slightly out of round after drying. Dry overnight.

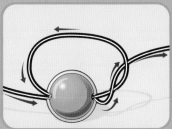

STEP 3 To rig, slip a bead onto your tippet, and then pass the end of the tippet back around and through the bead again, forming a loop. Pass the end of the tippet through the loop and cinch tight to secure the bead. Tie on a hook with an upturned eye to the tippet 1 to 3 inches from the bead. With the bead secured above the hook, it will look and drift more naturally, and the fish you catch will be hooked on the outside of the jaw. Fish this under a strike indicator.

NOTE It is against regulations to use a bare-bead, bare-hook combination in some fly-only waters. Check before you try this tip.

Match the beads you use to the size of eggs drifting in the river: 6mm for sockeye salmon, 8mm for coho, 10mm for kings. Fish may choose older-looking eggs over "fresh" ones, so stock up on a variety of colors.

179 TURN A KID ON TO FLYFISHING

Schooling your kids on flyfishing doesn't have to be as trying as helping them with their math homework. Start by limiting the time on the pond to a half-hour chunk. That prevents the kid from getting frustrated and the teacher from blowing a fuse.

Here's how to optimize those minutes.

KNOW YOUR STUDENTS Tailor your comments to your kids' age levels. A 14-year-old might understand what you mean by "feel the rod load," but an 8-year-old won't. Remember to bring your own rod so you don't take the rod from the kid; that feels like punishment. Don't wait for perfection. Instead, introduce new concepts quickly to battle boredom.

TEACH TIMING Start off with sidearm casts so that the kids can watch the fly line and better understand the physics of casting. Emphasize that fly casting is about timing, not strength.

MAKE A CASTING CALL Tell your kids to treat the rod like a ringing telephone: Bring the rod up close to their ear, say, "Hello, this is Drew Smith," and then set the "phone" down. That's the basic fly-casting movement: Sweep the rod back, stop it, let the rod load, and then make a forward cast.

KEEP THINGS ROLLING If the kids struggle with the basics, switch to roll casting for the time being. It's easier to learn, and with a bit of success, they'll be ready to tackle a standard cast.

TIME TO FISH Find a likely spot: Choose a time and place where the fish are willing. Bream beds are perfect.

GO PRO Do your kids bristle at every suggestion you make? Sign up for a casting school, or hire a guide for a half day and outsource the tricky parts.

CHOOSE A ROD A soft action helps kids feel the rod flex and load. Be wary of supershort rods, which can be difficult to cast. Go for an 8-foot, 6-weight, two-piece outfit.

CONSIDER LINE WEIGHT Overline the rod by one line weight for easier turnover.

GO EASY WITH FLIES Get a barbed fly stuck in your child's forehead and you can forget about him or her as a future fishing buddy. Only use flies with barbless hooks. For practice, tie orange egg yarn next to the fly to make it visible. On the water, cast big high-floating flies like Stimulators.

180 TRAILER A BOAT IN A HEAVY WIND

If you have to load your boat in a vicious crosswind, follow these steps for success.

STEP 1 Don't back your trailer too deeply into the water. You need firm contact between the hull and the bottom bunks.

STEP 2 Steer into the wind for control.

STEP 3 Approach the trailer at as close to a 90-degree angle as you can get, given ramp design. As you near the imaginary line that extends backward from the trailer, turn slightly toward the trailer.

The wind will catch the bow and move it toward a centered line with the trailer. Bump up the throttle so the bow enters the back of the trailer at an angle pointing slightly into the wind. Momentum will carry the boat into a straight line.

STEP 4 Apply enough power to push the bow eye to within 6 to 8 inches of the bow stop. Check your centering. Take a bow.

181 TRACK GRASSLINES WITH SONAR

Big Bass + Underwater Grass = Reel Bearings Shrieking in Pain. How to complete the equation in unfamiliar water? Follow what Texas guide John Tanner does:

STEP 1 "I look for coots hanging out in a cove or along the shoreline," Tanner says. "Ninety-nine percent of the time, they're over vegetation." Point the bow of your boat toward the birds and idle in. Keep a sharp eye on the console sonar. As the outer edge of the grassline begins to show on the bottom contour, cut the motor and turn the boat parallel to the grassline.

STEP 2 "Now I jump up front, drop the trolling motor down, and pick apart the grassline edge with the front sonar," Tanner says. You want to follow the very margin of the vegetation, so watch the bottom contour. If the sonar shows grass starting to get tall, steer away from it. If the grass gets sparse or disappears from the sonar, turn into it. Start fishing on the outside edge of the vegetation before working your way in.

182 FISH LIKE A BIOLOGIST

Knowing the life cycle of a mayfly will hook you more trout. In 1496, Dame Juliana Berners described fly imitations for about a dozen mayflies in her *A Treatyse of Fysshynge wyth an Angle*. And so it began. There are more than 500 species of mayflies known to North America, and no telling how many mayfly patterns. Learn to match the fly to the mayfly life stage.

NYMPH The body shapes of mayfly larvae differ. As nymphs feed and molt, they move about the stream and become dislodged in the current. Trout whack them.

EMERGER Mayflies beginning to hatch rise to the surface, crawl to the water's edge, or shed skin underwater. Trout key in on this vulnerable stage.

DUN The first adult stage is also called the subimago. They drift on the surface until their wings dry. Still weak, they fly to a protected area to molt a final time.

SPINNER This is the fully formed, final adult breeding stage. A "spinner fall" occurs when the dying insects fall to the water, wings outstretched. Trout go nuts.

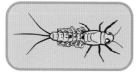

1 Pheasant Tail Nymph
2 Copper John

3 Klinkhammer
4 Emerging Para Dun

5 Sparkle Dun
6 Comparadun

7 Angel Wing Spinner
8 Krystal Spinner

This is when mending means the most. It will let you drift cleanly through riffles and runs.

Study the rise. If you see a trout head bulging out of the water, it's likely feeding on emergers.

If matching the hatch doesn't work, try an emerger. Trout will hit floating duns before they fly off.

Use a dropper rig with a larger fly as an indicator and a small submerged spinner as the trailer.

183 MIMIC THE TASTIEST CRUSTACEAN

Big trout can't resist the stop-and-drop flight path of a fleeing crayfish. Colorado guide Landon Mayer perfected this retrieve while targeting largemouth bass, and it's a coldwater killer as well. Use a weighted crayfish pattern for best results.

STEP 1 With the rod tip pointed at the surface of the water—or submerged as deep as 6 inches in the water—feel for tension on the fly. Then strip in 1 to 3 feet of line in a single, abrupt motion that lifts the fly off the stream bottom and into the water column, like a crayfish trying to escape a predator.

STEP 2 Pause long enough to feel tension from a strike or until you no longer feel the fly as it settles back on the bottom. The drop often puts up a little puff of sand, just like a crayfish hitting the dirt.

STEP 3 Repeat the abrupt strip. When a fish hits, set the hook with a pinch-lift strike: Pinch the fly line against the cork handle with your index finger and lift the rod hand sharply to a 45-degree angle.

184 READ TROUT LIKE AN UNDERWATER BOOK

Find glare-free viewing lanes of shade or darker colors reflecting on the water surface, such as shadows from streamside vegetation. These are windows of opportunity for sight-casting to trout. Got your viewing lane? Good. Here's what to look for.

WHITE "O" Analyze every speck of white on the stream bottom. An on-off glint of white is the inside of a trout's mouth. A broken pattern of white glints is a feeding trout (a).

MOVEMENT Look for a fish that moves slightly, then returns to the same location in the stream. That's a feeding fish (b).

SILHOUETTE Imagine a sketch of a fish with a heavy outline filled with color. Now remove the outline. That's the target: a ghostly underwater smear (c).

185 FISH A BREAM BED

For sheer action, few angling pursuits can touch spring-spawning bluegills. In ponds and lakes, look for sandy flats near deep water—they'll be Swiss-cheesed with beds. In rivers and streams, check out woody cover near hard bottoms and shallow water—a single dinner-plate-sized crater can hint at dozens more nearby. And no matter where you live, look for excuses to skip work on the full moons of spring and early summer, when bluegill spawning peaks and every cast can land a fish.

PRE-SPAWN 'Gills are suspended off shore of their spawning flats, so key in on creek channels near hard sloping ground and mid-lake humps. Back off into 5 to 15 feet of water and use small slip bobbers to suspend wax worms, wet spider patterns, and red wigglers in the water column. Retrieve a half-foot of line and then hold while the bait settles.

Fly anglers can trawl for pre-spawn bluegill with a weighted fly trailing a black ant.

SPAWN As water temperatures nudge 65 degrees F, the females move to the bream beds, followed by the bucks. Spawning will peak when the water reaches about 75 degrees F. You can't go wrong with crickets, worms, sponge spiders, hairy nymphs, tiny spinners, and crankbaits. The key is stealth. Stay as far from the beds as you can and still comfortably cast.

Cast to the outer edges of the spawning beds first and then work your way in.

POST-SPAWN Breeders need recovery time, and move into deeper water adjacent to the beds. Target tangles of roots, treetops, lily pads, and deep channels where the bottom falls steeply. Try weighted bobbers to detect the lightest bites. And don't give up when the bites go flat. Many bluegill spawn multiple times, so check bream beds as the next full moon nears.

One-pound trophy 'gills are not worried about bass predation, so you'll want to hunt for them on the outside edges of shady structure.

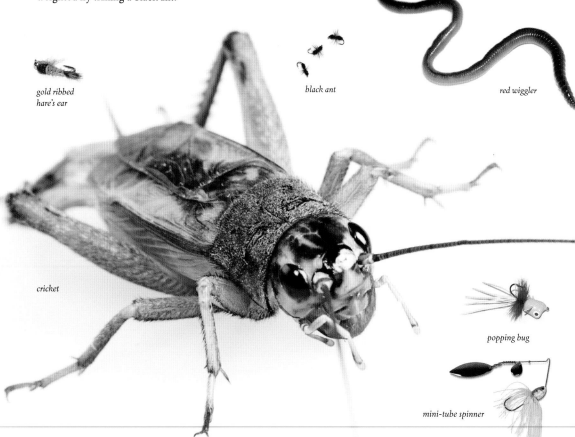

gold ribbed hare's ear

black ant

red wiggler

cricket

popping bug

mini-tube spinner

186 STORE BULK FISHING LINE

Most manufacturers will tell you that storing line for up to a year is no problem, but there are some significant caveats. First, long-term storage should always take place on bulk spools, not $1/4$-pound—or less—spools. The larger diameter of bulk spools will cut down on the problem of line memory, in which the coiled line retains loops that will snarl your casts come spring. You should also be careful about storing lines in a garage. Garages are often full of chemical vapors that can degrade monofilament and fluorocarbon lines, so you don't want your spools anywhere near cleaning agents, solvents, automobile fluids—just the kinds of thing you typically keep in the garage.

Equally important to line stability is a stable environment without large temperature fluctuations, so unless your garage is heated, it's better suited for beer than for bass string. A simple solution: Stack bulk spools in a couple of shoeboxes and jam them up on the highest shelf in the hall closet.

187 PATCH A KAYAK WITH DUCT TAPE

Launching kayaks off riprap landings and concrete boat ramps can be really hard on a boat. When this treatment leads to a cracked hull, here's how to fix that kayak and get back to chasing stripers in 30 minutes.

STEP 1 Stop the crack from enlarging by drilling a hole at each end of the split. Rub the cracked area with sandpaper, and clean it with a damp cloth. Let dry.

STEP 2 Heat the patch area with a hair dryer until it's nearly hot to the touch. Neatly place duct tape over the crack, overlapping it by 2 inches. Push out air bubbles. Now heat the patch with the hair dryer until small wrinkles form under the tape. Use a spoon to press as hard as you can, starting in the middle and working to the edges of the duct tape. Don't drag the spoon. Pick it up, press down, and roll toward the tape edge.

STEP 3 Repeat with three other layers, overlapping them by about $1/4$ inch.

FIELD & STREAM CRAZY-GOOD GRUB

188 FRY FISH STREAM-SIDE

You fish. You fry. This is the sacrament of the river trip, and here is how you get from a cooler full of fish to a riverbank communion.

At home, fill a break-resistant 1-quart plastic water bottle with peanut oil. Pour 2 cups of breading mix into a 1-gallon, zip-seal bag. Stuff it, along with a second empty bag, coffee filters, paper towels, and a baggie of Cajun spice mix, into a second plastic water bottle. Your fry kit is complete. At the campsite, it'll be quick and easy to put it all together.

STEP 1 Pour enough peanut oil into a skillet to cover the fillets' sides but not spill over their tops. Place the pan on two long parallel logs and build a fire in between. You don't need coals. For precise flame control, keep smaller branches handy.

STEP 2 Season the fillets liberally with Cajun spice and toss them into the empty plastic bag. Shake well. Add bread crumbs and, using your fingers, work the breading into the cracks. Shake off the excess. Now get ready—here comes the magic.

STEP 3 The oil should be almost smoking hot. Ease in a small piece of test fish. You want a rolling, sputtering boil around the edges. Nothing less will do. Gently add the other pieces but don't crowd the pan.

STEP 4 Give the fillets 2 to 5 minutes per side. When the fish turns the color of caramel, turn carefully—and only once. It's done when you can flake the fillet all the way through. Drain fillets on paper towels. Let the excess oil cool and then strain it back into its bottle using a coffee filter to reuse.

189 FISH LIKE A JAPANESE STREAM WARRIOR

Developed in Japan 200 years ago, tenkara fishing was introduced to American anglers in 2009. It involves using a very long fly rod with no reel; the line is tied directly to the tip. Using a truncated style of short-distance casting, anglers can use these rods to reach across conflicting currents and prevent a faster (or slower) current from pulling the fly and causing drag. Adherents are nearly worshipful of tenkara, which they say puts more emphasis on skill and less on gear.

Tenkara rods telescope, and some can extend to nearly 15 feet. With a base length of less than 2 feet, they're great for packing into tight headwaters. Use the longest rod you can. The limiting factor is how much canopy might impede the cast, not overall length. You'll quickly get used to the length, and you'll want the line control.

Lines are about the length of the rod and attach to the rod tip. There are two broad types: More traditional tapered lines afford a super-delicate fly presentation. Newer level lines are more easily altered on the stream but harder to cast. Lines are tipped with a short 3- to 4-foot tippet.

Most tenkara flies feature a reverse hackle in which the feather is brushed forward towards the hook eye. This gives the fly a pulsing, bloomlike profile, like a jellyfish opening and closing. Unlike traditional western flyfishing, tenkara places little emphasis on fly selection, and more on manipulating the fly to entice a strike.

190 CATCH A DINOSAUR WITH A ROPE

Longnose gar have been around for about 100 million years, skulking in freshwater with few predators. You can change that with a simple homemade rig. Cut 6 inches of yellow braided nylon rope and melt one end with a lighter or match. Unbraid the strands from the other end for two-thirds the length of the rope. That's your lure: a tooth-snaring garish yellow plug with no hook. Attach it to a stout leader with a slip knot and chuck it into gar water. When the fish strikes, give it slack so it works those fine teeth into the rope, shaking its head to snare it even more firmly. Only then should you apply pressure and bring the prehistoric beast all the way to the boat.

191 SHOOT DOCKS FOR CRAPPIE

Docks provide shade, baitfish, ambush cover, and even a little night mood-lighting, at times. It all comes together as super crappie cover—except for those pesky docks. There's no way to get a traditional cast in between all those boat lifts, finger piers, pilings, and gangways. You'll need to shoot your way in.

Shooting docks for crappie is where fishing meets bowhunting. You turn your rod into a bow and your grub into an arrow, shooting a jig deep into shady haunts beneath a dock. Look for old docks with wooden posts. Spool an open-face spinning reel with high-visibility monofilament in 4- to 6-pound test. Use a medium-light or even ultralight rod in the 5- to 7-foot range. Arm it with a soft-bodied crappie jig. You are locked and loaded.

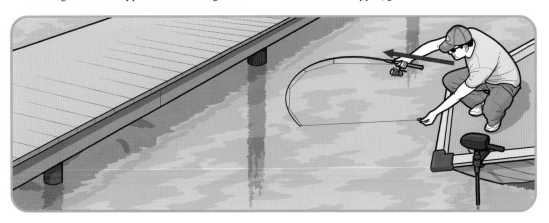

STEP 1 Point the rod tip up and open the bail. Release enough line so the lure falls to the bottom rod guide. Trap the line against the rod with the trigger finger of your rod hand. With your free hand, grasp the jighead between your thumb and your forefinger and middle finger with the hook point up and the rest of your fingers extended out of the hook's way. Holding the jig to your side, extend the rod tip toward your target zone. This creates a bend in the rod.

STEP 2 Keep the drawn line between the rod tip and the jig low and parallel to the water. You may need to crouch. The lure should start skipping just before the dock.

STEP 3 Let go of the jighead first, and in the next instant, release your trigger finger to allow the line to play out. To keep the lure from hitting the rod tip, pop the rod tip upward upon the release.

192 GIVE REDBREAST SUNNIES THE SLIP

One of the downsides of trying to fish and hunt for everything is that I miss being consumed by a single passion. On a trip to Florida's Suwannee River, I ran into a couple of codgers who fished for redbreast sunfish an incredible 75 days a year. They deep-drifted crickets with $\frac{1}{16}$-ounce bullet weights, but it was the bobbers they fussed over like kids with a puppy. They modified off-the-shelf 2-inch slip corks by removing the hollow inserts and pushing inserts from the next size up into the line channels. Monofilament slid twice as easily in those larger channels, allowing the crickets to attain deeper depths.

193 SURF CAST A COUNTRY MILE

Make a good "off-the-beach" cast, and the stripers beyond the breakers will learn to fear your truck. You'll need a shock leader of three times the test of your fishing line—as well as plenty of beach.

STEP 1 Face the water, with your left foot forward. Twist your upper body 90 degrees to the right, and look away from the water. Drift your rod tip back and let the sinker or lure drop to the ground at the 3 o'clock position. Move the rod to about the 1 o'clock position. Drop the rod tip down until your left arm is higher than your right. Reel in the slack.

STEP 2 Start with your right arm straight. With the sinker or lure on the beach, rotate your body at the hips, rod still behind you but moving in a smooth circular pattern, trending upward. Rotational energy fires the cast.

STEP 3 As your body straightens, shift your weight to the left foot, pull your left arm sharply down and in, and push with your right arm. Practice the timing of the release to straighten out a curve in the cast.

194 TOW A CANOE WITH A BOAT

Towing a canoe behind a motorboat is a neat trick, giving anglers a way to haul gear and have a boat ready to portage into remote waters. But a towed canoe can flip almost without warning. Make things go smoothly by towing with a harness that provides the pull from beneath the canoe's keel line.

STEP 1 Turn the canoe so that it will be traveling stern-first. This helps by putting the seat closer to the towing vessel. Use water jugs to provide 40 to 50 pounds of ballast behind the center thwart.

STEP 2 Attach a towline bridle to create a towing point at the canoe's keel. Tie a large butterfly loop in the rope; this is one end of the bridle. Wrap the bridle under the canoe and fasten the loop and one tag end to the seat thwarts. The knot itself should remain under the keel.

STEP 3 Connect the towing end of the rope to the midpoint of a Y-harness attached to the corners of the tow boat's transom. Retain about 30 feet of line between the tow vessel and canoe—enough slack so that you can fine-tune the length if needed.

STEP 4 Watch the canoe carefully, make gradual turns, and do not cross strong wakes.

195 CATCH EVERY FISH THAT BITES

Fish the first cast with as much focus as the sixth or seventh. People walk up to a pool and throw the line in. They're not ready. Make that first cast count, and when you're that close, treat all line tension as fish. Don't hesitate and think, "Oh, that's not a fish. Maybe next time." That was next time.

196 SURVIVE THE FROG CHOMP

Hollow-body topwater frogs are deadly on big bass in the pads, but if you watch a pro work one, you'll notice there's some finesse to the hookset. Most baits of this style feature two stationary single hooks on the back instead of treble hooks that dangle and pivot. By swinging the instant a bass crushes the frog, you are likely to score nothing more than a lure flying at your face. Giving bass time to eat a hollow-body frog is critical. It might take serious willpower to resist the set, but if you let the bass take the frog under and wait for the rod to load before you swing, you'll land more hawgs.

197 TIE THE NICKENS KNOW-NOTHING

I've been told that fish strike my Know-Nothing Shad Ball because they are insulted by such a simplistic offering. Whatever. I can tell you that it requires only four materials, and you have to know nearly nothing to tie it. It has caught hickory and American shad, stripers, bluegills, crappies, bass, and with the addition of a Mylar tail, Spanish mackerel, bluefish, and false albacore. What it lacks in fancy it makes up for in flash. Tie it with heavy eyes and fish it with a weighted line.

YOU'LL NEED
size-4 streamer hook • 6/0 white thread • dumbbell, nickel-plated eyes • krystal flash chenille body, medium

STEP 1 Secure the thread just behind the hook eye and wrap a thread base one-quarter the length of the hook. Tie dumbbell eyes on top of this base with crisscross windings. Don't crowd the hook eye; you'll need space to anchor the chenille. Add a drop of head cement to the dumbbell eye wrappings. Now run the thread wrap down the shank to just before the hook bend.

STEP 2 Tie in chenille at the hook bend, then wrap the thread back to the eye of the hook. Wrap the chenille forward up the hook shank. Wrap one winding in front of the other for a slimmer, faster-sinking profile, or double up the wraps to build a bulky body. Form a head by wrapping the chenille over the dumbbell eyes, using crisscross windings.

STEP 3 Secure the chenille to the hook in front of the eyes with a few wraps of thread. Build up a thread head, then whip finish the thread and dab with head cement. In an anchored boat on moving water, cast the fly straight across the current, then feed line and sweep the rod tip downstream as the fly sinks. Strip with short jerks all the way to the boat.

198

DYE BUCKTAIL LURES & FLIES

The most common natural material for lures and many flies is the tail of a white-tailed deer. Those long hairs are found in bucktail jigs, bass bugs, Clouser Deep Minnows, and many other fish catchers. Here's the 4-1-1 on preparation.

STEP 1 To skin the tail, split the underside with a fillet knife to within a few inches of the tip. Peel back the skin, wrap the tailbone with burlap, grasp it firmly, and pull the bone free. Continue the incision to the tip of the tail and scrape away all flesh and fat. Rub with salt or Borax and freeze.

STEP 2 To dye the hairs, soak the tail overnight in water and dishwashing detergent, rinse, and dry completely. Mix a solution of sugar-free Kool-Aid, water, and vinegar at a ratio of 2 ounces vinegar to 1 cup water. Pour this into a glass jar and submerge the tail. Place the jar in a larger pot of gently boiling water for 20 minutes to an hour or more. Check often for color. Remove the tail, blot, and tack to a piece of plywood to dry.

199 DRY WET WADERS

The only thing worse than going overboard in your chest waders is that sickening squishy sensation the next time you stick your tootsies into those cold, wet boots. Drying out chest waders can take forever because let's face it—not much air gets in there—unless you speed up the process with a few common household items.

FISH WRAPPER Wad up newspaper and stuff it into the boots. Replace frequently. Newsprint will soak up a lot of moisture and is much less expensive than paper towels.

HANG 'EM HIGH Fold the chest part of the waders down several times to expose the boots. Hang upside down in a closet or from a wall hook. Place a box fan on a chair under the boots so the breeze blows into them.

DIY BOOT DRYER Cut a 6-foot length of spare PVC pipe into two 3-foot pieces, using a diagonal cut. (You'll want pipe at least 2 inches in diameter.) Roll the chest part of the waders down over the boots. Insert the pointed end of a PVC pipe into each boot so that the open part of the pointed end faces the toes. Now turn the waders over and stand them up on a heat register.

200 PATCH WADERS ON THE STREAM

At best, leaky waders can turn a fishing trip into a bone-chilled, shivering torture test. At worst, they sink your trip completely. The patch kits for non-neoprene waders made of rubber, canvas, or breathable membranes will often require a full day to cure, but you can make your own on-the-stream emergency patch job with a piece of women's nylon hose and fancy adhesives. Here's your emergency patch kit.

YOU'LL NEED
• aquaseal • cotol-240 cure accelerator
• small piece of nylon hose • duct tape

STEP 1 Use the Cotol-240 to clean around the tear. Rub with a clean cloth to dry. Close the tear with duct tape on the inside of the material.

STEP 2 Cut a patch from the hose large enough to cover the rip plus ½ inch on all sides.

STEP 3 Mix 3 to 4 parts Aquaseal to 1 part cure accelerator. Stir with a clean stick.

STEP 4 Soak your patch in the Aquaseal, then place over the rip. Let the patch dry for 1 to 2 hours.

201 FISH A BUSH HOOK

In many parts of the country, bush hooking is a revered tradition. Using small boats and canoes, anglers rig set lines to limbs overhanging the stream, then while away the hours working one line after another. For hunters and anglers camping on or near moving water, it's a fine way to fill a frying pan while attending to camp chores or chasing other fish and game.

To fish a bush hook, find a stout sapling or limb that extends over the water a few feet upstream of a desired fishing location. Your best bets are strong eddy lines, tributary outfalls, and any deep holes beneath undercut banks. To tie the bush hook, attach a three-way swivel to 30- to 50-pound monofilament line. Tie one dropper line to an egg sinker, and another to the hook. Tie the bush hook to the sapling or branch, load the hook with a bait that will hold up to strong current—cut bait, live shiners, shrimp—and drop it into the water. You'll want to check it every couple of hours.

And check your local laws. Some states consider bush hooks as commercial gear, and may require the use of a cotton line or other specifics. Other states don't consider bush hooks as "sporting tackle." But to hungry hunters or drift fishermen, such distinctions fade away once you sink your teeth into a freshly caught catfish filet.

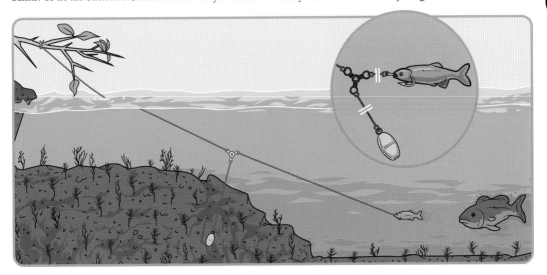

202 HOLD ON TIGHTLY

Inshore and surf anglers know to match the sinker to the fishing conditions.

PYRAMID SINKERS Perfect for holding a bottom rig in sand, these sinkers can get hung up in rock jetties.

SPUTNIK SINKERS These sinkers have wires that dig into the bottom for rough-weather holding power and release and fold against the sinker for an easy retrieve.

BANK SINKERS These sinkers, which are easier to retrieve than pyramids, have a bit of bottom hold, so they are good in calm-water but will move around in currents.

HATTERAS OR STORM SINKERS These sinkers will hang tight in swirling bottom currents.

Sputnik Sinker

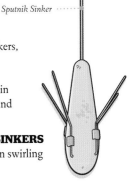

203 TAKE A JAW-DROPPING FISH PHOTO

No matter where you land your fish of a lifetime, here's a fool-proof way to capture the moment. Talk your partner through these steps and then smile for the camera:

SET THE SCENE Move away from water muddied by the fight, and keep the fish in the water as much as possible, moving it gently back and forth to keep fresh water washing through its gills. Position the lure in the fish's mouth the way you want it to appear, or remove it. And clear the scene of clutter—drink cans, extra rods and reels, anything bright that will draw the viewer's attention away from the fish.

MODEL BEHAVIOR Have the angler remove sunglasses and hat, or, at least, tip the hat up a bit to prevent a dark shadow on the face. A shirt with color will add pop to any photo, but avoid muted greens and blues that might blend in to foliage or a big sky.

FIRE AWAY Have the angler kneel in the water, supporting the fish with both hands. Meter off of the fish and then have the angler dip the fish into the water. Take a shot as the fish comes up out of the water, streaming droplets of water. Try it again with the flash dialed in to the fill-flash setting.

willow leaf blade

Colorado blade   *Indiana blade*   *willow leaf blade*

204 CHOOSE THE RIGHT BLADE

The configuration of spinnerbait blades dictates how the lure moves through the water. And that, of course, dictates in large measure whether a bass will ignore your lure or suck half the pond into its gullet during a boat-swamping strike (which would be a good thing).

There are three basic configuration styles. Round Colorado blades are akin to pimping your spinnerbait ride: They pump out tons of vibration, which makes them a go-to choice for stained water, and they impart the most lift to the lure, so they'll run more shallow than others. Willow-leaf blades create more flash than vibrating fuss, so you'll want to use them for clearer conditions. Willow blades also spin on a tighter axis, so they'll clear weeds more cleanly than others. Indiana blades are a compromise; they look like an elongated Colorado blade. Or a roundish willow-leaf. Nothing simple when it comes to bass fishing.

205 BACK A TRAILER WITHOUT LOOKING LIKE AN IDIOT

Backing a boat trailer down a ramp isn't all that hard, but like establishing proper lead in wingshooting, it takes practice. The key fact to bear in mind is that the trailer will always go in the direction opposite the tow vehicle. This causes a great deal of confusion and is one of the main reasons you see guys jockeying up and down the ramp with a trailer that seems to have a mind of its own. Here's an easy way to master the maneuver.

STEP 1 Find a big empty parking lot where you can learn to gain control over your trailer without worrying about a long line of irate fishermen behind you. After you shift into reverse, place your left hand on the bottom of the steering wheel (remove fly-tying vise first!). When you move your hand to the right (which turns the steering wheel and front tires to the left), the trailer will move to the right (a). And when you move your hand to the left (which turns the steering wheel and front tires to the right), then the trailer will move to the left (b).

STEP 2 Move slowly. Most beginners back up too fast. If the trailer starts to move in the wrong direction, stop. Pull up, straighten the trailer, and start again. Trying to correct a wayward trailer will only make matters worse. Once you master the parking lot, you're ready for the ramp.

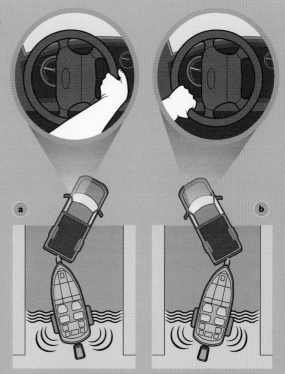

It takes a little getting used to (and your brain will fight you at first), but it works.

206 STICK A SHORT-STRIKING SALMON

Short-striking fish can drive a fly angler batty, a situation well-known to landlocked salmon fishermen who must contend with conflicting currents in larger rivers. What to do when you don't have a fly with a trailing hook handy? This: Let the accidental back cast level out behind you and then forward cast to the same spot where the fish spat out your lure. Keep the line fairly taut but let the fly drift and sink naturally, as if it were mortally wounded by the original chomp. Give it 5 seconds and then give it a good twitch. That's often enough to entice a salmon to show up for a second helping.

FIELD & STREAM-APPROVED KNOT

207 TIE A RAPALA KNOT

The Rapala knot is a winner because the wraps, which are ahead of the initial overhand knot, relieve stress where the standing line enters the rest of the knot. Also, line passes through the overhand knot three times, which serves to cushion the standing line.

STEP 1 Tie an overhand knot six inches above the tag end of your line. Thread the tag end through the lure eyelet and then through the overhand knot.

STEP 2 Next, take the tag end and wrap it three times around the standing line.

STEP 3 Pass the tag end through the back of the overhand knot.

STEP 4 Run the tag end through the new loop you formed in Step 3.

STEP 5 Lubricate and tighten by pulling on the tag end, main line, and lure.

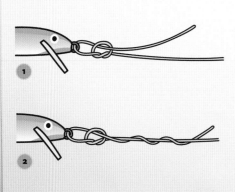

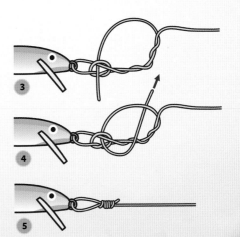

208 SKIN A CAT IN A JIFFY

Don't pout when a catfish pounces on your jig. Cleaning Mr. Whiskers is not as difficult as some people think.

STEP 1 Hold the catfish belly down and make two shallow slits through the skin: one should nearly girdle the fish's head from pectoral fin to pectoral fin, and the other should run from the top of this cut past the dorsal fin and down to the tail.

STEP 2 Grasp a corner of the skin flap firmly with pliers, and pull down and across the body all the way to the tail. Repeat on the other side.

STEP 3 Remove the head by bending it first toward the tail and then the stomach and then pulling it free of the body.

STEP 4 Remove the entrails by opening up the body cavity with a knife.

STEP 5 Fry and eat with a smile.

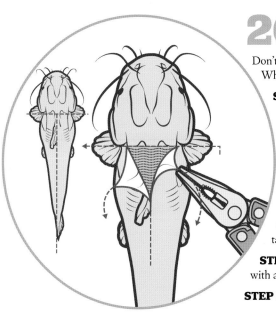

209 DRAG FISH OUT OF A CAVE

They are deep and dark as Grendel's lair, which is why Grendel-size trout, snook, and redfish like to hole up in undercut banks. Follow these tips to foil a cave dweller.

Cast a plastic tube bait, lizard, or other light lure with an embedded hook point onto the bank a few feet upstream of the undercut. Jiggle it into the water and let the current carry it under the bank. Leave a bit of slack so the lure sinks, reel in quickly, and jerk the rod tip to impart action. Stop to let the lure slow down, enticing a strike.

210 SKATE A FLY WITH A RIFFLE HITCH

A riffle hitch can be a very effective tactic. It is a knot that enables a fly to skim and skitter across the water surface, leaving a V-shaped wake that often results in a strike. That's called "skating a fly," or, as it is otherwise known, "Holy moley! Why haven't I tried this before?"

STEP 1 Your first line of action is to attach tippet to the fly with an improved clinch knot.

STEP 2 Next, you're going to want to add a half-hitch behind the eye of the hook, taking care to pull the tag

end of the leader straight down. Add a second half-hitch in front of the first one. Pull the tag end of the leader straight down and snip. The half-hitches can be placed as far down the fly as the gape of the hook for a variety of actions on the water.

STEP 3 Cast down and across. The fly floats higher in the water column and will skate across the surface film. Spincasters can use this technique with the addition of a casting bubble.

211 UNHOOK YOURSELF

Depending on how deeply you've sunk the barb into your own flesh, your choices are good, bad, and worse. If the barb protrudes from your epidermal layer, removing the hook is a snap. Just cut the hook shank below the barb and back the hook out. If the barb is embedded but is still close to the skin surface, it's time to grin and (literally) bare it: Push the hook point the rest of the way out, cut it off behind the barb, and then put it in reverse. A deeply embedded hook point requires a nifty bit of macramé, line lashing, Newtonian action-reaction physics, and a quick, courageous yank. It's not so bad. Really.

Here's how. First, double a 2-foot length of fishing line (at least 10-pound test) and slip the loop around the midpoint of the bend in the hook. Hold the line ends between the thumb and forefinger of one hand and wrap the line around the opposite wrist, leaving a few inches of slack. With the free hand, press the hook eye down against the skin to keep the barb from snagging. Don't let the hook shank twist. Grasp the line sharply, line it all up nice and straight, breathe deep, and yank. Really.

212

FLY CAST UPSIDE-DOWN

Well, sort of. Learning to cast underhanded will soothe a number of tricky flyfishing situations. It's a good way to cast into a wind. It'll slip a fly under overhanging brush. And it's a go-to cast for a bow angler situated where a traditional cast might bang the fly against a tall console or pierce a friend's earlobe. The loop in the fly line actually travels under the tip of the rod. Here's the drill.

213 DETECT LIGHT BITES

Even experienced anglers struggle with the light takes of walleye. It's especially tough with jigging. Nine times out of 10, a jig bite feels as if you're nudging weeds or about to get hung up on something. The rod just loads up a bit and feels a little heavy. That's likely to be a walleye, but people will end up pulling bait away from fish half the day. You're better off setting the hook. If it's a fish, you're a genius. If not, what did you lose?

To catch the bite, hold the rod at a 45-degree angle away from you, not straight out in front. Hop that jig as you bring the rod from the 45- to a 90-degree angle and then reel back to the original 45-degree angle again. This step is critical. Why? Because if you hold the rod straight out, you can't see the line hesitate or the rod tip bump.

214 CAST INTO A TORNADO

Heavy lures require a rod at least 7 feet long, with action in the tip to help load the forward section. Here's how to launch into a gale.

STEP 1 Holding the rod with both hands, bring it all the way behind you and stop when it is parallel to the water surface. Keep the rod horizontally behind you, knuckles up, and chill. Now, let 'er rip.

STEP 2 Right-handed casters should have their weight on the right foot. Shift your weight to the left as you begin to power the rod tip overhead. Instead of carving an arc in the air, shift your right shoulder forward to flatten out the top of the stroke. Accelerate through the cast, arms extended out. Then hold the pose, Madonna. It'll take a while before the lure lands.

KEEP TO THE BOW This is the go-to cast for a bow angler situated where a traditional cast might hook a friend's earlobe.

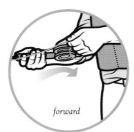

forward

backward

STEP 1 Start with a side cast, with the rod held nearly horizontal to the water surface. Turn the rod grip almost 90 degrees so the butt rests against your forearm. This gives you leverage.

STEP 2 Begin your false casting. At the end of each forward and backward stroke, you need to lift the rod tip up slightly. This will form the essential upside-down loop.

STEP 3 Deliver the fly with a strong forward cast. This should be powered with a strong flick-and-stop of the forearm; the motion is as if you were throwing a Frisbee™.

215 FLIP A LURE THE FLORIDA WAY

When most people flip for bass, they let the line go, it hits the water, and if a fish hits the lure on the way down and then releases it, the angler never feels the bite. It's especially problematic in heavy grass—unless you know how to tighten your line before the drop. Cast right into the middle of a weed mat and let the lure drive a hole into the hollow beneath. But the real key is this: As soon as the lure hits the water, apply slight thumb pressure to the spool to control the drop of the lure. Don't let it free-fall to the bottom. Set it on the mat and lower it with your thumb. That gives you the chance to feel even the slightest take on the drop.

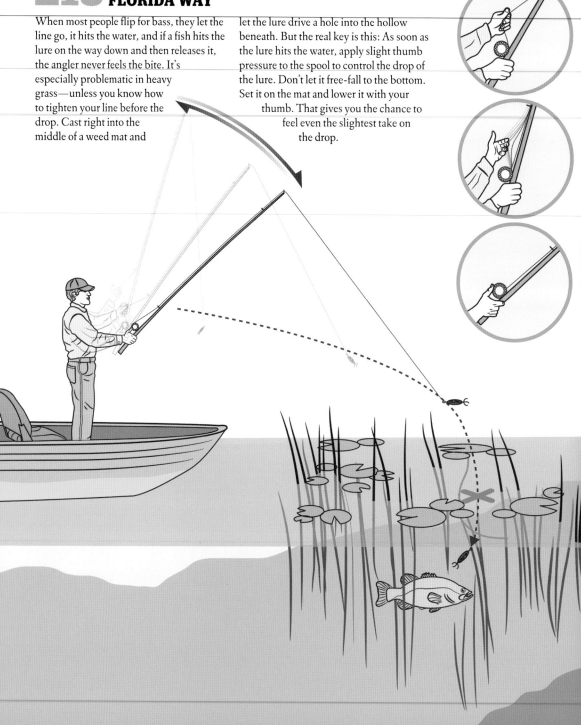

216 FISH WITH A SHINER

Florida is famous for its wild live shiner fishing. "The fish chase those shiners to the surface," says fishing guide Todd Kersey, "and, oh, man, the world blows up right in front of you. It's very exciting." Not in Florida? You can get in on the thrills wherever bass lurk.

GEAR UP Use a 4/0 live-bait hook and a standard egg bobber, and large baits—shiners between 6 and 10 inches. It's a handful, especially since the trick is to always keep the shiner right above the grass. Sometimes you need $^1/_8$ or $^3/_8$ ounce of lead to keep the shiners down, but if you use lead, make sure you've got a real kicker for bait. The minnow needs to spook and run because bass love to attack a moving target.

WORK IT The trick is in working the bite. A bass can eat a big shiner only headfirst—if it goes down tail first, the shiner's fins will get hung up in his throat. What happens is this: The bass blows out of the water, grabs that shiner, and starts buzzing drag off the reel. Your first instinct—to lock down and let him have it—is the worst thing to do. You have to let the fish run, and when he stops to turn that shiner around in his mouth, that's when you hit him. Sometimes it's 5 yards. Sometimes it's 35 yards. You never know.

FIELD & STREAM CRAZY-GOOD GRUB

217 TRY A BEER-POACHED FISH

A cold one is the 11th essential on a good fishing trip. Besides being the beverage of choice after a long day on the water, it also can be used to help you cook your catch. Any kind of beer is perfect for poaching fish, and the recipe is simple.

STEP 1 Build a good fire.

STEP 2 Lay out a sheet of heavy-duty aluminum foil that is two and a half times longer and deeper than your biggest fish. Drizzle the bottom of the foil with olive oil and then add a $^1/_2$-inch-thick layer of sliced green onions. Add a cleaned fish to the top of the pile and souse it with the first few ounces of a fresh beer. The rest of the can is for you. Roll up the foil, sealing the fish, onions, oil, and beer in a tight pouch.

STEP 3 Place the pouch near hot coals for about 15 minutes for a decent eating-size walleye. The onions will char. The beer will steam. The fish will flake with a fork. You will eat and drink like a king.

218 PRANK SOCIAL MEDIA PALS

Social media can turn you into a fishing hero or a former employee who's fish pics got you outed as a work-at-home poser. Here's how to post fish photos that supersize your catch while downplaying the fact that you boogied out early on a Friday afternoon.

GET RELATIVE Every fish looks bigger when photographed beside a toy-sized rod and reel. Pack one of those mini-micro-ultralight spinning or fly outfits to prop beside your catch. Turns a 6-inch bluegill into a true titty bream.

DELAY THE GAME When you post pics on the go, everyone—boss, spouse, buddies—is alerted that your nose is off the grindstone. Resist the temptation to post in real time. Lay down fake bread crumbs while on the water. "Deadline crunch today—hope I make that 3 P.M. cutoff!" and "Buried in this project for hours but light in the tunnel now!" will keep your pals from bugging you

since you are obviously sweating for The Man. Then hit 'em with that 8-pound hawg shot just past sundown. Use Instagram's "Hefe" filter to add sunset highlights, or throw them off the time trail completely with an artsy black-and-white filter.

HIDE THE SPOT Want to rub your big fish in your friends' virtual faces but without tipping them off to your favorite farm pond? Use the tilt-shift feature in the Instagram edit mode to blur out landscape details. Or haul in an inflatable palm tree for background foliage. The monkey gets them every time. "Man, that looks like Fred's pond, but I don't think there's a palm tree out there. And I would remember that monkey for sure."

219

MASTER THE ORVIS KNOT

Use this knot for tying small flies to light leader tippets, or spinning lures to light- or medium-size nylon monofilaments. It is usually 20 to 30 percent stronger than the popular improved clinch.

STEP 1 Extend 6 to 8 inches of line through the hook eye. Form a large loop with the tag end on the far side of the standing line.

STEP 2 Form a second loop by bringing the tag end around the standing line and back underneath and through the first loop.

STEP 3 Bend the tag end to the right and make two turns around the second loop. These turns must start from the far side of the second loop.

STEP 4 To tighten the knot, first pull in opposite directions on both the hook and the tag end. Then pull on the standing line to bring the knot firmly against the hook eye.

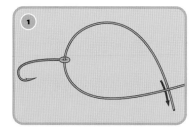

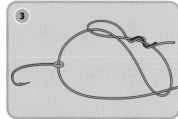

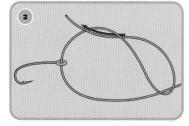

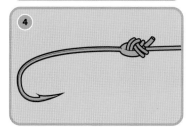

220

SCHOOL A KID ON FLY FISHING

Teaching your kids how to fly-cast doesn't have to be as trying as helping them with math homework. Approach the task like training a puppy: short, fun sessions with plenty of opportunities for success. Using kid-friendly gear is a huge bonus. Here's what to look for.

A soft action helps kids feel the flex and load. Resist the temptation to choose a super-short rod, which can be difficult to cast. Go for an 8-foot, 6-weight outfit.

Overline the rod by one line weight to make for easier casting and ability to feel the rod load.

Get a barbed fly stuck in your child's forehead and you can forget about a future fishing buddy. Only use flies with barbless hooks. For practice, tie orange egg yarn next to the fly to make it visible. On the water, cast big high-floating flies like Stimulators.

221 | TRICK LUNKERS WITH A LANTERN

For several million years, there was only one way to fish at night: Hang a trusty double-mantle, white-gas-burning Coleman lantern over the water and get to it. The lantern hissed gently, its glow attracting baitfish and their bigger brethren, as well as hordes of mosquitoes held at bay with metal-melting concoctions of 100 percent DEET. That's how your granddaddy night fished, and his'n and his'n. And guess what? It still works today.

222 FILLET THE BONIEST FISH THAT SWIMS

The Y-bones embedded in the dorsal flesh of a northern pike prevent many anglers from dining on one of the tastiest fish around. Learn to remove them, and you will never curse when a 3-pound pike bashes your walleye rig.

STEP 1 Fillet the fish, removing flesh from the ribs as you would with any other fish.

STEP 2 Find the row of white dots visible midway between the spine and the top of the fillet. These are the tips of the Y-bones. Slice along the top of these dots, nearly through the fillet, following the curve of the bones.

STEP 3 Next, you'll want to slice along the bottom of the Y-bones, following their shape, while aiming the knife tip toward the first incision.

STEP 4 Connect the two cuts above the fish's anus. Remove the bony strip. Get the grease popping.

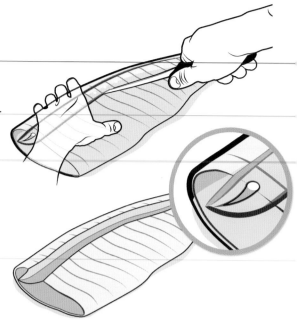

223 TAKE THE FIGHT TO THE FISH IN SMALL WATER

Big fish are so strong and tough in tight quarters. Two things are crucial to landing monster fish in small rivers. First, as soon as you know the fish is hooked well, go to the head of the pool. Put some distance between the rod and whatever rapids and logs and rocks are jumbled up in the tailout. Second, once you have some room, it's critical to make the fish go through at least two runs against the drag. Don't be afraid to wave your arms above the water if you have to. You simply must get the fish to work and tire out.

Instead of fighting with the rod held straight up and down, turn it at a 45-degree angle, and sweep the tip to the left or right to lead the fish into the current or into deep runs. You may need to steer a big fish into shallow water so it will get nervous and make a break for the current. If it just sits in the stream, holding, do something to get it moving again. Take control of the action.

224

FLY CAST IN CIRCLES

When brush or high ground limits your back cast, break the rules with a lob cast.

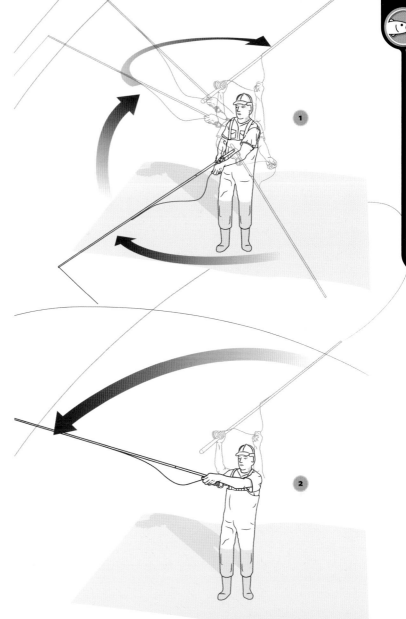

STEP 1 Strip the line in so you have the leader and about 10 feet of line in the water. Point the rod at the fly and then pick it all up, right out of the water at once, and make a big, fast, clockwise, circular pass overhead. The reel should actually move in a half-circle above your head.

STEP 2 Stop the rod behind at the position where you would stop a traditional back cast, feel it load, and then fire all the line out with one forward shot. You can seriously launch a heavy fly or sink-tip line this way.

225
CATCH BAIT WITH A SABIKI RIG

Sabiki rigs are ready-to-fish dropper lines festooned with small hooks trimmed with reflective materials and sometimes bucktail. These rigs are great for catching marine baitfish, but freshwater baits like white perch and small bream will suck in the hooks too. (Check local regulations before using.)

In freshwater, you're going to want to go for the smallest hooks you can find. Attach a 1- or 2-ounce weight, and jig slowly up and down with a long rod over likely structure. Don't make the mistake of bringing it in with the first strike. A hooked fish will move the hooks around and attract other fish.

To store your sabiki rig, wrap the rig around a wine cork, sticking each hook into the cork as you wrap.

"*A man may not care for golf and still be human, but the man who does not like to see, hunt, photograph, or otherwise outwit birds or animals is hardly normal. He is supercivilized, and I for one do not know how to deal with him.*"

—Aldo Leopold

The Thrill of the Hunt

The gun was a Remington Model 700 BDL Varmint Special, chambered in .22-250, and we fed it hot handloads that could flip a groundhog backwards out of its burrow at 300 yards.

If you could hit the target.

This was 40 years ago, and it was with that gun that I learned how to shoot a rifle. I learned through equal parts humiliation and determination. My mentor, Keith Gleason, was a former U.S. Marine who didn't coddle the newbie. We cruised dirt roads in the rolling foothills along the New River where it stitches back and forth between North Carolina and Virginia, trading shots at whistlepigs in greening pastures. You got one shot. After that, hit or miss, you had to hand over the rifle. If I blew my chance, well, Gleason didn't care that I was a 13-year-old kid and he was a trained sharpshooter. Try harder, he'd say. And I would.

And I've never stopped. Trying harder, that is, because hunting is a pursuit not only of wild game but of better and more efficient and more rewarding ways to pursue wild game. And the pursuit itself counts for much, for it is the pursuit that binds us to a favorite opening in the woods or a particular bend in a river. All hunters have felt this. Ojibwa and Shawnee. Seminole and Creek. The Georgia swamper and the Midwestern farm boy and the weekend warriors who flee the city for weekends in the woods.

Try harder. Tighten up the shot group. Fine-tune the turkey call. Get the hide off more cleanly. Learn a new knot. No hunter ever tires of this. Young or old, we're never as good as we could be if we just run a few more rounds through the rifle.

Even today, nearly 40 years after I last held that old groundhog rifle, I can be at a gun shop, glancing down a line of 50 used firearms, and the first thing that catches my eye are those familiar white spacers between the stock and the butt plate, and Remington's distinctive fleur-de-lis flourishes in the grip checkering. All of a sudden, I'm back on the New River, crosshairs wobbling around a woodchuck burrow, counting heartbeats and squeezing the trigger between each throb. A lot has changed since then, but one thing hasn't: It's the first shot that matters.

226 EARN THE RIFLEMAN'S MERIT BADGE

The official Boy Scouts of America Rifle Shooting merit badge is a prestigious one, conveying the hallmarks of practice, marksmanship, and respect.

Acing this badge's test means that you possess those fundamental skills required for shooting game—both big and small—in every corner of the continent: breathing control, trigger control, body positioning, and follow-through. There's a written essay test that leaves no doubt as to whether you know the difference between a squib and a hangfire. You had better bone up on rifle cleaning, gun safety, and local laws, too.

That's before you even pull a trigger. And pull it you will. The Boy Scout test involves 40 shots. Not a one can be a clunker. No wonder the test put many a young man in a cold sweat. It's not easy, whether your scouting days have just ended or are only a misty memory. Mop your brow, and get started.

This is a three-part challenge—shooting a tight group, adjusting the sights to zero, then punching high-scoring holes in an NRA bull's-eye.

STEP 1 Decide on a preferred shooting position, either from a benchrest or supported prone, and set up an NRA smallbore or light rifle target 50 feet away. You have to fire five groups, with three shots per group, each of which can be covered by a quarter.

STEP 2 Adjust the sights to zero in the rifle. Get ready to sweat.

STEP 3 Fire five more groups, with five shots per group. No fliers and no excuses—every single shot has to meet or exceed these scores:

• NRA A-32 target: 9

• NRA A-17 or TQ-1 target: 7

• NRA A-36 target: 5

CHALLENGE YOURSELF Stand up and man up. Get off the bench and shoot your group from a standing position.

227 BRIGHTEN YOUR RIFLE SIGHT

When the front blade of a rifle's open sights goes dull, brighten it up with a bit of sandpaper or emery cloth. Polish away the bluing from the top of the front blade and paint it with fluorescent paint or even nail polish. Now you have a bright spot to settle into the rear notch.

228 SHOOT WITH TWO EYES

Closing the weak eye robs you of depth perception and slashes field of view dramatically, which means you can miss important variables, such as wind gusts at the target's location . . . or the fact that an even larger buck stepped out of the woods 10 feet away. If you shoot with one eye closed and then open both eyes, it will take a few seconds for your brain to sort out the differentiated views and those few seconds can be critical. And perhaps most important, shooting with one eye closed leads to what Gunsite Ranch founder Jeff Cooper calls "getting lost in the scope." You see the animal with both eyes, pull the gun to your shoulder, and then waste valuable seconds waving it around trying to find the target. For those who have shot one-eyed for years, opening both eyes is easier said than done. The off-season is the time to kick the habit.

METHOD

AT THE RANGE Start off with two strips of masking tape on the outside of the nondominant-eye lens of your glasses. This helps to prevent the double image that is so bothersome to shooters. As you get used to keeping both eyes open, switch to frosted tape, then try a smear of petroleum jelly. Gradually reduce the amount until you need none.

AT HOME Back up range practice by dry-firing your rifle. Mount the rifle, acquire the target, then shift your attention between the view in the scope and the other eye, to pick out all the details of the environment surrounding your target. The trick is to do this while maintaining a strong "cheek weld"— never lifting your face from the stock.

229

SAVE YOUR EARDRUMS FOR A QUARTER

I keep foam earplugs stashed in my hunting jacket pockets, blind bags, and gun cases. The low-pressure polyurethane memory foam is made to compress easily and re-form in the ear canal for a tight fit that blunts any sound. Covered with a skin of slick material, they are easier to insert and much more comfortable to wear than the bargain-basement PVC stopples. They offer a noise reduction rating (NRR) of up to 32 decibels, and they make high-repetition shooting safe and comfortable. I make sure to plug up any time I share a blind with a ported gun.

The trick is getting the plugs deep enough into your ear canal. You can't just stuff them in like shoving letters into a mail slot. Here's the drill: Roll the plug in between your thumb and your first two fingers. Be careful not to roll a wrinkle into the plug. Roll it gently with increasing pressure until it's a third the original size.

Start with your right ear—hold up the plug in your right hand while still gently rolling it tightly between your fingers. Reach over the top of your head with your left hand and pull the tip of your ear lobe upward to open up your ear canal. Now, insert the small end of the ear plug deeply, retaining enough of the larger end to easily grasp and remove.

Repeat with the other ear. And don't wait. Proper insertion takes two hands and more time than you have when the ducks are coming.

230 BUILD A GUNSMITH BOX

I keep a basement table cleared off and dedicated for gun cleaning. (It's an old family heirloom—a gorgeous walnut drop-leaf—please don't tell my mother.) At least one gun cradle is deployed at all times, which makes after-the-hunt cleaning sessions much more convenient. Here's a list of items I store in the gun cradle or in a nearby tote.

TOOLS AND BASICS
- Gun cradle or two. Maybe three.
- Wheeler Deluxe Gunsmithing Screwdriver Set. The absolute foundation.
- #1 Phillips-head screwdriver for removing recoil pads. The Wheeler set with the interchangeable tips has a flange that prevents its use for this.
- Large flat-blade screwdriver
- Socket wrench with extension for removing stock bolts
- Roll pin punches
- Allen, Torx, and hex wrenches
- Needle-nose pliers
- Rotary tool with attachments
- Old toothbrushes
- Pointed cosmetic swabs. Not ear swabs, but the pointed ones made of denser cotton.
- Cleaning rods, brushes and wool mops
- Cleaning patches
- White hand towel. Useful as a mat on which to place small parts.
- Small flashlight
- Nut pick
- Small mountain of rags
- 0000 steel wool

GADGETS AND GIZMOS
- Trigger-pull scale
- Boresighter
- Scope bubble level

SPRAYS, GOOPS, AND LUBES
- Gun oil in various forms—spray and bottle
- Solvents in various forms—spray and bottle
- Choke-tube grease
- Bore-cleaning compound
- Break-Free CLP
- Loctite Threadlocker Blue
- AquaSeal for sealing recoil pads and screws on a duck gun's synthetic stock and adding grip to gun slings.
- Cans of compressed air
- Lens cleaner and tissues
- Lighter fluid

231 MAKE A DIY TARGET STAND

This target stand holds a pair of furring strips upright for easy target attachment. Assemble as shown. For a more permanent stand, glue the PVC pipes into place with PVC glue. For an easily transportable stand, toss all the components into a bag and push the pieces into place once you're out on the range. Staple the cardboard to the furring strips and attach targets.

It is, literally, a snap.

YOU'LL NEED
2-inch PVC pipe cut to these lengths: four 16-inch pieces, two 20-inch pieces, two 26-inch pieces • 4 PVC elbow joints • 2 PVC T-joints • two 1-by-2-inch furring strips • one 24-by-36-inch piece of flat cardboard

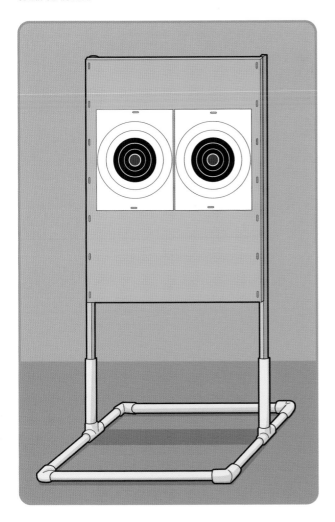

232

MAKE A TRAIL TAPE DISPENSER

By the midpoint of the hunting season, most hunting packs will contain messy wads of surveyor's tape. The stuff is indispensable for marking trails and tracking wounded animals, but the rolls unroll, twist, and get caught in pack zippers, and they become a nuisance when you're trying to fish out a small strip. Create a quick fix with an empty 35mm film canister: Stuff the canister with surveyor's tape, cut an X into the top, pull a tag end of the tape through the slit, and cap off the canister. It will work just like a box of tissues: You can pull out what you need, and no more. And they're small enough to stash in a shirt pocket or hip belt pocket, where it's ready to go.

233

STOP GUN-SLING SLIP

Nylon and paracord gun slings are light, but slippery. Add in traction with bands of a silicone sealant such as Seam Grip or Aqua Seal.

234 CAMO PAINT A GUN STOCK

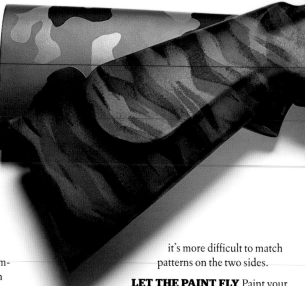

Think your old synthetic rifle or shotgun stock could use a modern face-lift? It's a snap for you to camouflage a stock with easily available hardware store spray paint and stencils you pluck from your hunting land. Instructors at the North Carolina Montgomery Community College Gunsmithing School dolled up these beauties and gave us their step-by-step plan. All you need is spray paints in three or four flat finishes (many hardware stores stock camouflage spray paint), a little bit of paint thinner, some paracord, and a few handfuls of leaves, pine needles, and grasses.

GATHER AND GLEAN Collect three species of local vegetation to use as custom stencils: a few medium-sized leaves; some pencil-thick vegetation, such as fern fronds; and finer materials, such as thin reeds and pine needles. Especially with pine needles and grasses, make sure there's plenty of open structure for the paint to get through.

PREPARE THE STOCKS Remove the barrels, actions, and sling swivels from the stocks. Degrease with a wipe of paint thinner. Use some masking tape to mask off areas that shouldn't be painted, such as the barrels' bedding channels and any action ports. Use a sharp X-Acto blade for precise cuts. Make a clothesline of paracord out in the workshop or backyard, and hang the stocks for painting. You can also paint them lying flat on some newspaper, but you'll have to wait till the paint dries to flip them over, and

it's more difficult to match patterns on the two sides.

LET THE PAINT FLY Paint your entire stock black. Let dry. Now use the natural stencils. Start with the medium-sized leaves and a medium-dark paint, such as brown or olive green. Hold that vegetation very still up against the surface of the stock, and spray with a light back-and-forth action with the can about 6 inches away. Rotate the camo vegetation in all directions to prevent striping—everything in nature is random. Next, use your thin grasses and pine needles with a bit of light brown or khaki paint for added depth. Use just enough paint to get the desired effect; too much, and thick paint globs will crack upon drying. Finish with a coat of clear flat acrylic sealant.

235 CLEAN A TRIGGER WITH A TOOTHBRUSH

We fuss over our barrels and actions, but we give too little thought to the first line in a firearm's offense: the trigger. A gunked-up trigger might be, at best, cranky to pull and the root cause of a missed shot and, at the worst, the culprit of a shot that fails to go off at all.

Cleaning a trigger is as easy as degreasing it with lighter fluid, which doesn't harm the plastics, bluing, stock finishes, or epoxy. Lighter fluid flushes out the crap and leaves behind a slight residue that provides just enough lubrication for a trigger.

There are two ways to apply. The quick and easy way

is to remove the bolt from a rifle, squirt the lighter fluid into the trigger assembly, and work the trigger as all that evaporating liquid works its magic. For a truly gunked trigger, such as a duck gun that's been hard at work all season long, remove the trigger assembly from the receiver. Flush it with lighter fluid, using an old, clean, toothbrush to flick out the grime. After it dries, use a can of compressed air to blow junk out of all the little nooks and crannies. Repeat as necessary.

236 HOLD BINOCULARS ROCK STEADY THREE WAYS

It's not easy holding binoculars steady over the course of a long glassing session for mule deer, pronghorn, and other open-country game. Here are three tricks to keep your glasses from shaking—and your arms fresh for holding a rifle.

ⓐ **RIFLE SLING** Use a long, wide binoculars strap like a rifle sling for some stability. Hold the binoculars horizontally, so that the single strap loops down towards the ground. Then, one at a time, insert your hands through the loop far enough that your elbows are inside the loop. Hold up the binoculars in a typical grip. The strap should wrap around the outside of your arms at your triceps muscle. Now spread your arms apart, tightening the strap across upper arms and chest.

ⓑ **HAT TRICK** Adjust a baseball-type cap so it fits a bit tighter than normal. Hold binoculars in a regular grip, then extend each middle finger over the cap brim and grasp firmly.

ⓒ **RECYCLE A HOCKEY STICK** Developed in Finland, a "finnstick" is a device that allows you to keep binoculars at eye-level without needing your hands. Make one out of a forked branch about 2 to 3 feet long (depending on your height). The fork holds on to the center barrel of the binoculars, while you hold the other end of the stick at waist height. In another nod to their Finnish roots, many birders use broken hockey sticks as DIY finnsticks.

237 FIX STOCK DINGS WITH AN IRON

If you view the minor dents and dings in a wooden rifle or shotgun stock as badges of field honor, then skip ahead to the next skill. If not, then grab a wet cloth, a clothes iron or soldering iron, and prepare to raise a little grain. By carefully steaming the dent you will cause the wood cells to expand, minimizing the blemish. This process works best on porous oil-based finishes. Lacquer finishes may need to be removed first, however.

STEP 1 Clean the dent to keep from steaming dirt permanently into the wood grain.

STEP 2 Wet a corner of a towel or cleaning patch with hot water. Place the wet cloth directly over the dent, and press with the tip of a clothes iron or soldering iron.

Don't overdo it. A few seconds of steaming is enough.

STEP 3 Repeat as necessary. Depending on the dent and the wood, you might need to repeat twice, thrice, or a dozen times. Let the wood dry completely between treatments.

STEP 4 The steaming process tends to raise the wood's grain, so hit the raised grain with steel wool to buff it down.

238

PICK THE RIGHT RIFLE CALIBER

Most opinions about cartridges are formed by a combination of shuck, jive, ad copy, and friends' ill-informed advice. On these pages you will find the truth, always unglamorous, sometimes downright ugly. And one of the ugliest facts is this: Choice of cartridge ranks fairly low in determining whether you will succeed as a hunter. If you're a good shot, it doesn't matter much what you use. On the other hand, choosing the wrong round can screw you up royally. With that contradiction firmly in mind, here are top choices in each category.

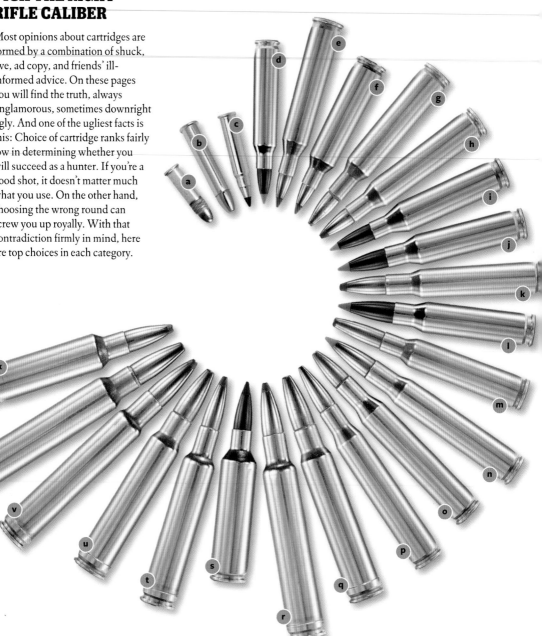

SMALL GAME Light in the hands, easy on the wallet, these rimfire rounds are the perfect choice for hunting squirrels and rabbits. These are also used on short-range varmints.

a .22 Long Rifle

b .22 Winchester Magnum Rimfire

c .17 Hornady Magnum Rimfire

VARMINTS Long-range, flat-shooting, hyper-accurate calibers with light recoil.

d .223 Remington

e .220 Swift

f .22/250 Remington

VARMINTS AND BIG GAME Heavier bullets than straight varmint rounds make these a choice for deer hunters as well.

g 6mm Remington

h .257 Roberts

i .243 Winchester

BIG GAME: THE LIGHT KICKERS These calibers are powerful enough to drop deer in their tracks but light enough to shoot enough to make you accurate enough to do it.

j 7X57 Mauser

k 7mm/08 Remington

l .308 Winchester

m 6.5X55 Swede

BIG GAME: THE ALL-AROUND ROUNDS For everything in between antelope and moose, these calibers excel.

n .30/06 Springfield

o .270 Winchester

p .280 Remington

q .338 Winchester Magnum

BIG GAME AT LONG RANGE These calibers are ballistically capable of killing elk and bear some four football fields away. They demand similar capabilities from whoever pulls the trigger.

r .300 Weatherby Magnum

s .270 Winchester Short Magnum

t 7mm Weatherby Magnum

HEAVY OR DANGEROUS NORTH AMERICAN GAME These are large, tough calibers for large, tough game. Warning: They kick both ways.

u .338 Winchester Magnum

v .338 Remington Ultra Mag

w .340 Weatherby

x .325 Winchester Short Magnum

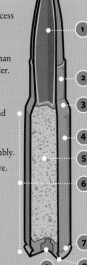

1. BULLET The construction of the projectile has a major influence on the success of the cartridge.

2. NECK Holds the bullet in place and aligns it with the rifling.

3. SHOULDER Modern cases have sharper shoulders–30 degrees or more–than older ones. It's thought that this gives a cleaner, more efficient burn to the powder.

4. CASE Always made of brass. There's nothing better.

5. POWDER It can be either spherical (ball) or extruded (log) and ranges in burning rate from fast to slow, depending on the bullet weight, case capacity, and case shape.

6. TAPER Modern cases have very little body taper; older ones have a lot. Low taper makes room for more powder, but cases with high body taper feed more reliably.

7. RIM Rimless cases have rims that barely extend beyond the extraction groove. Rimmed cases lack the groove and have wider rims.

8. BASE The base of the case carries the primer pocket and the headstamp, which designates caliber and make.

9. PRIMER Composed of a cup, anvil, and a small charge of explosive compound. Primers come in several sizes, and there are some with longer-sustaining flames, for magnum charges of slow powder.

239 DECOY A PRONGHORN ANTELOPE

There might not be any more exciting archery hunts than decoying a lust-crazed prairie goat ready to stomp the life out of the life-sized decoy you are hiding behind. During the late-summer rut, dominant pronghorns gather harems of does during a brief 2- to 3-week period and chase away any other bucks that may horn in on their love nest. Even the less-dominant bucks are ready to fight at the drop of a decoy and run out across the plains—literally—for a no-holds-barred smackdown. Here's how you can dupe that goat with a decoy.

GO WITH A PAL Decoying works best when one person handles the decoy and a rangefinder while the other is dedicated to getting the shot. Trade off positions during the course of a day.

MAKE IT VISIBLE You have to be seen to be charged.

Set the decoy up on a ridge or swell where it will show up against the sky, or place it out in a flat open spot where there is minimal vegetation.

BE READY Your decoy might bring in a goat from the next county over or from just out of sight. As soon as the decoy is up, get on your knees and nock an arrow. Have your partner range a few clumps of brush or rocks so you'll have a rough idea of distance. It can happen that quickly.

DROP DOWN Speaking of knees, practice shooting from them, and practice shooting while leaning to one side to replicate working an arrow around a decoy.

GET AGGRESSIVE If a pronghorn buck is distracted by females, feeding, or another goat, go ahead and stalk close, hiding behind the decoy.

240 PACK STRING WAX EVERY HUNT

Place a big glob of bowstring wax on the E- or C-clip of your bow axle and you'll help to prevent a trio of noise problems. It stops the clip from rattling, it keeps debris and water out of the axle, and it will give you a handy supply of surplus wax in the field. Nick your string on a tree step or in some briars, or if dealing with a rest that suddenly develops a squeak, and you can reach up and grab a little wax to take care of the problem right in your stand.

241 CUSTOMIZE YOUR BOW SIGHT

Smaller .010 sight pins are all the rage, as they cover up less target surface than larger, more traditional .019 pins. But many shooters with less-than-perfect eyesight find the smaller pins tougher to shoot with, and some do find that they aren't bright enough in low-light situations.

Luckily, you don't have to take the one-size-fits-all approach. Many bow sight manufacturers offer models that take pins of multiple sizes. Set the sight up with larger pins on top and smaller pins below. That way you get the advantage of the smaller pin size at longer distances when the target picture is reduced, while retaining the brighter pin at the shorter distances you're more likely to shoot at in low-light scenarios. And while you're on the range, mix and match the pins. You might find that the smaller sized pin actually works better at super-short ranges of 20 yards or so. It's all about the individual shooter, and the right bow sight will give you all the flexibility you need.

242 READ A BLOODY ARROW

It's a very fortunate archer who recovers a bloody arrow, but now the tougher part begins: finding the deer and turning all that luck into steaks and roasts in a freezer. The first step is to examine that arrow for clues about where it passed through the deer. Find a strong source of light—sunlight or flashlight—and take a close look from nock to broadhead.

BLOOD Bright pink-red blood from tip to nock indicates a hit in the vitals. Frothy bubbles can suggest a lung hit. No bubbles indicates a heart shot. Dark red blood with no bubbles could indicate a liver hit.

HAIR Coarse brown hair can indicate a good shot if the arrow entered in the vitals. White hair suggests a low hit. Wait several hours before tracking.

BROWNISH OR GREENISH MATERIAL An arrow streaked with any brownish or greenish material is a bad sign. An arrow from a gut-shot deer might be flecked with stomach contents such as green leaves or little bits of any partially digested corns or soybeans. Lift it up to your nose and smell for a strong odor. This typically indicates a gut-shot deer. If gray or brown hair is on the arrow, that could mean a higher hit than white hair.

FAT Greasy streaks of fat or tallow can be a clue that the arrow passed through the deer's back or haunch.

243 MASTER THE GROUND-BLIND SHOT

The growing popularity of pop-up ground blinds has changed the game. Deer bowhunters are down from the trees, now joined by a growing number of gobbler hunters. But there's more to hunting from these blinds than simply sitting on a bucket with a bow in hand. Here's how it's done.

FIND YOUR BLIND SPOT Set up your blind between tree trunks and break up the horizontal outline of the blind's roof with cut brush.

GET BACK TO BLACK Wear a black facemask, gloves, and shirt or jacket to blend in with the blacked-out interior of the blind.

KNOW YOUR WINDOWS OF OPPORTUNITY Open the windows at 12, 3, and 6 o'clock. Sit in the back and raise your bow as the deer passes from an open side window toward the front.

BE A STRAIGHT SHOOTER Concentrate on keeping your back straight. Many shooters rely more on arm and shoulder strength than back muscles while sitting, so dialing down 5 or 10 pounds can help. And a shorter draw length can make it easier to reach full draw from a bucket.

244 USE SUPERGLUE

Servings that can hold peep sights, nock points, nock loops, and other aftermarket items will fray with hard use in the field. When they do, wandering sights or flapping serving threads will kill your accuracy. Toss a little tube of superglue into your hunting pack for instant field repairs of loose servings. Grasp the loose end of thread between thumb and forefinger. Pull taut and then place a drop of superglue on the serving. Once the glue sets, snip off the tag end and keep hunting.

245 USE CONFIDENCE DECOYS TO ARROW A DEER

How many times have you seen deer feeding calmly amidst a flock of turkeys? It might be time to take the hint. Turkey decoys are getting more and more realistic, with details from fully fanned tail feathers to wobbling heads. Using a fake turkey as a confidence decoy for deer hunting, especially while bowhunting, could give you the edge you need. Some hunters report that deer seem to be relaxed while in the presence of a confidence decoy, while others figure that it can hold a little bit of the deer's attention, thus making it easier to draw the bow undetected. In a field, crow decoys work, as well. But it is vital to keep those decoys scent-free—spray with scent killer and handle with gloves.

246

SHOOT TIGHTER GROUPS AT EVERY DISTANCE

It might sound counterintuitive, but archery field tests prove that a slim grip—or better yet, no grip at all—is a better grip. A thick, cushy bow grip feels great in your hand, but all that hand-to-bow contact creates opportunities for greater bow torque when you release the arrow. Shoot a few groups while your bow grip is on, then remove it and shoot a few more. You just might be surprised at the difference.

The hardest hunting lesson I ever learned was a result of missing the biggest deer of my life. My guide and I found a monstrous mule deer bedded down just within bow range of a cliff top. After a 90-minute barefoot stalk, I had the bowstring nearly anchored for a 15-foot shot—and then the really big deer snorted 40 yards away. Now, had I spent more time behind the binoculars and less time mentally clearing wall space in my office, I'd have seen both deer. Using this grid system would have done the trick.

STEP 1 Divide the field of view into an imaginary grid pattern. Begin reading it like a line of type: Move your eyes slowly from left to right along the uppermost grid cube until the horizontal line intersects with a vertical line. Move down slightly, then glass from right to left. Repeat this pattern till you complete a grid. Mounting binoculars on a tripod can be a huge help.

STEP 2 Between grids, give a quick look to open areas where any movement may be obvious. As the sun comes up, pay attention to west-facing slopes that stay in shade. Muleys will feed later in the morning if they can stay out of the sun.

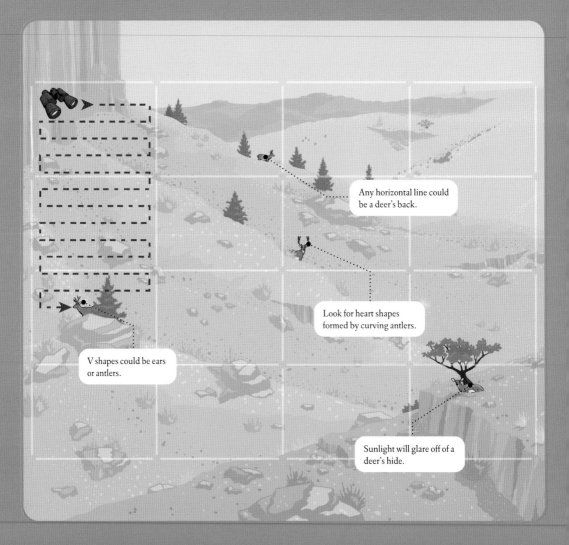

Any horizontal line could be a deer's back.

Look for heart shapes formed by curving antlers.

V shapes could be ears or antlers.

Sunlight will glare off of a deer's hide.

248 HOMEBREW DEER SCENTS

You can buy fancy commercial scents to lure out those big bucks, or you can make your own. Here are a few options.

EASIEST Stuff a pillowcase one-third full with aromatic vegetation from your hunt area, such as green leaves, pine needles, pieces of bark, moss, acorns—even dirt. Tie a knot in the top. Prior to a hunt, dampen the pillowcase with water and toss it in the clothes dryer with your clean hunting duds.

EASY Gather ½ gallon of acorns; add in a double handful of green pine needles if pines occur in your hunting area. Boil them gently in 1 gallon of water for 30 minutes. Let the mixture cool. Remove the nuts and needles, mash them, and boil again in the same water. Let the mixture cool, then strain it through cheesecloth. Store the liquid in a refrigerator. To use the cover scent, pour into a spray bottle.

NOT-SO-BAD Snip off one leg from a pair of hose. Remove the tarsal glands from a buck's hind legs by cutting around each gland, lifting it with rubber-gloved fingers, and then separating the connective tissue under the skin. Use a 10cc hypodermic syringe and needle to remove urine from the buck's bladder. Place the glands in the hose and knot closed. Squirt them with the urine and store in a sealed plastic bag in a freezer. Hang it by your stand during the hunt.

HARD Remove the tarsals from a buck, following the directions above. With a leather needle, thread the end of a 5-foot length of heavy monofilament through a gland; tie it off. Tie a loop in the other end of the line. Vacuum-pack the glands separately and freeze them. Before a hunt, thaw one out, then spritz it with urine scent and use it as a scent drag.

HARDEST Collect enough pine needles to fill a 5-gallon bucket. Boil in a large kettle with 6 to 7 gallons of water. Strain the needles out, then pour the liquid into a washing machine set at the lowest load setting possible. Toss in clean hunting clothes, and wash using the presoak cycle for a very intense pine scent. Clean the machine by washing a few old towels in hot, soapy water.

249

STICK A CALL TO YOUR COAT

Put a small, lightweight grunt call to your hunting jacket and you'll be able to call deer with a minimum of movement. Sew or glue a small strip of Velcro to the top of your jacket sleeve or upper chest, and then glue a corresponding patch to a grunt or bleat call. Now just a slight turn of your head will put that call into your mouth and keep both of your hands on the gun or bow.

250

MAKE A DRAG RAG

That first deer of the season will provide much-needed burger and backstrap, but if you're smart, it will also provide a pair of tarsal glands that will up your chances at tagging more deer. Remove these dark tufts of hair and skin with a sharp knife, wearing rubber gloves to keep them free of human scent. Toss in a zippered plastic baggie along with 6 feet of paracord, and store in a refrigerator or freezer. To use, simply tie a cord to the tarsal gland and knot it off on one of your belt loops. Drag it behind you on the way to your stand. Once near your hunt location, hang the tarsal gland from an upwind branch. You can get a couple of weeks of usage out of fresh tarsal glands by recharging them with a few drops of commercial doe urine.

251 KNOW WHAT YOUR BULLET IS DOING

Dime-size groups fired on the range are one thing, but hitting game under hunting conditions is quite another. What you see here are some of the practical problems involved in the latter. The cartridge involved is one of the most effective long-range rounds available, the Federal version of the .270 WSM, loaded with 140-grain Nosler AccuBonds—real-world velocity in a 24-inch barrel, about 3,100 feet per second, or fps.

MOA = MINUTE OF ANGLE

MEDIUM DISTANCE What applies to 100 yards applies here. The problem is one of appearances. Two hundred yards looks much farther than 100 yards and causes people to compensate for range and wind when they don't need to.

IN CLOSE At 100 yards, you don't need to think about ballistics. The trajectory is flat, and even a strong crosswind is not going to move the bullet enough to matter. All you have to do is pick an aiming point and not aim the rifle at the whole deer in general.

THE SHOOTER Offhand shots are sometimes a necessity, but always try for a rest or a more stable position. Only a fool shoots offhand past 100 yards.

SIGHTING AND AIMING The best system of all, for those without range-compensating reticles, is to sight in 3 inches high at 100 yards. With the .270 WSM, that will give you an effective point-blank range of 300 yards, or a bit more. If you want to shoot at 400 yards, you had better get a reticle with mil dots that will allow you to avoid the horrors of holding off target.

*bullet drift 2.2 inches

MOA 2-inch group

*bullet drift 0.6 inch

MOA 1-inch group

200 yd.

100 yd.

SEEING THE TARGET A deer-size animal looks very small at 400 yards; that is why variable-power scopes that magnify up to 10X were invented. Here is what the typical whitetail looks like with the scope cranked to 9X.

More magnification means more reticle movement with each twitch.

0 yds   100   200   300   400

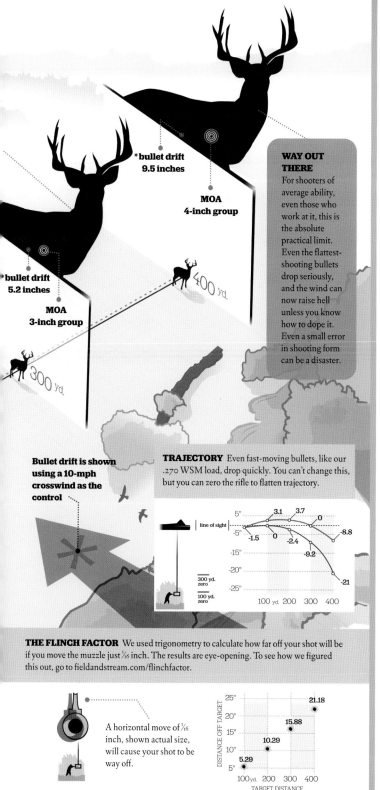

**bullet drift
9.5 inches**

**MOA
4-inch group**

WAY OUT THERE
For shooters of average ability, even those who work at it, this is the absolute practical limit. Even the flattest-shooting bullets drop seriously, and the wind can now raise hell unless you know how to dope it. Even a small error in shooting form can be a disaster.

**bullet drift
5.2 inches**

**MOA
3-inch group**

400 yd.

300 yd.

Bullet drift is shown using a 10-mph crosswind as the control

TRAJECTORY Even fast-moving bullets, like our .270 WSM load, drop quickly. You can't change this, but you can zero the rifle to flatten trajectory.

line of sight

5"
-5"
-15"
-20"
-25"

3.1 3.7 0
-1.5 0 -2.4 -8.8
-9.2
-21

300 yd. zero
100 yd. zero

100 yd. 200 300 400

THE FLINCH FACTOR We used trigonometry to calculate how far off your shot will be if you move the muzzle just 1/16 inch. The results are eye-opening. To see how we figured this out, go to fieldandstream.com/flinchfactor.

A horizontal move of 1/16 inch, shown actual size, will cause your shot to be way off.

DISTANCE OFF TARGET

25" 21.18
20" 15.88
15" 10.29
10" 5.29
5"

100 yd. 200 300 400
TARGET DISTANCE

252
PLANT A MICRO FOOD PLOT

Farm and beaver ponds are perfect for seeding with Japanese millet strips, which ducks relish. It's easy and cheap and very effective. Here's how.

SCHEDULE IT Summer heat will often draw pond levels down, or you can lower the pool with flashboard risers. Millet matures in about 60 days. Plan with opening day in mind. Stagger the planting over a few weeks; plant deeper areas first and then move up the bank. That will keep the feed coming for a month.

RAKE IT If you're seeding mud, simply broadcast on the surface. For drier soils, use a steel rake or an ATV rake to score.

SEED IT Plant Japanese millet at the rate of 20 pounds per acre. You want to plant the seeds about an inch and a half apart. Plant it too densely and you'll stunt the growth of the new stems.

FEED IT Use one bag of 13-13-13 fertilizer per bag of seed and fertilize when the millet is 12 to 18 inches tall.

253 MAKE A BUCK BED WITH A CHAIN SAW

Savvy big bucks are all about shelter. They like a thickly brushed spot with a view, just the kind of microhabitat you can create in 15 minutes with a chain saw. This is especially effective where an open oak flat offers little bedding cover. Provide a dense spot of brushy cover on the edge, and it's likely a buck will take up residence to scope out does feeding on the acorns.

It's easy. Locate two or three trees about 6 to 8 inches in diameter and growing 10 to 15 feet apart. Decide which direction you want each tree to fall.

To hinge-cut, use a chain saw to create a downward cut at a 45-degree angle on the side of the tree that is opposite of the direction you want it to fall. Make the cut at waist height or slightly higher. For larger trees, loop a rope around the trunk as high as you can reach, and have a buddy pull on the rope to prevent the saw blade from pinching. Such a helper can be useful even with smaller trees—the less that you cut through the trunk, the more future growth the tree will be able to maintain, which will keep the bed not only thickly vegetated, but provide browse.

254 STEER DEER WITH BUCKETS

When television host and Outdoor 3-D Archery World Champion Travis "T-Bone" Turner wants to steer a buck to his bowstand, he hits the woods with a stack of 5-gallon buckets. Bowhunters are often advised to learn exactly where a buck enters a field and sit just downwind. But not all bucks are so accommodating as to approach from the same spot every night. "He might show up within 100 yards of a certain tree, trail, or field corner," Turner says, "but that doesn't help very much when you're shooting a bow."

So Turner steers these deer to his stand with

buckets. Yes, buckets. "They stack like traffic cones for easy toting, and to a whitetail they say, Detour— go that way." If a certain deer tends to show up anywhere along a 100-yard stretch of a field edge, Turner places a line of four or five of his 5-gallon buckets parallel to that stretch, 100 yards or more into the opening. He then hangs his stand along the edge of the woods, lined up evenly with the farthest-downwind pail. "When the buck comes out, he'll spot those buckets, be leery, and instead of marching into the field, he'll hug the edge and, with luck, walk right to you."

255

MAKE YOUR OWN SCENT DRIPPER

Scent drippers work on a physical principle we all learned back in grade school: heated air expands. Sunlight hits the dark cloth, warms air trapped in the bottle, and pushes the scent out of the tube. Here's how to make your own. It's quick and cheap, so it's perfect for public land locations where some scofflaw could take a liking to your scent dripper and take it home.

YOU'LL NEED

a small glass bottle with cap • bubble wrap • tape • a power drill • 12 inches of ¼-inch outside diameter rubber tubing • zip ties • epoxy • string • dark cloth—maybe an old T-shirt you can cut up • flat spray paint in a dark color

AT HOME Wrap a small glass bottle with bubble wrap and secure it with tape. Drill a hole in the bottle top the same size or slightly smaller than the diameter of the tubing. Fasten a loop into the rubber tubing with a zip tie, leaving approximately 1 inch of the tubing extending below the loop. Thread the other end of the tubing through the bottle cap till just past flush. Epoxy in place. Once dry, wrap the bottle in black cloth and secure with string. Spray paint the bottle cap and tubing.

Experiment at home with how much scent to place in the bottle. Start at a quarter-full and place in sunlight conditions—ratio of sun to shade—that mimic those where you plan to hang the dripper.

IN THE FIELD Fill the bottle with the correct amount of scent. Hang from a limb. Return with rifle and gutting knife.

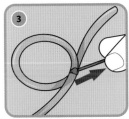

256

PRUNE AN APPLE TREE FOR DEER

Many overgrown farmsteads hold apple trees. When neglected, they produce few fruits. With a little pruning, however, they can churn out deer chow. Do it in late winter, just before the new spring growth. And then make it an annual event because the sucker shoots (skinny, whiplike branches) grow back.

CLEAR THE GROUND Remove all of the brush and saplings that are around the tree, at least to the canopy's drip line.

CUT THE DEAD WOOD Remove all dead wood, using a chain saw if necessary.

TRIM IT BACK Remove any and all sucker shoots. They sap growth, siphon off any needed nutrients, and will stymie the tree's ability to produce its fruit.

GET VERTICAL Remove any branches that grow horizontally, as the burden of apples can shear these off.

WEED OUT WEAKLINGS Pick the healthiest-looking branches to save, and remove some or all of the rest.

FEED THE TREE Fertilize with tree spikes made specifically for fruit trees.

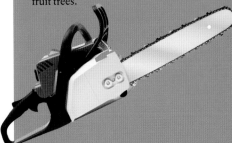

257 SOUND LIKE A DEER

Calling deer adds an exciting element to whitetail hunting. Here are the most important deer sounds for hunters. Each can be duplicated by commercial calls, and each requires practice to make it field-ready.

BUCK GRUNTS The deer grunt establishes dominance and signals aggression, often in the presence of a doe, so the right buck grunt at the right time can provoke a buck to move toward your position. Use a soft grunt to get a buck to move out of cover or take a few steps from behind a tree. "Tending grunts" are deeper and more urgent, often used when a buck is trailing a hot doe.

BLEATS Doe and fawn bleats can be ordinary contact calls or alarm signals, and deer will often investigate out of pure curiosity. A "doe estrous bleat" is a louder, drawn-out bleat made when a doe nears peak breeding time. A can-type estrous bleat call can be a deadly buck tactic during the rut.

DISTRESSED FAWN BLEATS Used to target does for the meat cooler, these high-pitched, urgent calls can also pull in curious bucks who want to see which does respond to an anxious fawn.

BUCK SNORT-WHEEZE This contact call is heard when two bucks rub shoulders over a food source or a hot doe. Use it during the rut's peak to troll for a mature buck or to pull in a buck that comes to a grunt call but hangs up out of range.

BUCK GROWL-ROAR Calls to replicate the growl-roar are among the newest whitetail tactics. As a buck trails a hot doe, its state of arousal climbs. Some bucks turn a tending grunt into a rapid-fire vocalization with a bawling, growling sound. Other bucks will investigate the scene of such intense activity.

258 MAKE RATTLING ANTLERS

Cut off brow tines and antler tips. Sand sharp edges or burrs. Drill a small hole at the base of each antler. Thread the ends of a 3-foot-long piece of black parachute cord through each hole and tie a stopper knot at each end. The week before opening day, toss the antlers into water to replenish lost moisture for the perfect tone, and paint a tine or two blaze orange.

259 GET INTO A BUCK FIGHT WITH RATTLING ANTLERS

Rattling up a buck works best in areas with a healthy, almost even, buck-to-doe ratio. Here's the drill.

STEP 1 Factor in the breeze. Most bucks try to approach a fight from downwind. Set up with the wind at your back, overlooking open woods or a field.

STEP 2 Start slow. Rattle antlers lightly for 90 seconds. Wait five minutes and then repeat with louder rattling for up to two minutes. Sit tight for a half-hour.

STEP 3 Scrape the antlers against a tree and the ground and then rattle again. Give it another 30 minutes and then relocate.

260 SHOOT WITH A "CHING SLING"

Shooting instructor Eric Ching's Ching Sling does away with the multiple loop adjustments and shoulder gyrations associated with the traditional military-style strap. It's essentially a standard rifle sling with the addition of a short strap on a sliding loop, and a number of shooting accessories companies make the slings. You'll need to add a third swivel just ahead of your trigger guard to use it, but that's it.

When you're ready to fire, insert your support arm (the left arm for a right-handed shooter) through the loop in front of the short strap, snug the short strap tight against your upper arm, and rotate your forearm back under the main strap to grip the forestock. Quick. Intuitive. Solid.

261 SIT LIKE A KING ON A STYROFOAM THRONE

Nature's call can be a cruel song at 10 degrees below zero. One deer camp's savvy members have taken the edge off the frigid encounter between a bare bottom and the outhouse plank. First, they lined their john with three layers of cushy inch-thick Styrofoam and beveled the edges of the toilet seat for maximum comfort. Upon entering la toilette, you light a Coleman lantern, which provides light and heat. The lantern handle is raised upright for a makeshift towel rack. A baby wipe is draped over the handle. Voilà—a warm and soothing end to the business at hand. Or is that the end at hand?

262 HANG NASTY WET BOOTS FROM THE RAFTERS

WHAT YOU'LL NEED

- PVC cement
- One 10-foot length of 1-inch PVC pipe, cut into the following sections: 8 @ 10 inches, 6 @ 2 inches, 1 @ 24 inches
- Three 1-inch four-way PVC pipe connectors
- Six 1-inch 45-degree PVC pipe elbow joints
- 1 No. 8 bolt, 1 inch long, with two nuts
- 1 eyebolt
- Clothesline or parachute cord, long enough to reach from your waist to the top of the tallest ceiling in your camp and back
- 1 large washer

DIRECTIONS

STEP 1 Cement the pipe pieces, connectors, and joints as shown in the photo.

STEP 2 Attach the bolt to the bottom end of the PVC frame.

STEP 3 Drill a hole through the top of the PVC frame. Attach the eyebolt to the ceiling and then run the clothesline through it and back down to the PVC frame, tying it off at the drilled hole. Tie the washer to the clothesline at a location that will stop the PVC frame at about waist height.

STEP 4 Raise the PVC frame like a flag and hook the washer over the bolt head at the bottom of the frame to hold it aloft.

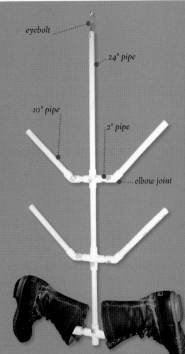

eyebolt

24" pipe

10" pipe

2" pipe

elbow joint

263 KILL A WILD PIG WITH A KNIFE

For centuries, Hawaiian natives dispatched wild pigs with little more than gumption and a 6-inch blade. As wild pig populations explode across the country, hunting them with dogs and a knife is growing in popularity. Here's the drill—if you dare.

STEP 1 Approach the pig from the rear, while it's focused on the dogs. Move slowly and avoid getting between your quarry and anything that would prevent you from backing away.

STEP 2 Grab the pig's hind legs just above the hooves. Lift the animal up like a wheelbarrow. The pig will fight for a few seconds and then stop. Flip him over on his side. Have a buddy secure the dogs away from the pig.

STEP 3 Let go with your knife hand and get a knee on the pig's shoulder. Unsheathe your knife. Sink it low and behind the shoulder, so it enters the heart, and then remove the blade immediately. Keep your weight on the pig until the deal is done. Pull this off correctly, and it takes mere seconds.

264 DISSECT THE WIND

Wind patterns are insanely complicated. One common mistake hunters make is misreading how currents react to landscape features. Missouri whitetail guide Kevin Small takes wind patterns apart with surgical precision.

It doesn't take a canyon wall to make the wind do flips. A hill, a ridge, a line of thick timber—all of these can have a dramatic effect on wind direction. Pick apart a buck's travel routes to find the one narrow window at which the wind is temporarily wrong for his nose but he has no other travel option. In this scenario, a west wind can work against you.

WIND WAVE When a breeze comes into contact with a large landscape obstruction, the wind will rise and then roll back over itself.

COULD BE TOO GOOD TO BE TRUE In theory, this is the perfect stand location (a) when dealing with a west wind. "But the wind will be rising at this point," Small says. "It will pick up your scent here and bring it right back to the bedding cover and the trails. You'll be busted 99 percent of the time."

SWEET SPOTS The only time to safely hunt these trails is in a north or south wind. In a north wind, hunt here (b). In a south wind, hang a stand here (c).

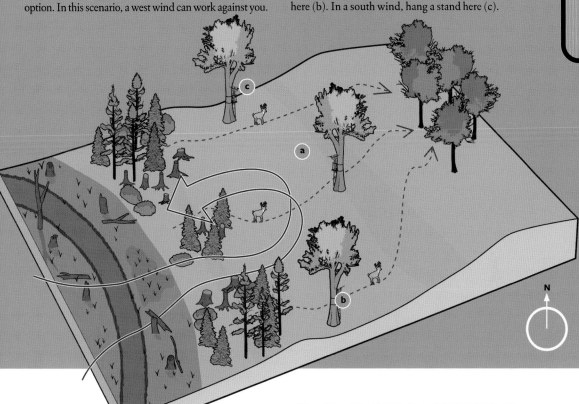

265 WALK LIKE A DEER

Moving whitetails generally stop on odd-numbered steps—three, five, seven, and so on. It's an irregular cadence that you should try to duplicate when tracking over crunchy snow, tricking deer into thinking that the intruder has four legs instead of two.

266 LET A YOUNG DUCK HUNTER CALL DUCKS

Duck species that routinely whistle include bluewing and greenwing teal, pintail, wood ducks, and wigeon. But mallard drakes will also make a sharp, single- or double-noted whistle, and, though the call is typically tied to breeding, it's a deadly finisher for shy greenheads during hunting season. For early-season teal hunting, a five-peep whistle is the go-to call. Since it's easy to learn, duck whistling is a great way to get a kid started.

267 RAISE A LADDER STAND SAFELY

It is physically impossible to put up a ladder stand alone if you follow certain manufacturers' instructions. And what if you want to move an old ladder stand? But here's how a two- or three-person team can get it done.

READY IT Lay the ladder out with its base approximately 3 to 4 feet from the base of the tree for a one-person stand, or 4 to 5 feet for a two-person stand. The side of the stand that will touch the tree faces up. Tie a stout anchor rope to each back corner of the stand platform. The ropes should be 10 feet longer than the stand's height.

RAISE IT One person goes to the base of the stand and braces his feet against the ladder's bottom, holding an anchor rope in each hand. The others raise the platform end overhead and walk the stand up as the anchor person stays put and pulls in the slack on the ropes, keeping them tight so the ladder rises straight overhead.

RATCHET IT With the stand against the tree, crisscross the anchor ropes behind the trunk and tie them tightly to the bottom ladder rung. One person climbs the ladder, attaches a ratchet strap to the base of the platform, and secures it tight.

268 MAKE THE BEST JERK CORD IN THE WORLD

Tired of lugging motorized decoys, remote-control units, and cumbersome mounting poles into the duck swamp? Then go retro with the best jerk cord you'll ever see in action. It gives up to five decoys a surprising amount of motion, with a minimum of movement on your part. The whole rig fits right in your pocket and goes up in no more than five minutes. And it's as deadly as it is simple.

You'll need 85 feet of decoy line, 15 feet of ⅛-inch black bungee cord, and six large black snap-swivels. Using overhand knots, tie five 6- to 8-inch-long loops into the last 20 feet of decoy line. These should be about 2 to 3 feet apart. Tie a snap-swivel to the end of each loop. Then tie one end of the bungee cord to the end of the decoy line near the last loop. Finally, tie the last snap-swivel to the other end of the bungee. To set up the rig, pass the bungee cord around a tree or sturdy stake (or a heavily anchored decoy) and hook it to itself using the snap-swivel. Run the decoy line to your blind and clip decoys to the loops. Pull the slack out, until the bungee cord just begins to stretch. A short, swift jerk will set the birds in motion, appearing as if they're splashing, content . . . and happy to have company.

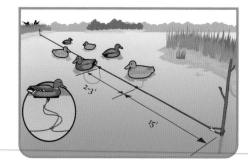

269 IDENTIFY A BUTTON BUCK AND HOLD YOUR FIRE

Many hunters want to protect buck fawns, those inglorious "button bucks." Identifying button bucks can be tough, but you can do it. Button bucks often travel alone; adult does rarely do. Buck fawns are squarish in body shape, whereas mature does are more rectangular. Glass the deer's head. Even if you can't make out the antler buds, a buck's head is flat between the ears compared with a doe's more rounded skull.

270 DROP THE FOLLOW-UP DUCK

What's the toughest shot in waterfowling? "It's the follow-up shot in a big wind," says Missouri duck guide Tony Vandemore. After that first volley, birds have their wings out, and they're catching serious air. "It's an optical illusion. They're facing you, but actually moving backward." These directions are for a wind coming from the right; switch for a wind from the left.

If you're quick on the follow-up, put the bead to the left of the bird's butt and pull the trigger. You're trying to put shot in front of the bird's tail, not the head. For the next shot, the birds are traveling faster and could be starting to turn. "They look like they're flying straight away, but they're banking to the left and gaining velocity." Increase the lead but keep shooting below the birds at the trajectory of their butts.

271 HUNT A CROSSWIND

The standard advice is to still-hunt with the wind in your face. But this isn't always best. Bucks like to bed at the edge of cover, with the wind at their backs, so they can see what's coming in front of them and smell what's behind them. By hunting at right angles to the wind, you have a better chance of getting the drop on a bedded buck before it either sees or smells you.

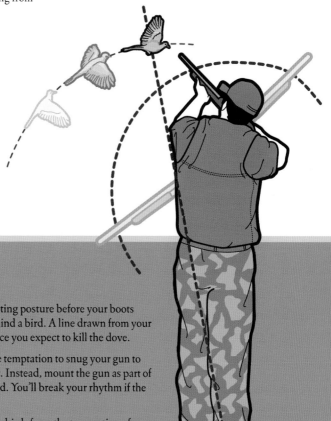

272 SET UP FOR A DOVE SHOT

WATCH YOUR FEET Think about good shooting posture before your boots tangle in cornstalks and you empty the barrel behind a bird. A line drawn from your rear heel to your front foot should point to the place you expect to kill the dove.

GET IN THE SWING OF THINGS Resist the temptation to snug your gun to your shoulder when the birds are 75 yards distant. Instead, mount the gun as part of the same fluid motion you use to swing on the bird. You'll break your rhythm if the buttplate hits your shoulder too soon.

KEEP YOUR HEAD DOWN Watch incoming birds from the top portion of your peripheral vision. That way your head will already be lowered when it's time to put your cheek to the gunstock.

273 USE A LINEMAN'S BELT

A linesman's belt, or climbing belt, will not only make climbing trees and hanging tree steps, sticks, and stands much easier, it will make this inherently dicey activity much safer. Typically, the belts are a loop of rope, webbing, or sometimes leather, with a carabiner at each end. The belt encircles the tree at a height just above your waist, and then connects to loops on a safety harness. This not only provides a safety catch should you slip, but allows you to lean back and work with both hands. You'll need a safety harness built to accept a linesman's belt, but

most have the two required connections, as do many harnesses specifically made for tree stand hunting.

To use a linesman's belt, put on a safety harness. Attach one end of the belt to a harness loop above the point of one hipbone. Swing the other carabiner around the tree, grab it, and clip it into the harness loop on the other hipbone. Lean back and the loop supports your weight. Many belts come with a set of Prussik loops that allow you to adjust the angle of lean. The most comfortable will be between 25 and 30 degrees.

274 MAKE YOUR OWN SCENT-KILLER

Even if you shower in no-scent soap right before your hunt, the little bit you sweat going to your stand will turn into a powerful stench to deer. That's why many hunters compulsively use commercial scent killers. The problem is that their cost can make you apply them sparingly, which is like putting deodorant on only one armpit.

Here's a simple homemade scent killer. Hydrogen peroxide kills the bacteria and fungi that turn sweat into a deer-busting funk, and baking soda deodorizes whatever sneaks by.

YOU'LL NEED

2 cups (16 ounces) 3% hydrogen peroxide • 2 cups (16 ounces) distilled water • ½ cup baking soda • 1 ounce unscented shampoo or unscented hunter's body wash

MIX Gently combine all of the ingredients in a large bowl until the baking soda dissolves. Next, pour this mixture into a 1-gallon container with a lid, such as a milk jug. Let it sit for three days with the lid on loosely to allow gases to escape.

BOTTLE Fill a plastic bottle that has a trigger sprayer with the scent killer. It must be clean, so buy a new one from a hardware store or online.

WIPE To make your own scent-killing wipes, place plain brown multifold paper towels—the kind that come in stacks, not on a roll—in a small plastic tub with an airtight lid. Cover them with your scent killer and let it soak in. Pour out excess liquid and replace the lid. Now you can wipe down boots, bows, and stands, and even use a towel or three to neutralize the sweat that you'll produce while shinnying up that perfect white oak.

275

MOUNT A MEAT GRINDER FOR EASIER GRINDING

Hand-cranked meat grinders are efficient and last forever, but they do require a very sturdy attachment to a very sturdy table. If you don't want to permanently bolt a grinder to a table, you can easily mount the grinder to a separate board, then C-clamp the board to an existing table. Voila—an instant grinding station.

For a mounting board, avoid cutting boards made of multiple wood pieces; all those forces exerted by the grinder chewing through gristle will split them easily. Go for a solid cutting board, or better yet, a good solid 1-inch-thick polyethylene cutting board or kitchen laminate such as Formica or Arborite. Place the grinder on the board. Leaving room for four C-clamps that will attach the mounting board to your table, mark the foot holes, and drill them out. Use machine screws with lock washers and bolts to attach the grinder to the board. Now you can C-clamp the grinder to a kitchen table, deck railing, or work bench, and never buy sausage again.

276

PROTECT YOUR TURKEY-CALL STRIKER

The plastic caps that come with cheap ink pens are perfect for capping the tip of a turkey-call striker, protecting it from dings and chips in you vest pocket, or oil from your hands.

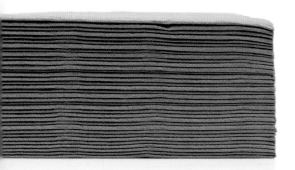

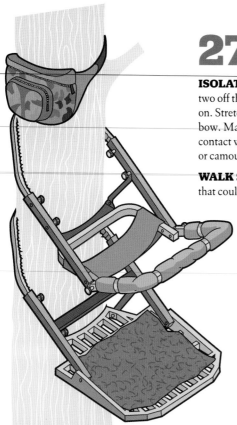

277 SILENCE YOUR TREE CLIMBER

ISOLATE THE PROBLEM At home, attach your stand to a tree a foot or two off the ground. Wear hunting clothes, grab your gun or bow, and climb on. Stretch your legs. Shoulder your gun and twist to each side. Draw your bow. Make a note of every place where metal or hard plastic comes into contact with the stand. Insulate the offending places with closed-cell foam or camouflage tape.

WALK SILENTLY Secure loose cables, buckles, and other noisemakers that could spook deer on your walk into the woods.

LUBRICATE MOVING PARTS Lube all squeaky hinges, welds, and joints with scent-free oil.

WAX SLIDING RAILS Run a scent-free candle across all rails that slide into larger-diameter tubes to dampen the sound of adjusting the stand.

LAY DOWN CARPET Glue a layer of marine carpet to the stand platform to silence scraping feet.

MINIMIZE ACCESSORIES The more gadgets you carry in your pockets, the likelier you'll sound like spare change clinking in the trees. Extra ammo, flashlights, and other small items should go into a daypack, to be fastened around the tree or hung from your stand.

278 CHOOSE YOUR WEAPON FOR SQUIRRELS

Rimfire or scattergun? The decision is as much about philosophy as it is about ballistics. On the one hand, the squirrel is as sporting a .22 target as exists. On the other, they are tasty. Match the tool to the task.

USE A .22 RIFLE WHEN

• Hunting in a light rain. Stalking squirrels in the wet woods is a true joy.

• Hunting a dense population. Use .22 short ammo. It packs enough wallop out to 50 yards, but its softer report will keep squirrels active after a shot.

• Hunting fox squirrels. Slower and more prone to walk along the ground, these trophy-sized squirrels deserve a Boone and Crockett category of their own. Sniper them from 75 yards or better.

• There's a 48-hour *Rambo* marathon on television. Pack a semiauto and get it out of your system.

USE A SHOTGUN WHEN

• You hunt the early season. Leafy foliage makes rifle hunting exasperating.

• There's wind. Breeze-blown branches jack normally squirrelly squirrels into a level of physical schizophrenia unknown in the animal kingdom. Your only hope is a wide pattern.

• You want to walk. Follow creek banks and logging roads deep into the lair of the delicious tree rat. Shoot quickly and don't stop till something's falling.

• You're hungry. A hankering for squirrel is nature's way of telling you to forget sport and go big-bore.

279 MAKE BUTTONS AND ZIPPER PULLS FROM A DEER RACK

Racks too small to show off are sized perfectly for handmade buttons and zipper pulls.

To make a button, use a hacksaw to cut off a tine at the diameter you need.

STEP 1 Using the tag end of the tine as a handle, sand the cut surface. Use 80-grit sandpaper first and then 120-grit. Next, saw off a disk about ³/₁₆ inch thick and buff the other side.

STEP 2 Drill thread holes with a ³/₃₂-inch bit, spacing the holes evenly.

To make a zipper pull, saw off a tine about an inch long.

STEP 1 Smooth the surface with sandpaper and drill a small hole into the center of the antler, about ¹/₂ inch deep. Fill this with a few drops of five-minute epoxy and thread a small screw eye into the hole.

STEP 2 Attach the pull to the zipper with a small loop of rawhide or ribbon.

280 MAKE YOUR OWN SCENT WIPES

Make your own scent-killing wipes and use them to wipe down everything from body parts to binoculars.

INGREDIENTS

2 cups 3 percent hydrogen peroxide
2 cups distilled water
¹/₄ cup baking soda
1 oz. unscented shampoo (larger chain drugstores will carry this item.)

In a large bowl, mix together the hydrogen peroxide, distilled water, baking soda, and unscented shampoo. Stir, pour into a one-gallon milk jug, and loosely cap the jug. Let the mixture sit for three days.

While that's marinating, fill a small, lidded tub about two-thirds full with plain brown multifold paper towels—the kind that come in stacks, not on a roll. Cover the paper towels with your homemade scent killer and mush it all around so the paper towels absorb the liquid. Squeeze out the excess scent killer and replace the lid. You're good to go—undetected.

281 ENTICE A SHY BULL

When bull elk give Wyoming guide Terry Search the silent treatment, he turns to a cow estrous call. Here's his plan:

STEP 1 When bugles are few and far between, listen for a distant bugle, a closer grunt, or a bull horning a tree. Get downwind, settle into a spot, and make an estrous-cow call just loud enough to be heard.

STEP 2 No response? Wait at least 15 minutes. It's all about

discipline now—do not call. Still no response? Make sure you can move without being seen by the elk and then relocate at least 30 yards away. You can move farther, but a 100-yard relocation, Search says, "would be pretty radical." Settle down and call again.

STEP 3 Play cat-and-mouse for two hours, calling and relocating every 15 to 30 minutes. If nothing happens in that time, back out carefully. The elk should remain close by as long as it has food, water, and shelter. Return later in the day or the next morning.

282

PULL OFF A BUNNY HUNT ON YOUR BUCK LEASE

You have a deer lease but no bunny dogs? Now that whitetail season is over, you may be sitting on a world-class rabbit hunt in the making. Post a message on Craigslist (craigslist.org) or your favorite online message board saying that you'll trade access to your whitetail heaven in return for a rabbit hunt. The setup: You bring a couple of buddies and let the hound handler do the same. It's a win-win for everyone (except for the rabbits). Use your deer sense to fine-tune the rabbit hunt.

DRAINAGE DITCH Dominant bucks use these dense corridors to move across an open landscape. Rabbits will use the subtle trails as an escape hatch or a place to wait out the heat. Toss the dogs in or thrash through on your own.

BLOWDOWNS These were prime bedding spots, and you stalked close, moving as slow as molasses. Now, forget stealth: Jump on the trunks, bang on the limbs—even if the dogs have passed by.

LOGGING ROAD This was a scrape-line mecca during deer season. Use dirt roads and ATV trails to get standers into position without much noise.

SWAMP Just like deer, rabbits take refuge in the most tangled messes on the property. Use your hound pack to dislodge them from their safe places.

INNER WOOD'S EDGE Bucks love to rub saplings along the edge of pine thickets and open hardwoods. It's a great spot for standers as rabbits dash out of the thick pines to pour on the speed.

GROWN-OVER CLEAR-CUT This is core bedding cover for whitetails, and bunnies use it for that and more. Work it over thoroughly, and not just with the dogs. Get in there and worm your way around too.

ng guide Ron Dube walks softly but keeps a ʌgm call in his mouth all the time. His advice: When ʌmp an elk, call instantly. Call if he's seen you; call if he Call even if you've shot at him. "Often I make this bugle scream," Dube says, "nothing fancy, just rip a

lot of air across the diaphragm so it screams, like th beginning of a bugle without all the chuckles. I'll sc I'm out of breath and scream some more. I'll call lou long until he's either dead or gone. I've had elk stop being shot at twice. It's extremely important to call ʌ elk has been hit by an arrow. Many times, that buglє will stop him and rather than go charging off, he'll jɯ little bit and bleed out."

FIELD & STREAM-APPROVED KNOT

284 TIE A GETAWAY KNOT

Hunters on guided horsepack trips can help the wrangler out by knowing how to tie up their own mount. It doesn't sound like a very big deal until there's a game animal getting away and your guide has to deal with his horse, your horse, and whoever else's horse while you're all standing around. Learn a good hitch knot like the old getaway knot.

Start at chest level so the horse can't get a leg over the rope, and tie the horse with no more than 2 feet of rope slack between the halter and the tree.

STEP 1 Pass the rope around the tree on the right side (or over a rail).

STEP 2 As you bring the tag end of the rope around the tree, form a loop by passing the rope over itself. Lay the loop over the standing part of the rope.

STEP 3 Reach through the loop on the outside of the standing part and pull another loop of the working end through.

STEP 4 Snug the knot up to the tree.

STEP 5 To release the hitch, all you have to do is pull on the tag end and go.

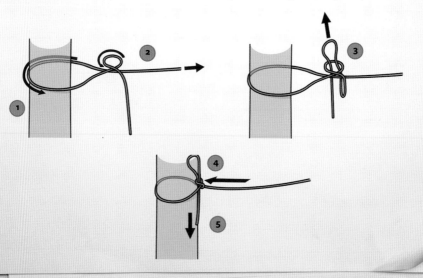

285 MASTER THE RUT

This is it. Thirty days to give it your all. When does are ready to breed, bucks are ready to do whatever it takes to line up a hot date. When they drop their guard, be ready to drop the hammer.

Pre-Rut Bucks are getting antsy as their testosterone levels rise and the amount of available daylight plummets. Mature deer move out of their swamp and thicket hide-outs and nose around for does.

TACTIC–FIND A CORRIDOR Find a place where thick cover with food value, like greenbrier, edges into open woods near doe-feeding areas, such as crop fields or oak flats, and climb a tree. You might spot a buck doing a little pre-scouting on his own. Or put doe meat in the freezer before the rut kicks in.

Seek-and-Chase Does are coming into estrous right and left, and bucks are in pursuit. Deer will literally be running through the woods, all day long.

TACTIC–SIT TIGHT Does are like rabbits—they don't like to leave familiar habitat. If a buck chases a doe past you without giving you a shot, don't move. They could make another swing by, or, better yet, a bigger buck might storm the scene, ready to brawl. Scent bombs and other estrous scents can improve your chances.

Breeding Deer seem to have evaporated from the woods, because bucks and does are pair bonding. They might spend 24 to 48 hours together and move very little.

TACTIC–GO MOBILE Glass the edges of bedding cover thoroughly, looking for coupled bucks and does. If you find antlers, plan a stalk. You might also troll for bucks in between hot does by setting up in a funnel and using an estrous-bleat call.

Post-Rut Most bucks—but not all—are worn out and holed up in dense cover, seeking a safe haven where they can rest and refuel for the coming winter.

TACTIC–GO DEEP AND NASTY Put up a stand that overlooks swamp edges, the backsides of clear cuts, or steep brushy gullies where bucks feel cloistered. And check out old scrape lines. Does that didn't breed initially are coming into a second heat, and a few bucks will be on the prowl for their last dance of the year.

286 TRACK AN ELK

Tracking bull elk is primal and addictive. It requires all the woodsmanship, intelligence, and endurance you can muster. It's always possible that after you've hiked many miles, you'll be left staring at the tracks of a spooked elk that's already in the next county. But what makes it worth it is the feeling that comes with knowing that 1 mile down the trail stands an animal worthy of all your efforts. Here is a six-step game plan for tracking elk. Be warned: Once you start, you won't ever want to stop.

START IN THE PARKS Open parks and other sunny clearings in the timber are great places to find tracks. Elk feed and bed in these exposed areas only at night, pawing through light snow to search out sedges. The animals will be gone before dawn, but you will have a good chance of finding fresh tracks at first light. To make sense of the mess of prints you will find there, move a few yards back into the timber. Here you'll find where the trails funnel together, and you'll be able to isolate specific bands of animals.

TEST THE TRACK In powder snow, during a cold snap, or in deeply shaded areas, a three-day-old track may look fresh to the untrained eye. A hoofprint left in melting snow that quickly refreezes stays cookie-cutter sharp, though the animal that made it is long gone. Conversely, a recently made print drifting in with snow can appear old. Rely on your sense of touch instead. In powder, the edges and midline will set up and feel firm within an hour or two of the animal's passing. Fresh droppings are shiny, soft, and emit an organic, sweetish smell (a). Fresh lances of urine give to the slightest pressure. Crusty urine streaks, or pellets that crumble when squeezed, mean the trail is cold. Don't forget to use your nose. Elk beds retain a rank, barnyard odor that can fool even an experienced hunter, but a faint, clean scent of elk usually indicates a hot track.

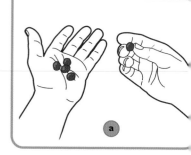

b

c

30 yards

30 yards

SIZE UP YOUR PREY It's difficult to predict the sex or size of an elk by looking at just hoofprints. More telling is the story that a trail writes in the snow: A large track accompanied by a small one invariably means a cow and a calf (b). A small band of elk, say five to six, will often include a spike but seldom a mature bull. A herd of 10 may indeed have a 6-point bull among it. Big bulls like to travel in pairs, so two sets of good-size tracks are always worth following. A lone track can be a bull or a cow, but if it's a bull of any size, you'll see where his antlers have made him skirt low-hanging branches. If a lone trail covers a lot of country but switches directions without apparent purpose, it likely has been made by a 2½-year-old bull. Young bulls will often stand from their beds and then hesitate before bolting away, affording the careful tracker a shot.

HEAD THEM OFF Elk rarely give hunters a second chance—and damned few first ones—so you need to follow them without alerting their acute senses. To better the odds, anticipate where they are heading. Often, elk heading to bed down for the day will walk along the side of a forested slope and then climb and circle back on a higher contour before lying down—choosing flat spots on side ridges where they hold the high ground on three fronts. They tend to divert from their course and feed before bedding, so look for circular depressions where they have punched their noses into the snow.

Don't be discouraged if you come to a freshly departed bed but the tracks don't indicate that the elk was spooked. A

bull will often lie down awhile and then move off to find a better bed somewhere nearby. There's a good chance he's within range of your rifle.

SNEAK INTO THEIR BEDS When the track starts to waver and go uphill, slow way down because the elk is most likely preparing to bed. Stay 30 yards or so to the side of the track, cutting into it just often enough to stay on course (c). If you hunt with a partner, have one hunter take the track while the other takes a contour at a higher elevation, keeping the tracker just within sight. Try to circle and work down to the bedding elk from above. More often than not, you'll guess wrong, but a direct approach along the trail, no matter how carefully you place your feet, tilts the odds in the elk's favor.

TAKE THEM WHERE YOU FIND THEM If you finally catch up to elk, they're likely to be in heavy cover, revealing themselves only as pieces in a larger puzzle. Your eye may linger on a patch of color that resembles a peeled log, or a branch stub cocking at an odd angle might trigger a second glance. Then, like a trick picture, the animal comes into focus. If you've been scanning every inch of forest as it enters your view, the elk will be near the outer limit of your vision, its body striped by a picket of tree trunks. Don't try to stalk closer. Either you'll lose sight of the elk, or the elk will catch sight of you. This is why a powerful rifle with a good scope is a tracker's best choice. A lot of things can go wrong when tracking. The shot that ends the hunt shouldn't be one of them.

287 USE A POV CAMERA

Point-of-view cameras have transformed the outdoor experience, and hunters have latched onto these pocket-sized dynamos. Here's a grab-bag of tricks from GoPro engineers that go beyond the instruction manual. They range from common-sense tips to high-tech insights, and they'll make you a better videographer.

CARRY IT RIGHT Transport the camera with its battery separate. If you don't, then the camera or its WiFi can accidentally, and easily, turn on.

FIGHT THE FOG Waterproof housings are great, but be vigilant. Moisture captured inside the housing can cause the lens to fog, and it doesn't take a deluge. Damp fingers, humid air, and hot breath can all fog the inner surface of the lens. If available for your camera, carry anti-fog pads.

GET CLOSE Most of the time, closer is better, so put the camera right into the action. Let the dog lick and sniff it. Set it in a cooler and then toss in the ducks. A point of view 2 or 3 feet away from the subject is not too close for many shot opportunities.

CENTER IT If there is a large sweep of horizon in the shot, it is often best to try to have that horizon line in the center of the frame. That will keep the horizon line straight, instead of bowing with the wide angle.

CONTROL TIME Learn how to take and edit time-lapse sequences. Opinions vary about ideal intervals between shots, but do the math to figure out how long you'll need the photo capture to run in order to get the desired seconds of "video" out of the time-lapse clip. For example, at 30fps video playback, and taking a photo every 2 seconds, you'll get 1 second of video for each minute of photo capture.

ADJUST FRAME RATE In low light conditions, adjust the frame rate to allow the camera to capture more light per frame. In decent sunlight, 48fps is a standard setting, but don't be hesitant to crank it down to 24fps.

RELAX Don't let the camera get in the way of your fun, or your quarry. Practice at home so you can seamlessly integrate the camera once you're in the field.

288 USE GPS TO RECORD GAME TRAILS

The "track-back" or "path" mode in a GPS is one fantastic tool to mark both human and animal trails on your favorite hunting grounds. While scouting, turn the mode on as you walk any linear feature. Choose one color for human features, such as logging roads, ATV trails, and property boundaries. Choose another for game features, such as rub lines, primary trails, and faint buck trails. Now you will have a features map that makes it easy to plan entry and exit routes to your hunting locations.

289 CONTROL A SPINNING TURKEY

When it comes to turkey decoy movement, there can be too much of a good thing. Those super-lightweight foam decoys bob and dip in a slight breeze, but a decent puff of wind can send them weathervaning to all points of the compass—and spook any gobbler that's giving them a look. To rein in a spinning turkey decoy, tie twine to the tail and stake it loosely to a tent stake or nearby sapling. If you're caught in the turkey woods without twine, jab a pair of sticks into the ground a few inches to the left and right of the decoy's tail. That will give it plenty of room for lifelike motion without spinning like a top.

You can't keep up with all the advances in trail camera technology until you learn the language.

BLACK FLASH Typical infrared sensors emit a dull red or orange glow that can be detected by game; a black flash supposedly doesn't.

BURST MODE This setting shoots multiple images in quick succession when triggered.

DETECTION ZONE Cone-shaped area formed by the maximum distances at which the camera's sensors can detect an animal and shoot a photo.

MP Stands for megapixel. High-MP cams can produce higher-quality photos, but other factors also affect picture quality.

PIR Passive infrared sensors can detect the heat and/or movement of an animal and activate the camera.

RECOVERY RATE How long it takes a camera to rearm before taking the next photo.

TRIGGER SPEED Time elapsed from when a camera's sensor detects an animal to when a picture is taken. Speeds vary greatly, and fast is almost always better.

291 FINE-TUNE TRAIL CAMS

Here's how to snap a picture of a bruiser buck.

STEP UP Place each camera 6 to 8 feet high in a tree, with the lens angled slightly downward. Wedge a stick behind the camera to get the correct angle. You will get a much better field of view and also increase your chances of picking up bucks in the background. Plus, there's less chance of alerting deer with the camera flash.

QUARTER ANGLE One of the most common mistakes is to aim a camera perpendicular to the trail. A quartering angle is best for maximizing the time the deer stays in frame.

BUCK SHOT Place an additional camera on your stand tree, facing behind you, to capture savvy bucks skirting field edges and moving parallel to established deer trails.

TIME TRAVEL If your camera will run in both time-lapse and motion modes simultaneously, switch on both modes.

CHECKMATES Always carry spare memory cards and surgical gloves when you check cameras. It's quicker to swap cards than remove the entire camera, and surgical gloves will keep cameras and trees free of human scent.

292 TARGET SHOP AT WALMART

Looking for fun targets to shoot with a .22? Take a stroll through the aisles of your local superstore. There are plenty of cheap, reactive targets that will add pizzazz—not to mention a mini-explosion—to your next rimfire shooting session.

- Condiment packs
- Charcoal briquettes
- Animal crackers
- Eggs
- Kool-Aid ice cubes
- Figurines
- Sandwich baggies filled with white flour
- Cheap cookies
- Poker chips
- Baby carrots
- Cheap soda
- Golf balls

293 TURN A PISTOL INTO A SHOTGUN

Ranchers in serious snake country are known for toting revolvers loaded with rat shot for those too-close encounters with Mr. No Shoulders. There are plenty of myths and misinformation about shotshells for handguns, so here's what you need to know before plugging away with pint-sized shotshells.

MICRO-SHOT Pistol shotshells are loaded with tiny shot. In .22 and .22 Magnum, most shells are filled with tiny No. 11 or No. 12 shot. Step up to the larger calibers—9mms, .38s, .40s, .44s, .45s—and the shot size can creep up to No. 9. That's still pretty lightweight stuff.

BARREL BASHING It's a misconception that shooting rat shot in a rifled barrel will ruin the barrel. Lead shot won't damage a steel barrel. Shoot a lot of the stuff, however, and lead and plastic fouling could be an issue, so clean barrels with a bronze brush after firing rat shot.

SEMIAUTO PAINS It's true that the plastic-topped rat shot is a questionable load for your semiautomatic pistol. Even if the round cycles, there's a chance that the feed ramp or any other metal parts might tear the plastic cap and allow all the spilled lead shot to dump into the inner workings of a handgun. That's no good.

BOTTOM LINE Rat shot from these calibers is a decidedly short-range, very-small-game load. The shot cups spin from the rifling, so the pattern opens quickly. And the shot itself is too small to do much damage. They're great for bumblebees on the wing, blackbirds at 20 feet, and rats, mice, and snakes at super-close ranges. Not so much for something as tough as a squirrel.

294 CHANNEL THE SONG DOG

Learn to blow a coyote howler, and you can avoid getting busted when leaving a deer stand at night. It happens all the time: Hunt till dark, and then deer appear in the field, pinning you in your stand. This season, practice making like a coyote. Carefully climb down from the stand, and knock out a few howls. Now move down the field edge with an irregular gait, stopping and starting, and howling every now and then. Deer may slip away, but they rarely bolt like they do if they see a human walking out of the woods.

---

295 TRAIN FOR A DEEP WOODS DEER DRAG

One of the most significant dangers for hunters comes when it's time to drag a heavy animal out of the woods. To prevent blowing out knees—or worse, your heart—train with a simple dead-weight drag. This exercise is part aerobics, part brute leg-strength workout. Start with a 20-pound bag of dog food or grass seed, and work your way up.

HERE'S WHAT YOU NEED:
- Loop of heavy rope or, better yet, webbing, long enough go over one shoulder and around your torso.
- Carabiner.
- Plastic decoy sled, snow toboggan, or hard plastic tote with a rope attached.
- Heavy bags of dog food, grass seed, horse chow, or even concrete mix.

Drape a webbing loop around one shoulder and torso. Clip a carabiner to the back of the loop, and attach it to the rope handle to the sled or tote. Load the sled with heavy bags, and start pulling along a 50-yard loop around the backyard.

296 COUCH DRILL FOR THE SHOT OF YOUR LIFE

Television hunts might be fun to watch. After all, you see deer wandering all over, taking their time about everything. Not in the real woods. When you get that chance at a once-in-a-lifetime buck, you need to make sharp shot decisions, and you can practice while sitting on your sofa.

To help train your mind, flip through a hunting magazine, look at the pictures, and compute the angles for a shot. Tell yourself: If this was my deer, I could shoot there and there and there. Now, flip through it more quickly. If that was your deer, where would you put the bullet?

FIELD & STREAM CRAZY-GOOD GRUB

297 COOK A DEER ON A ROCK

Before there were porcelain-coated grill grates and ceramic infrared burners, there was a hot rock with a hunk of meat on it. Cooking thin medallions of venison backstrap on smoking-hot slabs of once-molten earth is still a great way to channel your erstwhile Cro-Magnon.

STEP 1 Build a hot fire down to a good coal bed.

STEP 2 Find a flat rock that's less than 2 inches thick. Avoid shale, sand-stone, and stream rocks, which can explode in a fire. Wash the rock and place it near the coals for 15 minutes to preheat, which will lessen the chances of it cracking. Move the rock to a shallow nest scooped into the coals.

STEP 3 When the rock is hot enough that a drop of water sizzles and vaporizes, brush on a film of flavored olive oil and plop on backstrap medallions and onion slices about ½-inch thick. Season with cracked black pepper. Cook the venison and onions for about 2–3 minutes. Remove to a plate. Turn the rock over, brush away the ashes and drizzle with more olive oil. Place the medallions and onions on the fresh, hot surface, and top each medallion with an oil-packed sun-dried tomato. Cook another 2 minutes. Stack an onion slice on the meat and tomato, and serve.

298

MAP YOUR SPOT

Buy a U.S. Geological Survey (USGS) topographic map of your hunting camp. Or, better yet, print a topographic map or a satellite photograph from Internet sources.

STEP 1 Glue the map to a single sheet of foam-core board (a cardboard and Styrofoam laminate available at arts-and-crafts supply stores).

STEP 2 Mark the heads of pushpins with the initials of hunt club members.

STEP 3 Each hunter should mark his stand location with his pin upon arrival and remove it upon departure.

FIELD & STREAM CRAZY-GOOD GRUB

299 ROAST A DEER HAUNCH

The 17th-century English poet and soldier of fortune Gervase Markham had this advice: "Stick it with cloves all over on the outside . . . larde it either with Mutton larde, or Porke larde, but Mutton is the best: then spit it and roast it by a good soking fire, then take Vinegar, bread crummes, and some of the gravy, which comes from the Venison, and boile them well in a dish: then season it with sugar, cinamon, ginger, and salt, and serve the Venison fourth upon the sauce when it is roasted enough."

Of course, Markham was writing in the England of 1615, when six servants were assigned to every respectable kitchen. Here's an easier way— if you're looking for an imaginative main course for your Christmas dinner, you can't do better than this.

INGREDIENTS

1 haunch of deer	3 tbsp. ground cumin
3 tsp. garlic powder	Dried diced cherries
3 tbsp. brown sugar	2 tsp. ground red pepper
Toasted pecans	3 tsp. ground ginger

2 tsp. Chinese five-spice powder (enough diced dried cherries and toasted pecans to fill the bone cavity; will vary)

Cut the shank off the hind leg of a dressed deer and bone out the haunch. Stuff the bone cavity with a 50-50 mixture of diced dried cherries and toasted pecans. Tie haunch with kitchen twine. Roll it in a spice rub made of the cumin, brown sugar, ginger, garlic powder, red pepper, and Chinese five-spice powder. Roast the meat at 350 degrees F until a meat thermometer reads 140 degrees F (rare) to 160 degrees F (medium).

Slice and bask in your own glory.

300 CLEAN YOUR KNIFE

Fixed-blade knives need only a quick wipe down with a damp cloth after each use and a light application of honing oil on the blade.

Folders and multitools collect blood and dirt at pivot points and locking mechanisms. If the tool has a plastic handle, immerse it in boiling water for one minute and then put it in a pot of warm water (so that quick cooling doesn't crack the handle). Scrub nooks and crannies with a toothbrush, working pivot points back and forth, and then air-dry the knife before oiling. Use compressed air to blast out gunk.

Wipe away surface rust with an oily cloth or 0000 steel wool. Carbon blades naturally discolor with use. Bring them back to near-original luster by rubbing them with a cork dipped in cold wood ashes.

301 TAKE A KILLER TROPHY SHOT

Tired of boring, dark, fuzzy photos of your best deer? Here's how to create a photograph every bit as memorable as the moment you fired.

STEP 1 Arrange the antlers in front of an uncluttered background. Situate the hunter to one side, holding the antlers with both hands. A big mistake is photographing a rack against the pattern of a camouflage shirt.

STEP 2 Stuff the deer's tongue inside the mouth or cut it off. Tuck the legs under the body. Cover wounds with your gun or bow. Wet the nose. Wipe away all blood. The final touch: Slip glass taxidermic eyes over the buck's eyeballs. They work like contacts and prevent those ugly glowing orbs. They're cheap and reusable.

STEP 3 Take some pictures with a flash, especially at midday. This will help light shadows, such as from a hat.

STEP 4 Try something different. Lie on the ground. Stage a photo of the hunter dragging the buck out. Experiment with unusual angles.

302 AGE DEER IN A BIG COOLER

Not all hunters have walk-in coolers, and a lot of us kill deer when it's still 70 degrees F outside. Here's a way to age whitetails for four to five days even when you're wearing shorts in the backyard. All you need is a whopping big cooler and a supply of 2-quart juice bottles or 1-gallon milk cartons washed out, filled with water, and frozen solid.

STEP 1 Decide whether to keep the hide on or off. Keeping the hide on prevents some moisture loss, but you'll have to contend with hair on the meat due to quartering the animal with the hide on.

STEP 2 Remove the tenderloins, which don't need aging. Saw off the front legs at the knees and then remove the legs at the shoulder joints. Remove both rear quarters in one piece by sawing through the backbone just ahead of the pelvis—you'll lose just a bit of backstrap. Remove the lower shanks. You're left with four pieces: the double hams, two front quarters, and the rib cage and backbone.

STEP 3 Place four to five 2-quart bottles or cartons of ice in the bottom of a large cooler; the absolute minimum size cooler you should use would be 160 quarts. You can use bags of crushed ice or small blocks of ice instead of cartons or bottles, but you'll need to monitor water levels carefully, and drain meltwater to keep it off the meat. Arrange the deer in the cooler—the double hams go in first and then the rib cage. Then, work the shoulders around them. Now tuck a few more cartons of ice in the space around the meat. Cover the cooler with a couple of blankets or sleeping bags for extra insulation.

303 BE THE CAMP BIOLOGIST

Every deer camp should have a jaw puller to use to estimate the age of deer, if for no other reason than to have something else to talk about. Two tools are required: a pair of long-handled pruning shears and an inexpensive jaw extractor.

STEP 1 First, you'll need to lay the deer on its back; then, insert the jaw extractor between the incisors and premolars. Pry the mouth open.

STEP 2 Work the extractor along the lower jawbone, pushing down hard to separate cheek tissue from the jaw.

STEP 3 Use the pruning shears to cut the jaw as it curves upward behind the last molar. Place the cutting bar to the outside of the jaw and keep the handles parallel with the roof of the mouth.

STEP 4 Push the extractor through the cut. Put a foot on the deer's neck and then firmly pull the extractor out of its mouth. It will slide along the lower bone. At the front of the jaw, rotate the extractor 90 degrees to separate the jaws. Remove the freed jawbone.

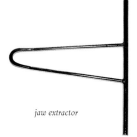

jaw extractor

304 TAKE THE TENDERLOINS

These are the long fillets that run parallel to the deer's backbone inside the rib cage, under the saddle. They are the most tender cuts and deserve the most tender care. All that is required is a sharp knife to remove them, a quick rinse, and a trip into a plastic baggie fast to prevent drying. Besides that, they simply call to be sliced into medallions, pan-seared in real butter seasoned with black pepper and rosemary, and eaten with the fingers.

305 SHARE THE BIRDS

You know it, and your buddies know it: One side of the blind is the King Daddy seat—the coveted downwind edge where the shooting is easy as the ducks drift in with wings spread a mile wide. Don't hog it. Seat placement can make the difference between fast shooting and hard feelings, especially when three or more gunners are in the blind. If there's an obvious hot spot in the blind, rotate the seating.

306 STOP A RUNNING BUCK

A low grunt or bleat will stop a close-in deer most of the time, but you'll need to minimize your movements. Make a call holder by sewing a loop of elastic cord on one side of the upper chest part of your jacket. Slip a grunt call under the loop, and you can easily reach it with your mouth. If you can't risk even that movement, try making a squirrel-like tch, tch-tch with your mouth. Have your gun or bow up and ready. Beyond 50 yards, a short, loud whistle sounds enough like a natural sound—a bird call, perhaps?—that it holds deer in place, intrigued but unalarmed, while they try to zero in on the source. If you can't produce an ear-splitting whistle with your lips, buy a referee's whistle and slip it on your grunt-call lanyard. Caught without a whistle? Holler "Stop!" and hope for the best.

307 WET-AGE A DEER

Aging venison allows naturally occurring enzymes to break down the structure of collagen and muscle fibers. That helps tenderize the meat and gives it distinctive, complex flavors. But early-season deer hunters—and deer hunters all season long in the sunny South—have a tough time hanging deer when the outside temperatures are warm enough for short sleeves.

To age venison in balmy weather, try wet-aging. Cool the carcass with ice for at least 12 hours; butchering a deer before rigor mortis sets in can turn even tender cuts chewy.

While butchering, remove as much silverskin and connective tissue as possible; keep whole muscles as intact as you can. Drain off any blood, pat the cuts dry with a paper towel, and then package cuts of butchered meat in vacuum-sealed bags. Store in a refrigerator for five to eight days. After aging, freeze the cuts as they are or finish butchering them into portion sizes.

Wet-aging won't give your venison the complex, concentrated flavors that would accrue during a week in a frosty barn. But even in the fridge, enzymatic action will go to work on silverskin and tendons, turning a warm-weather September buck into a meal worth bragging about.

308 SEE IN THE DARK

If you've ever wished that you could see in the dark, you're in luck! With these simple steps, you'll soon be able to maneuver in low-light conditions.

PROTECT In the critical minutes of dawn and dusk, shield your eyes from the sun. When moving your field of vision, allow your eyes to travel below the horizon line or shut your eyes as you move them. Before dawn, use the least amount of light required for the task; a low-level red or green light is best. Practice walking at night to increase your comfort level and clear favorite trails so you won't need a flashlight.

BOOST Use peripheral vision by focusing to the side of an object. Scan when you can; when your eyes linger on a particular object, they will adapt to whatever light is available. Try to get lower than the target to see its contours better.

309 TAN A DEER HIDE

Tanning a deer hide with the hair on is work but it is manageable. Here's the drill.

Stretch the skin over a 2x6-foot board. With a dull knife held at 90 degrees to the surface, scrape off all remaining muscle, sinew, and membrane. Rub copious amounts of noniodized salt into the flesh side, roll it up, toss it into a plastic bag, and freeze. Two to three days later, let the skin thaw, flesh it again, and wash out the salt.

Prepare a tanning solution of 4 gallons of water, 1 pound of granulated alum, and 1 pound of salt. Soak the hide in the solution for a week, stirring once a day.

Remove it from the tanning bath and squeeze it dry. Lather the flesh side with neat's-foot oil; let this soak in for a few hours. Stretch the wet hide over a hard, straight edge such as a sawhorse or table, and work it back and forth over the edge, as hard as you can, to soften it.

Use a rounded dowel or butter-knife handle for the hard-to-reach corners. If you think you're finished in less than eight hours, you're not.

310 HELP A KID GUT A FIRST DEER

Now it gets tricky: You have a deer on the ground and a kid at your side with a face white as biscuit batter. Think carefully about how you introduce a young hunter to the labor of turning what was once a living, breathing animal into bundles of neatly labeled meat.

Don't make a fuss. Approach the animal as next year's supply for spaghetti and stew, and you'll send a subtle message: What happens after the shot is just another part of the process. Gutting and skinning is nothing to dread. It's as much a part of hunting as lacing up your boots, so treat it that way.

Don't push it, either. On the other hand, recognize that the notion of removing the organs and severing joints from an animal with a saw is not exactly a stroll through Candy Land. Go easy. You're not out to prove a point or toughen up a soft kid. Also, if you think you might have crippled an animal, get your child out of the picture immediately. Dealing with a wounded animal is difficult under the best conditions, and watching while you dispatch your quarry at close range might just be enough to send a kid into early retirement from hunting.

Be methodical. Talk through every step, pointing out the animal's body structures. And give your child a job. Even if she (or he) is too young to handle a knife, she can hold a leg while you open up the body cavity or pull back the rib cage as you remove the lungs and heart.

See it through. The learning experience shouldn't end with field dressing. Involve your child in butchering, freezing, and other preparation tasks. If a pile of bloody meat gives your kid pause, then assign another task. Ask for help running the vacuum sealer, turning the grinder handle, or loading the freezer. Help your child understand that a large part of killing an animal is devoted to sustaining another life—their own.

311

STICK IT TO DOWNED GAME

Pick up a long stick and approach a downed big-game animal from behind. Watch for the rise and fall of the chest cavity. Closed eyes typically indicate a living animal. Never lay down your gun or bow until you use the stick to touch the animal's open eye. If it doesn't blink, you're good: Break out the skinning knife.

312 HOIST A DEER

I used to dread the backbreaking task of getting a buck up and over the truck tailgate solo. Until I discovered this trick.

STEP 1 Throw one rope over a branch. Tie one end to the rack and the other to the trailer hitch. Tie a second rope to the rack and toss the tag end over the branch.

STEP 2 Pull the truck forward to lift the animal off the ground. Secure the free end of the second rope to a tree or another object strong enough to hold the deer.

STEP 3 Untie the first rope from the vehicle. Back up, untie the second rope, and lower the deer into the truck.

313 TAKE A KILLER SELFIE

Taking a great selfie with your latest big buck is practically impossible unless you use a camera with a self-timer. Not all smartphone cameras come with a self-timer function, but many do, and those that don't can accept inexpensive self-timer apps. Add a small smartphone tripod and you'll be armed for taking boss self-portraits with your trophy.

This classic setup of the hunter approaching a downed deer is a snap. Focus on the deer's head and move back a few dozen feet for a more staged approach. That should put the deer in sharp focus and the hunter slightly out of focus for a dramatic

view. This is one of the few times that having the hunter "skylined" against a light background is a good thing.

A shot as you drag the deer out of the woods can tell you an important part of the story. Use a small tripod to affix the phone to a sapling or tree branch. Frame up shots as you drag the deer towards the camera and away.

Another good shot that showcases headgear in a subtle way is attaching a permit to the deer's antler or punching a tag. Prop the smartphone on a pack or use a small tripod to frame up a shot of just your hands, a knife, the permit, and the deer's rack.

314 IDENTIFY TRACKS BY GAIT

Language teachers have discovered that the fastest method of learning a foreign tongue is to focus on phrases rather than attempt to translate each word. Tracking is similar. Studying the details of a single print in order to identify its source can be a daunting task. Instead, noting the pattern or "phrasing" of the tracks, which reveals the traveling gait of the animal, as well as the overall shape of the impressions helps you narrow the possibilities.

Note that animals use many different gaits; what is shown are their most common.

DIAGONAL WALKERS-TROTTERS (deer, elk, moose, wolf, coyote, fox, mountain lion, bobcat, lynx)

bobcat

deer

coyote

WALK   **TROT**

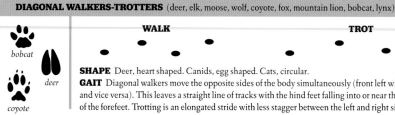

SHAPE Deer, heart shaped. Canids, egg shaped. Cats, circular.
GAIT Diagonal walkers move the opposite sides of the body simultaneously (front left with rear right and vice versa). This leaves a straight line of tracks with the hind feet falling into or near the impressions of the forefeet. Trotting is an elongated stride with less stagger between the left and right sides.

PACERS-AMBLERS (bear, raccoon, badger, skunk)

black bear

WALK   **AMBLE**

SHAPE Boxed-off toe with fuzzy leading edges and an elliptical rear (humanlike).
GAIT Pacers have wide bodies and move the feet from the same side of the body simultaneously. The impressions of the front and rear feet are roughly side by side. In a leisurely amble, a common pace, the back foot oversteps the front foot.

FULL BOUNDERS OR HOPPERS (tree squirrel, ground squirrel, chipmunk)

tree squirrel

FULL BOUND

SHAPE Star-shaped. **GAIT** Full bounders keep their rear feet side by side and their front feet side by side. The rear feet land ahead of the front feet.

HALF BOUNDERS (rabbits, hares)

cottontail

HALF BOUND

SHAPE Front round, rear oblong. **GAIT** Half bounders place their hind feet side by side, whereas their forefeet are staggered. The rear feet land ahead of the front feet.

GALLOPERS (most weasels, including marten, wolverine, ferret, mink, fisher)

fisher

4X4 GALLOP

SHAPE Front foot is box-shaped, with the rear foot longer. **GAIT** In galloping, the rear feet swing around the front feet and usually fall in front of them. Think of it as skipping. Tracks are composed in a group of patterns; the 4x4 group pattern is shown, but 3x3 and 2x2 are also common.

315 HOIST ANY LOAD WITH A BACKCOUNTRY BLOCK AND TACKLE

Maybe you're all alone and need to lift an elk quarter off the ground, hoist a food bag beyond the reach of bears, or hang a deer. Maybe you should know how to rig a backcountry block and tackle using nothing more than rope or parachute cord and a couple of lightweight rock-climbing carabiners.

STEP 1 Find a tree with a strong, live branch that is at least 2 feet higher than you want to suspend the load. Throw a rope over the branch. Tie a loop in the rope about 5 feet from the standing end by making an overhand knot and pulling a short section of standing line through. Clip a carabiner to this loop.

STEP 2 Thread the running end of the rope through a second carabiner and then through the first.

STEP 3 Pull the end of the rope that goes over the branch until the first carabiner is near the branch. Tie this end of the rope to the tree trunk.

STEP 4 Clip the heavy object to the second carabiner. You may need to fasten a rope around the object.

STEP 5 Haul the load as high as required, using the tree as a block by passing the hauling end of the rope around the trunk. Pad it with a jacket or pack to lessen friction. Last, tie the hauling end of the rope around the tree.

316 SHOOT YOUR OWN BIRD

Doubling up on one bird is the mark of the rank amateur—and a mistake even seasoned waterfowlers make too often. You and your partners need to discuss a strategy to avoid pulling the trigger on the same duck or goose. The gunner on the left might agree to take birds on the left of the flock or to shoot the trailing bird in a pair. Based on wind conditions and your decoy spread, figure out where the birds are most likely to fly and then hand out the shooting assignments accordingly.

317 SNEAK A RIDGE READY TO SHOOT

When you're stalking over a ridge, think a few steps ahead. First, stop just below the crest. An inch is as good as a mile, so get as close to the top as you can. Get your breath under control there, not when you're looking through the glass at your prize. Next, look for a clump of grass, a rock, anything to break up your outline as you ease your head up. Take your hat off, chamber the rifle, and pull a small pack or some other rest along with you as you slowly take a look. If that muzzle is waving around, back down, get your head right, and get your breath under control, because you can't put that bullet back in the gun once you pull the trigger.

318 SKIN A DEER WITH A GOLF BALL

No hair gets on the meat, and this method stretches the deer out and lays it right down on clean plastic. It's like taking its pajamas off. Don't laugh, because it works.

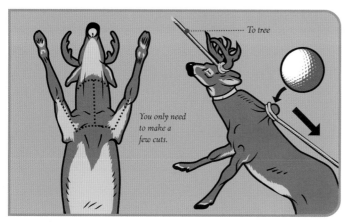

To tree

You only need to make a few cuts.

STEP 1 Lay the deer belly-up on a sheet of plastic or plywood. Make an incision through the skin all the way around the deer's neck about 6 inches below the ears. Make another incision from the neck cut down to a point between the front legs. Continue this incision out the inside of each front leg as far down as you want to skin the carcass.

STEP 2 Working from the top of the deer, free about 6 inches of skin between the top of the shoulder blades, and insert a golf ball or golf ball-size rock under the skin.

STEP 3 Tie the deer's head off to a sturdy pole or nearby tree. Make a slipknot in one end of another rope and cinch it over the golf ball, making sure it holds the deer's hide firmly. Attach the other end of this rope to your vehicle's tow hook.

STEP 4 Now just strip the hide from the deer by easing the vehicle slowly away from the carcass.

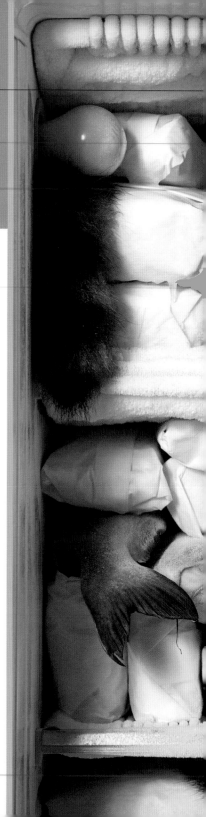

319

FREEZE ANY GAME FOR CHEAP

You need two things to properly freeze game meat: a vapor barrier and a constant, supercooled environment. Here's the cheap, easy way to ensure a fine meal of venison or grouse come next summer.

Place small animals such as squirrels, doves, quail, and ducks into gallon-size resealable plastic freezer bags, and place the bags in a sink. (Many big game cuts, such as steaks and tenderloins, also fit.) Fill the bag two-thirds of the way with ice water—chilled water will hasten the freezing process—and swirl the meat gently to release any trapped air. Now press down slightly. While water spills from the bag, seal it tightly. You've created two barriers to freezer-burn-producing air: the plastic bag and a cocoon of protective ice.

So far, so cheap. Now you need to freeze those bags—quickly. The longer the freezing process, the larger the ice crystals that form, and large ice crystals will damage the cell walls of muscle tissue and degrade meat. A free-standing freezer is far superior to the traditional refrigerator freezer, which may or may not produce temperatures below the recommended 0 degrees F. Spread the packages out with at least two inches of air space between them. (Once frozen, they can be stacked.)

If your freezer sports wire grate shelving, line the shelves with newspaper to prevent the bag corners from drooping through the shelf grate and freezing into an icy hook. And don't freeze more than a quarter of the freezer's capacity at a time. Locked in ice, birds should keep six months or more; larger cuts last up to one year. By then you'll need to throw a wild game dinner party to clear out the freezer for a fresh delivery.

320 REALLY, REALLY TICK OFF YOUR HUNTING PARTNER

A duck-hunting buddy finally caves in to your ceaseless whining and takes you to his new honey hole. It's on the back side of public land, so of course you cross your heart never to set a wader boot on the pond without him. And you don't—at least until you line up another hunt with someone else. There is nothing illegal about such two-timing promiscuity, but it is patently immoral. Such disloyalty may (or may not) be forgiven. But it is never forgotten.

321 MAKE YOUR OWN DEER DRAG

Prevent rope burn and your own heart attack by using a homemade deer drag. You'll need two black plastic pallet sheets in good condition (try getting them from a warehouse), a grommet tool, 20 feet of parachute cord, and 10 feet of drag rope.

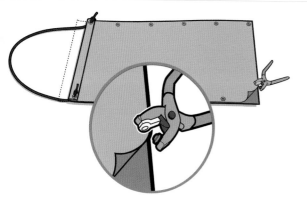

AT HOME Stack the two pallet sheets one on top of the other, slippery sides facing down. Attach them with grommets spaced about a foot apart all the way up both sides. Next, double over 2 inches of one of the short ends; secure with two grommets. Fasten the drag rope onto this reinforced edge with stopper knots.

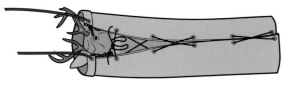

IN THE FIELD Place your deer on the plastic sheeting. Use parachute cord to lace the plastic around the deer, just like lacing up a shoe. Get dragging.

322 SPOOK THE BULL YOU'RE HUNTING

One of the most common mistakes hunters make is trying to sound like a big bull. Throwing in half a dozen ringing grunts and a lot of chuckling at the end of the bugle might impress your hunting partner, but a herd bull's usual response is to round up his harem and nose them away from the intruder.

323 GREEN-SCORE A WHITETAIL RACK

To gain entry into the Boone and Crockett (B&C) record book, your deer must be measured by an official B&C scorer after a 60-day drying period. But you can get your own score by using any measuring tape. It's called green scoring, and here's the formula for a typical whitetail. (All measurements are to the nearest $\frac{1}{8}$ inch.)

Measure the length of the longer main beam. Then measure the inside spread of the main beams; if this is less than or equal to your previous notation, it's your first number to keep. But if it is greater, discard it and use the original figure instead. Call whichever you retain A.

For each antler, add up the following: length of main beam; length of each normal point (the beam tip counts as a point, but do not include its length in your measurements here); the circumference at the smallest place between the burr and the first point; and the circumferences at the smallest places between the first and second, second and third, and third and fourth points (or halfway between the third point and beam tip). Add the two antler totals together to get B. Take A plus B to get your gross subtotal, C.

Now for the deductions: Take the differences between the corresponding measurements of each antler—that is, beam and point lengths, and the various circumferences. For example, if the right beam is 2 inches longer than the left one, write down that amount. Do the same for each individual measure; total them. To this figure, add the lengths of all abnormal points—those tines that don't project from the top of the main beam, or that don't have a matching tine on the other antler. This is D. Subtract D from C for the score.

324 WORK A BEAVER POND OVER FOR DUCKS

Hunting a beaver pond starts with finding the right one. Young ponds and flooded swamps are a hunter's best bet, because rich, flooded soils produce a flush of edible plants, from duckweed to wild rice.

If your favorite pond seems to be drawing fewer ducks, look up and down the watershed for places where beavers have recently migrated.

Even older ponds, however, can produce a fine duck shoot. The surrounding trees produce more and more mast as they grow, a wood duck bonanza. As a beaver pond ages, it also tends to expand as the beavers add to the dam. The deeper waters stay ice-free longer and can be a late-winter magnet when surrounding spots freeze up.

Always scout in the morning, not the evening. An older beaver pond or swamp that fills with ducks roosting at sunset might be empty of birds just a few minutes past legal shooting light as they depart for distant feeding grounds.

This two-person team (1) is set up near a creek channel. They have 8 to 10 decoys out in front of a blind, but they've moved back, temporarily, to the creek to shoot the first-light wood duck flights that follow the stream.

These hunters (2) are hunkered down for the long haul: well camouflaged in a fallen tree, comfortably seated at angles to each other to provide 360-degree views of the sky and using a jerk cord to create decoy movement.

This pair of hunters (3) is working birds that have lighted just out of sight of their decoy spread. One guy is in the blind, gun ready to mount.

His companion is stalking mallards on the far side of dense brush and blowdowns. They're doing what is called a pinch maneuver: When the stalker flushes the birds, they'll fly over the guy still in the stand so he can easily get a clear shot at them.

325 MAINTAIN A MOUNT

Ol' Bucky not as impressive as he used to be? Lifeless eyes, dull hair, nostrils stuffed with cobwebs? Time to take 10 minutes and buff that deer mount into museum quality again.

STEP 1 Don't grind in dust and grime with a cloth. First, vacuum the entire mount with a shop-vac using a stiff bristly dusting head attachment. Go lightly, and move in the direction of the hair. Clean out the ears and nostrils.

STEP 2 Clean ear cavities, nose cavities, and open mouths with a blast of canned compressed air.

STEP 3 Wipe down antlers with a wet rag, let dry, then go over with linseed oil or a touch of non-yellow liquid floor wax.

STEP 4 Starting with the head, give the hide a light wipe down with spray furniture wax.

STEP 5 Clean glass eyes with glass cleaner and a pointed-tip cosmetic swab. Available at most drugstores, these swabs holds less liquid and reduce the chances of wetting the eyelids. That is a no-no, for ammonia in the glass cleaner can dry out those tissues.

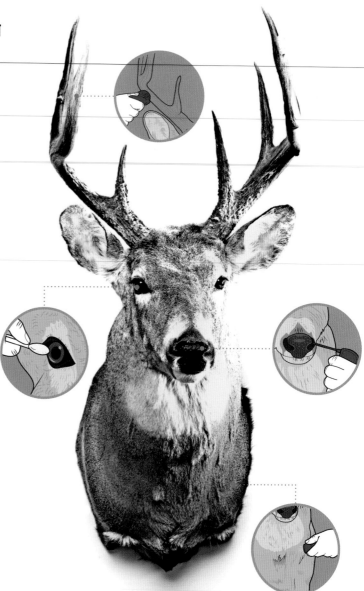

326 MAKE JERKY WITH A PENCIL

Here's an easy way to make jerky without using a dehydrator or smoker: Line the bottom of an oven with foil, spray the racks with cooking spray, and drape jerky strips over the racks. Dry at about 180 degrees, and prop the door open with a 3-inch pencil stub so the moisture can escape.

327 PACK A FIELD-DRESSING KIT

Store-bought field dressing kits often include a bunch of unnecessary items for a hunter who's faced with gutting a deer and getting it home. This DIY kit fits into a gallon-size plastic zippered bag, which also serves as a handy place to put down a knife while you're wrestling with a transcending colon. At the truck, stash 3 gallons of clean water for rinsing out the body cavity, and a hatchet if you want to open the pelvis.

(1) DEER DRAG Store-bought deer drags have a handle that makes them too bulky for this kit. Tie a loop in each end of an 8-foot length of 9mm climbing rope. Now you can slip a choker loop around the doe's neck or buck's antlers and cinch the other end of the rope around a sturdy stick for a handle. **(2) LATEX GLOVES** Lots of field dressing gloves go up to your armpit, to turn blood away from clothing and any open cuts. But wrist-high gloves have a better feel and grip and still prevent blood and nicked guts from infecting small cuts. **(3) PAPER TOWELS** I like to keep 15 paper towels, folded up, to use as cavity and hand wipes. **(4) PARACORD** Keep a 5-foot length of cord in the kit and use it to tie one leg to a sapling and hold it out of the way for easier gutting. **(5) BUTT OUT 2** It works. Enough said. **(6) IBUPROFEN** If I'm farther than a few hundred yards from the truck, I make my back happy with a dose of Vitamin I within minutes of pulling the trigger. **(7) ZIP TIES** Tie off the intestinal canal with one hand. Snazzy. **(8) HAND SANITIZER** Bring a small bottle for field treatment of knife nicks and overall cleanup. **(9) BANDAGES** Pack these for knife nicks. **(10) ZIP-SEAL BAGS** Have two gallon-size bags for the heart and the liver. **(11) GUT HOOK** Tons of small gut hooks have hit the market.

328 MOUNT A RACK ON A ROCK

For more than a year this 6-point rack, connected by its antler plate, had been relegated to a grimy corner of my basement. There it kept company with a few other racks that never quite made the mounting cut. But every set of antlers tells a story and deserves better treatment. One day, I kept telling myself, I'll do something with those horns. One day I did.

Turning that overlooked rack into a distinctive piece of sporting art took maybe three hours of work and less than $10 in supplies. I used a paving stone from a landscape supply shop. You won't believe how easy it is.

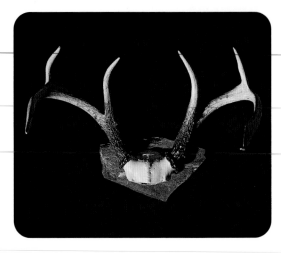

STEP 1 Cut away as much of the hide and flesh as you can, being careful not to score the bone with your knife. Soak the antler plate in a basin of water for two to three days. Scrape away as much tissue as possible.

STEP 2 Mix bleach and water in a one-to-one ratio, then carefully swab down or spray the entire antler plate with the liquid. Be very careful to keep it off the antlers or they will discolor. Repeat every 30 minutes or so until the bone is completely white. This might take one or more afternoons.

STEP 3 If the antlers have lost their color, use a woodstain to restore. Test it with a small spot on the back of the antler first, and use sparingly. Let it dry, then spray the finished antlers with a clear semigloss polyurethane.

STEP 4 Round off the edges and corners of the antler plate with a hand-held rotary tool, being careful not to breathe in the bone dust.

STEP 5 Drill two ¼-inch holes through the top of the antler plate, approximately 1 inch apart. Drill another pair of ¼-inch holes, about 1 inch apart, through the mounting board or stone.

STEP 6 Fasten the antler plate to the backing using a leather lace (wet it so that it dries tightly), tied on the back side with a very tight square knot. The lace also serves as a handy hanging loop.

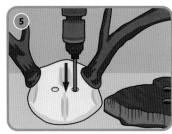

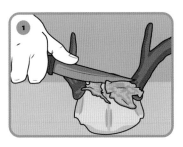

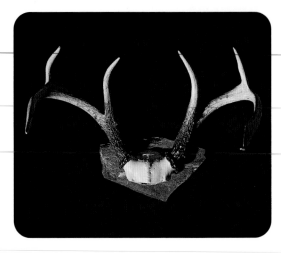

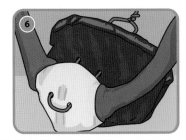

331

RIG A DEER DRAG

Have a few odd pieces of webbing and rope heaped up in the basement? Add in a carabiner to make a handy deer drag. First, lash the deer's front legs tight to the upper neck. Next, wrap a 6-foot loop of some webbing or rope around the antlers (if it's a buck) or its neck (if it's a doe), and tie an overhand loop in the end. Clip the carabiner onto the loop. Now run a 6-foot loop of wide webbing through the carabiner to form a pair of loops like butterfly wings. Slip a shoulder through each loop and stand up; the deer's head will lift up and off the ground. Head for home.

329

TRACK A BLOOD TRAIL

The same hydrogen peroxide your mother sprayed on skinned knees can help you track your next deer. The liquid will foam up on contact with blood as the peroxide reacts with the enzyme catalase, which is released when tissues are damaged. Take along a small spray bottle and you can use it to tell whether those tiny dark specks are blood from the deer you are trailing or just little leaf spots and pieces of dirt. Spray with a fine mist, and mark each positive result with surveyor's tape, because the hydrogen peroxide will remove small blood specks. It's a great trick for color-blind hunters.

330

LIGHT UP A HUNT

Stash a few glow sticks in your daypack. Down an elk or deer at dusk and it will soon get dark. Tie the glow sticks to branches to mark the blood trail. When the trail gets sparse, you can look back through the woods and the glow sticks will line up, giving you a general direction of travel. Once you find the animal, the glow sticks mark the route back to where you were when you shot.

332 REMOVE A BACKSTRAP WITH PRECISION

Many hunters ruin the best cut of venison. To avoid doing this, begin by hanging the deer from its hind legs and removing the shoulders.

STEP 1 Insert the knife beside the spine right in the middle of the deer. Keep the blade tight against the vertebrae and cut down to the neck. Turn the knife around and extend the cut to the hindquarters until the knife hits the pinbone of the hip. Repeat on the other side of the spine.

STEP 2 Insert your knife out in the curve of the ribs, 4 inches from where you think the edge of the backstrap lies. Carefully work the knife along the curve of the ribs and the bottom of the vertebrae to meet your long cuts.

Be sure to bring all the rib meat out with the backstrap.

STEP 3 Make the final cut across the backstrap at the pinbone, connecting the two long incisions.

333 RIG A PRUSIK-KNOT SAFETY ROPE

When it comes to danger, climbing into your tree stand could be said to rank right up there next to hunting rhinos with a pellet rifle. Learn to climb with a safety rope tied with a Prusik knot clipped to your harness, and you'll dramatically increase your chances of one day being a crotchety old fart. Tie off a rope to the bottom of the tree and then to the trunk above the level of your head when you're standing up in your stand. Tie a Prusik knot around this safety rope, and slide it up and down as you go.

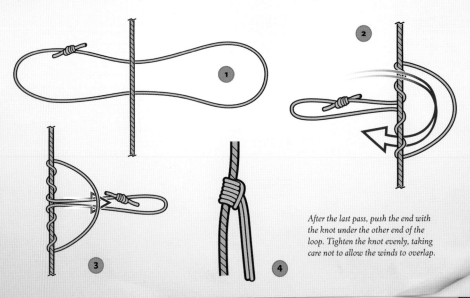

After the last pass, push the end with the knot under the other end of the loop. Tighten the knot evenly, taking care not to allow the winds to overlap.

334 ADJUST A SADDLE FOR AN ALL-DAY HUNT

After planning a horseback hunting trip for months, many desk jockeys finally arrive in big-game country barely able to walk, just due to the ride in. The secret to success is paying attention to the length of your saddle's stirrup leathers, which connect the stirrups to the saddletree. This is the primary factor that determines whether your trail will take you to lifetime memories or salty tears. Here's how to adjust your stirrups to fit your legs.

ON THE GROUND Get in the ballpark by running your hand under the seat to where the stirrup straps touch the saddletree. Adjust the length of the leathers so that the stirrup bottoms reach to your armpit.

IN THE SADDLE Fine-tune the fit by letting your legs hang down naturally from the saddle. Adjust the stirrup so the bottom of the tread is slightly below your anklebone. Now stand in the saddle. You should have a fist-size clearance between the saddle and your butt. If you're a greenhorn, it's wise to err on the shorter side.

IN YOUR MIND Adjust your expectations—riding over long distances hurts. There's an old saying: "If your knees are sore, your stirrups are too short. If your butt is sore, your stirrups are too long. If both your knees and your butt hurt like fire, then everything is just right."

335 HAUL YOUR DEER ANY DISTANCE

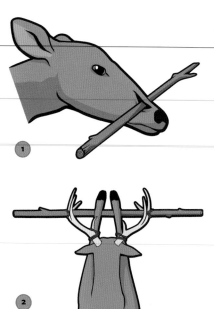

One tagged deer, no cart, no ATV, no dragging harness, and miles to go before you sleep. So what's the most efficient way to haul that animal out of the woods? Here are two methods to try. Both get your deer's head, neck, and shoulders off the ground, which results in less friction and easier dragging.

ONE-PERSON DOE DRAG Cut a sturdy stick of about ¾-inch diameter to an 18-inch length. Whittle a point on one end. Stab an inch-long slit through the animal's muzzle with your knife, just behind the black part of the nose and across the top of the nose bone. Work the knife blade under the cartilage and out the other side of the muzzle. Insert the stick into this slit. Grab the dragging stick with both hands behind your back.

TWO-PERSON BUCK PULL Pull the front legs forward and tie each tightly to the base of an antler. Then lash a stout 4-foot-long stick to the antlers at a crotch in the tines, leaving enough length protruding from either side for two people to stand beside the deer and pull, oxen-style. In addition to easing the burden, this method protects the cape from dirt and abrasion.

336 FACE A DUCK BLIND IN THE RIGHT DIRECTION

Sometimes there's no choice, but on a cloudless day, an east-facing setup will force you to shoot into the glaring sun during the critical first half hour of legal light. A front-lit blind also stands out from its surroundings more than a blind set in the dark shadows. Some hunters argue that drawing a bead on birds silhouetted against the light in the eastern sky is easier, but you'll disagree after five minutes of frying your retinas once the sun has topped the horizon.

337

TEACH A BIRD DOG TO POINT

Getting a bird dog pup to start pointing feathers has as much to do with training as instinct.

GET THE PUP IN FEATHERS For the first year, it's all about getting the dog into birds. You want your pup to find so many birds that he figures out there's no way he can actually catch them.

GET TO THE DOG Once the dog points, get there fast. Your pooch needs to see the bird shot in front of him. That's the positive reinforcement.

GET THE POINT ACROSS Never shoot at a bird that he hasn't pointed. Teach your dog that the only way he's ever going to get a bird in his mouth is to point it so you can shoot it.

338 SOUND LIKE A DUCK

A happy-sounding quack from a 10-pound hen is the foundation of duck calling, but there's more to it than blowing hot air. Blowing a duck call well requires forcing air from your lungs by pushing with your diaphragm, and using an open-throated calling style to get enough air volume to shred cattails. Here's the practice drill.

STEP 1 Learn to blow from your belly. Hold a small mirror a few inches from your mouth and fog it with your breath, blowing deep, sharp exhalations. Even the quietest clucks and quacks come from that hot, deep, fog-the-mirror air.

STEP 2 To open your throat, sit down, tilt your head back, and look up. Practice blowing a sharp quack straight up at the ceiling. Master one clean, happy-as-a-clam hen quack. This is the most essential duck call, and you have to get it right.

STEP 3 Once your craned-neck, staring-at-the-ceiling quack is solid, slowly bring your head forward a few inches at a time. Master the single quack in each progressive position until your chin is level.

STEP 4 When you can maintain an open throat in a normal posture, follow the single quack with a second clean one, then a third. Tone comes next: Use quacks to work your way from the bottom of the scale to the top, and back down.

339 DECIPHER FLIGHT PATTERNS

Keep an eye on wingtips—when the ducks stop flapping and sail for a second or two, they're looking for the source of the calling, which means you're doing something right. Don't stop now. If a duck's tail is lower than his head, he's cruising and looking, and you've got a good shot at finishing him. But if he levels up, your chances are getting worse. Back off the call. Pull that jerk cord. And call hard "on the corners" as the birds are starting to circle and all you see are tail feathers.

340 DECODE A DUCK QUACK

The best duck callers carry on a conversation. Here's what they're saying.

HAIL CALL Loud and nearly obnoxious, used when ducks are too far away to hear anything but the most raucous racket. Think Bourbon Street or spring break at Daytona.

GREETING CALL Warm and personal. "How ya doin'? What's going on tonight?"

COMEBACK CALL This is the party invitation. The gang's-all-here-and-you're-missing-it plea.

FEEDING CALL When ducks hear this, they should think about a bunch of guys scraping their plates with a fork.

HEN QUACK "Life is good, my friends. Grub a-plenty, and plenty to share."

341 KNOW WHEN YOU'VE SCREWED A SCOPE HARD ENOUGH

One way that you can avoid endless trouble is by degreasing the base screws on your scope mounts and screwing them in hard.

How hard is hard? Hard is when you're turning the screwdriver for all you're worth and the next thing you know you're lying on the floor and the dog is pawing at you and whining. Hard is when you're twisting away and everything turns purple and silver. You get the idea.

When tightening scope ring screws, however, you do not crank on the screwdriver until all the little blood vessels in your nose burst. You crank until, with a reasonable amount of effort, the screws will turn no longer. Then you stop. That's hard enough.

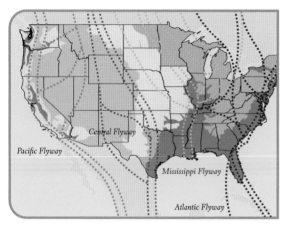

Central Flyway

Pacific Flyway

Mississippi Flyway

Atlantic Flyway

342 KNOW YOUR FLYWAY

Pouring down from the northern United States, Canada, Alaska, and the Arctic, migrating waterfowl broadly follow one of four migratory routes as they flee winter weather for their warmer southern wintering grounds. Knowing the flyway in which your favorite hunting spot is located will help you track the weather patterns that drive ducks south. Watch for big storm fronts bearing down in the northern reaches of your flyway. Ducks will be on the move. You should be packing decoys.

FIELD & STREAM CRAZY-GOOD GRUB

343 MAKE A TEAL POT

A duck dish made with pancake syrup and a can of cola? This is no joke.

INGREDIENTS
6 plucked and cleaned teal, or 3 to 4 mallards
One 12-oz. can cola
3 medium onions, quartered
Smoked sausage, 4 to 5 links cut into 3-inch lengths
Pancake syrup
Cajun spice blend

Place ducks breast side down in a large Dutch oven–style pot.

Pour the cola over the birds.

Add onions. Place one piece of smoked sausage inside each duck. Scatter the remaining sausage pieces in the pot.

Squirt each duck with a dollop of pancake syrup.

Shake Cajun spice blend over the whole batch.

Cover and bake in 300-degree F oven for 3 hours.

Serve with rice and spiced rum.

344 FLAG A DUCK

Your buddies might snicker when you bust out a duck flag in a timber hole, but soon enough they will be asking you, "Where can I get one?" Goose hunters have long used flags to pull honkers into gun range, but I've flagged ducks in open country and tight timber with very positive results. Don't forget the camo—head to toe, nose to fingertips. After all, you're asking those birds to practically look you in the eye.

GIVE A FLAP Grab the flag firmly, raise it over your head, and shake it vigorously as you flap it down toward the water. Picture your mallard back-flapping hard as it descends the final 10 feet to land. You can see the flash of those white underwings in even the shadiest corners of a swamp, and that's what you want to replicate. Repeat three times quickly.

PLAN YOUR SALUTE As the ducks begin to close the distance, they'll be looking right down at you. Similar to calling, you should work the flag only when the ducks are "on the corners" as they loop around the decoy spread. When the hunting slows down, however, you shouldn't be afraid to give the flag a hearty flapping every few minutes to grab the attention of cruising mallards you might not see.

DO THE WAVE If you and a buddy are hunting out in thick timber and beaver swamps, a pair of flaggers can mean an especially deadly strategy. Stand about 5 to 10 feet from each other, and shake the flags in a row-row-row-your-boat round style: As one flag nears the water, that's when the other flagger starts his turn. This sequence helps simulate one duck following another to the honey hole.

345 COOK A DUCK WITH A STICK

My hunting partners and I watched in amazement as our Athabascan Chipewyan guide cooked a whole duck on a stick. The bird self-basted in its own dripping fat, which scorched in the fire and sent seasoning plumes of smoke up around the meat. It is not required that you put on a moosehide hat that has been sewn by your mother while cooking a duck this way, but it doesn't hurt. Total cooking time will be about 20 minutes.

STEP 1 Cut a 1-inch-thick green stick 18 to 24 inches in length. Sharpen one end. Gut and pluck the duck.

STEP 2 Remove the feet and the wings. Our host left the bird's head on, an impressive but not necessary flourish. Butterfly the duck through the breast, not the back. To do this, insert a stout knife along one side of the breastbone keel, cutting all the way to the backbone (A).

STEP 3 Loosen up the bones and flesh by working the duck back and forth between your hands, like trying to break a stick. Place the duck on a flat surface and press with the palm of your hand (B).

STEP 4 Skewer the duck by running the stick in and out of the breast meat on one side of the keel, and then on the other. Anchor the stick in the ground at a 45-degree angle to the fire, 6 inches to a foot away from the heat source (C). Cook breast side to the fire first, and rotate once.

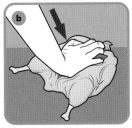

346

MAKE A DUCK HUNTER'S FLOATING TABLE

This floating table is a duck hunter's rip-off of the classic swimming pool beer pong table. All the pegboard holes drain any water that slops onto the table, so it will keep your shells, calls, gloves, and other items high and dry in a flooded swamp or timber hole. The pipe insulation serves as edge bumpers and keeps items from sliding off and provides a bit of outrigger flotation. Make the table long enough and it'll float a gun, as well. Pretty swanky.

YOU'LL NEED
a couple of pool noodles • a sheet of plastic pegboard in a dark color • black foam pipe insulation (the kind with the slit) • zip ties

STEP 1 Cut pool noodles into three pieces that are 4 inches shorter than the full length of your pegboard table top. Cut pipe insulation to the proper length to slip over all four table top edges.

STEP 2 Using zip ties, attach pipe insulation all the way around the pegboard.

STEP 3 Using zip ties, attach your pool noodle sections. Place one lengthwise down the center of the pegboard, and two other sections down the long edges. If more flotation is needed, simply attach more pool noodle sections.

347 SET MONSTER GANG LINES FOR BIG WATER DIVERS

Diving duck hunters often have to contend with extreme decoy-setting conditions. This heavily weighted gang line will hold decoys in place through Armageddon but still give hunters the option of moving them when the birds need tweaking.

Tie a 5- to 10-pound anchor to each end of 150 feet of decoy cord. (A tip for hunters with retrievers: Use lead-core line to keep this long mother line underwater and out of your pooch's paws.) Tie in 18-inch dropper lines for each decoy, spaced about 6 feet apart. Tie in a metal trout stringer clip to the end of each dropper. Set a number of gang lines parallel to one another and fill in the gaps with individual decoys.

348 KNOW YOUR NUTS

Nothing draws game like mast crops, be they oak, beech, or hickory. The trick is knowing which crop is which, and what critters can't pass them by.

WHITE OAK

In a good year, a mature white oak can produce upwards of 2,000 acorns. White oaks typically produce "bumper" crops every three to four years.

BEST FOR Deer, squirrels, turkeys, grouse, bears

CHESTNUT OAK

These sweet acorns are among the largest mast fruits in the woods and sprout soon after they fall. Deer can't eat enough of them.

BEST FOR Deer, squirrels, turkeys, bears

RED OAK

Red oaks are higher in tannin than white oaks, so deer target acorns of the latter first. But in years with a wet, cold spring or a late spring frost, white oak acorn production often plummets. A stand in red oaks pays off.

BEST FOR Deer, squirrels, turkeys, grouse

CALIFORNIA BLACK OAK

This western oak doesn't mind rocky slopes, thin soils, and dry climates. It's critical for muleys, and fawn survival rates are tied to its mast production. Look for pure groves loaded with acorns.

BEST FOR Mule deer, bears, quail

AMERICAN BEECH

Once the oily beechnuts are released from their prickly husks, smaller animals prize them. Wild turkeys will cover a lot of ground to find a good beech ridge; the extinct passenger pigeon once flocked to such spots.

BEST FOR Deer, squirrels, turkeys

SHAGBARK HICKORY

It's the sweetest hickory nut in the woods. Squirrels love them, and their gnawing sounds are a giveaway to knowing hunters. Wild turkeys swallow the nuts unshelled and let their gizzards do the hard work.

BEST FOR Squirrels, turkeys

349 SPATCHCOCK YOUR BIRD

You heard right. It's an Irish term that means to butterfly and nearly flatten a whole bird, so the meat cooks evenly. Use it to cook any gamebird over a fire.

Turn a dressed bird breast side down. With bird hunter's shears, cut cleanly up one side of the backbone and then the other, from neck to tail. Toss the backbone in the trash. Press the bird against a cutting board with the heel of your hand. Rub down with spices. Grill or spit it on a Y-shaped stick and roast it over the fire like a marshmallow.

350 GLASS WITH A PLAN

Big, open country requires hunters to spend quality time behind good glass. Use spotting scopes and binoculars to visually pick the landscape apart to find that one memorable animal that offers a good chance for success. And you can't just lean over a spotting scope and rubber-neck distant ridges. Have a plan.

MAKE LIKE A PIRATE Spotting scopes can produce eyestrain-induced headaches. Consider wearing a patch over the eye you're not using.

BRACE YOURSELF You might be glassing for hours, so get comfortable and get rock solid. A backrest is key.

HAVE A FORMULA Be sure to avoid letting your eyes wander. Use binoculars first to pick apart the obvious cover. Then work a spotting scope over the rest of the landscape. Pick a viewing pattern and stick with it. Don't forget to look away from the glass every couple of minutes. Your trophy might have walked right up on you.

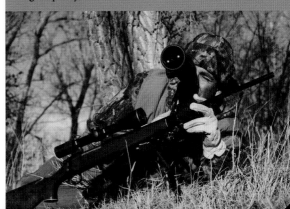

351 FOOL WOOD DUCKS WITH A SPINNING DOVE DECOY

Spinning wing dove decoys can pull double duty in a duck swamp frequented by woodies. To raise the spinner above the water, cut a length of gray PVC pipe and sharpen one end with an angled cut. Push the pipe into the mud, then insert the spinner pole into the pipe. Dove spinners are small and light, so you can easily fit one into a daypack for those dawn hikes into wood duck swamps.

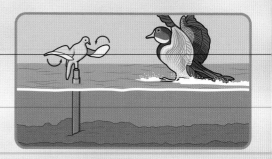

352

MAKE THE AWESOMEST DUCK WHISTLE ON THE PLANET

This loud, breathy whistle is a charmer for teal and wigeon. It's a snap to make with a few common tools and pairs of spent 12-gauge shells. Each requires either one low brass head shell (approximately 5/16 inch tall) and one high brass head (approximately 5/8 inch tall), or two low brass head shells. Whistles made from low or high brass heads will make different sounds, so keep a variety on your lanyard.

STEP 1 Heat up the brass head in the flame of a propane torch. Put on a work glove to hold on to the brass and gently remove the plastic case with pliers. Take out the plastic cup inside the brass head by reheating the brass, then scraping away the remaining plastic with a flat-tip screwdriver.

STEP 2 Place the brass head (with the primer down) on a 1-inch-thick stack of cardboard. Punch out the primer. Use your screwdriver to partially flatten the metal flanges that held the primer for each brass head. Hold the pair together and blow through the holes. The final sound will be louder and sharper.

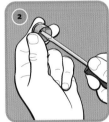

STEP 3 Widen out the rim of the high brass head to take the other head. Use a rotary tool to grind the rim of a 9/16-inch socket just slightly so that the ground rim will barely fit into the brass head. Lightly tap it with a hammer to widen the circumference of the brass, then remove. Lastly, tap one brass head into the other.

353 TRANSLATE A QUACK

Know a great duck caller? Have him turn a call around and blow his best hail calls and highballs with the insert against his lips. Now you know what to "say" into your own call.

354

SNAG DECOYS IN DEEP WATER

Pulling in dozens of floating decoys after a hunt is a task burdensome enough to make you forget all about the easy incomers you dispatched at dawn. But you can make quick work of the chore with these two tricks.

ⓐ GRAPPLE LINE Tie 30 feet of decoy line on to a 6- or 8-ounce lead sinker. Twist a half-dozen screws into the sinker at odd angles until each one protrudes by about 1/2 inch. To use it, toss the sinker at the decoys. All those screws will grab the onto the anchor line on the way to the bottom, and you can gently pull the decoy close.

ⓑ PADDLE PICKER-UPPER With a handsaw, a band saw, or a small handheld rotary cutting tool, cut a 1/2-inch angled slot 1 inch deep into each edge of your duck-boat paddle's blade. Slant the slots about 45 degrees away from the handle. File down the rough edges. The slots won't affect your paddle, and you'll be able to reach out from the boat and snag decoy lines from much farther away.

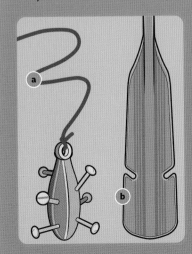

355 DISAPPEAR FROM DUCKS

With so much pressure on birds from north of the 49th parallel to the Gulf of Mexico, head-to-toe camouflage is critical for all but the earliest flights of the season. In a salt marsh or over open water, a shiny human face peeking over the blind is visible to ducks from a half mile or more away. In timber, ducks are doubly wary, and anything that looks out of place will send puddlers into the stratosphere. Why didn't they commit after a couple of passes? Take a good look at yourself. Hands, face, neck. Cover every inch, every time.

356 FILLET A DEER QUARTER

Boning out a deer quarter is quick and easy, resulting in tender cuts of meat void of bonemeal and marrow formed when cutting through bone with a saw.

STEP 1 Place the skinned hind leg of a deer on a sturdy table, with the outside of the leg facing up. Slice through the silverskin along the natural seam between the top round and the sirloin tip, and pull the muscle away from the bone. Cut the top round off at the back of the leg.

STEP 2 Remove the remaining silverskin. Cut the rump roast away from the top of the hip bone.

STEP 3 Turn the leg over. Using your fingers, separate the bottom round from the sirloin tip at the natural seam. Cut the bottom round from the bone. Then cut the sirloin tip from the bone. Slice the shank meat away from the bone and trim off connective tissue.

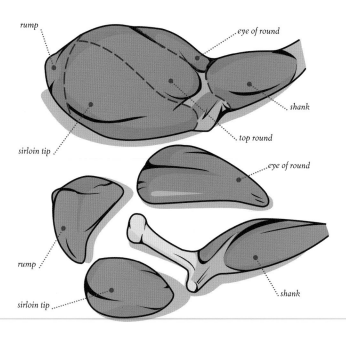

rump · eye of round · shank · top round · sirloin tip · eye of round · rump · shank · sirloin tip

357 WALK LIKE A SHADOW

Spring woods are noisy. A carpet of dead leaves and a winter's worth of ice-felled branches litter the forest floor. Learning how to walk silently will put you in a better position to call in the gobbler of a lifetime—and help you walk up to a hat-rack buck next deer season.

WALK LIKE A CAT Begin your step by lifting your foot straight up, toes pointing down to avoid snagging. Place the outside of your foot down first. Press the ball of your foot into the ground consciously, rolling from the outside in. Bring down your heel, then slowly shift weight to that foot. Be prepared to lift and shift whenever you feel any obstacle that might snap or crackle under your weight.

MAP YOUR STEPS To avoid having to watch your feet, make a mental map of the upcoming ground cover for the next 8 to 10 paces. Especially note where you might need to sidestep branches or high-step over fallen logs.

GO SLOW When looking for game, take three to four slow steps and stop. How slow? Three steps should take you at least 20 seconds.

HIDE YOUR NOISE Mask the noise of footfalls by moving whenever other sounds can muffle your own. Wind in the trees, moving water, and even airplane noise can all hide the sound of a human on the hunt.

358 TUNE-UP YOUR TURKEY SKILLS

Often even the sweetest-sounding box calls come out of storage sounding a little flat. It's easy to ruin a call through overzealous tuning, so the secret is to go easy.

STEP 1 Cleaning comes first, but be very careful not to change the contours of the call's lips and paddle. Forgo the sandpaper. Instead try a light touch with a plastic-coated sponge of the kind usually used to scrub pots without scratching them. The plan is to remove hand grease, dirt, and old chalk, not wood.

STEP 2 Once the wood is cleaned, re-chalk the underside of the paddle. Many call-makers prefer to use railroad chalk, the type that is used to mark the sides of boxcars, but now there are many brands that are sold specifically for turkey calls. Stay away from blackboard chalk or any type of chalk made with oil.

STEP 3 Play the call, listening for the desired tone. Shiny spots on the lid's underside indicate that oil or dirt is still present. Repeat Step 1 until you get the sweet notes.

STEP 4 Adjust the tension screw on the paddle as a last resort. On most calls, it's right where it needs to be. Your goal is just to get the screw back into its original position if it has worked loose. Start by tightening it a quarter turn and then test the call. Repeat if necessary until you feel that you are tightening the screw past the point where it was set. If you reach this point, back off.

359 STORE A DUCK IN PANTYHOSE

Don't be alarmed when your duck-hunting buddy breaks out a little lingerie while on your next trip to the marsh. Pantyhose can make a fine protective tote sack for ducks bound for the taxidermist, keeping their feathers slightly compressed and out of harm's way.

In the field, gently wipe off blood and soil. Don't worry so much about blood staining the feathers; the taxidermist can clean them up. Just mop off the excess. Gently tuck the head under the wing, and slide the entire bird into a section of pantyhose. You'll want a bit of excess hose on both ends, and don't tie off either end just yet. Store the bird where it will be protected on the way out of the marsh—in a cooler or rolled in a vest and tucked into a daypack.

At home, snip the foot end from the hose, roll it back slightly, and insert a wad of paper towel or a few cotton balls into the bird's beak to soak up any blood that might seep out during the freezing process. Gently tuck the head back into the hose and tie off with a knot. Wrap the feet in a damp paper towel and secure with a rubber band or twist ties. Tie off the feet end, and slip the duck into a zippered plastic bag. It should easily store in a freezer for six months. If you need to store it longer than that, take the bird out of the pantyhose and freeze the entire duck in a large plastic bag filled with water.

360 TUNE SHOTGUN SWING WITH A FLASHLIGHT

Proper shotgun mounting is critical to hitting targets consistently, and you can practice without ever firing a shot. Happily, a shotgun and the nearly ubiquitous Mini Maglite are all you'll need to kill hours working on shotgun technique that you might have otherwise wasted on yard work.

STEP 1 Check to make sure that the gun is unloaded. Check again. Put the gun down. Pick it up and check it again.

STEP 2 Wrap the shaft of a Mini Maglite with a single layer of duct tape and insert it into the gun barrel, lamp pointing out. The Maglite that uses AA batteries will fit a 12-gauge shotgun. The AAA-battery model works for a 20 gauge. Dial down the beam to its tightest point.

STEP 3 In a darkened room, start from the low ready position. Point

the light up at the place where two walls meet the ceiling. Next, mount the gun slowly. The goal is to have a smooth mount so that the light will stay centered on the spot.

STEP 4 Now practice your crossing shots by tracing the line where the wall and ceiling meet. Now, move the muzzle along the seam, bring the gun up to your face, and track a smooth line across the entire room. Shotgun mounting is purely a matter of muscle memory, so repeat it often, past that point at which any family members become alarmed at your behavior.

361 TURN AWAY TICKS

Spring turkey hunting season is a prime time for ticks, and long after your gobbler is in the refrigerator, these nasty bloodsuckers will still remind you that you should've used duct tape. To keep any ticks from crawling into your pants and up your legs, seal pants from cuffs to boots with duct tape (matte black or camo), or stuff the ends of your pants into your socks and then seal up the seam with a strip of duct tape.

362 DISAPPEAR WITH ZIP TIES AND CLOTHESPINS

Make handy vegetation clips for camouflaging blinds and boats with zip ties and clothespins. Insert a zip tie through the opening of a clothespin spring, and cinch down handfuls of raffia, marsh grass, or holly twigs with the zip ties. Now you can clip instant vegetation to any surface grasped by the clothespin.

363 MAKE A EUROPEAN MOUNT DUCK SKULL

Here's how to turn a greenhead—or any other duck or goose—into your very own miniature European mount, complete with crossed upper leg bones and, if you're lucky, a snazzy bird band to bling it up.

I've used two methods of preparing the duck skulls: The first involves soaking the bones in hot water for days, painstakingly scraping away the flesh, then gluing the parts back together. Once I discovered the second, super-easy way, I'll never go back. It starts with a friendly phone call.

MEET THE BEETLES Flesh-eating dermestid beetles can clean off a duck skull in a matter of days. Plenty of museums and nature centers keep a colony or two of the dermestid beetles, and a modest contribution—say, $25—can often win you a spot in their beetle box. You will first need to skin the upper legs and then cut away most of the muscle, and skin the skull and cut out the tongue, but the bugs will do the rest. Another option: Inquire with a local taxidermist if you and your buddies

can toss a few duck skulls and leg bones in with a load of deer skulls being prepped for European mounts. Tell the taxidermist there's no need to go through the degreasing process. You will do that yourself in the next step.

DEGREASE THE BONES Once the bones are back from the beetles, degrease them by soaking them in warm water and Dawn dishwashing detergent for a few hours. Rinse well. Dry in the sun. To further whiten the bones, soak overnight in hydrogen peroxide and set in the sun to dry. Use small dabs of wood glue to strengthen any loose joints. Brush bleach on stubborn brown spots, or go all natural. If you want, add a yellow bill with acrylic paint.

COME TOGETHER Cross the leg bones and use hot glue to hold in place. Once they're dry, build up a few layers of glue in the concave underside of the bill for a flat base, then attach the crossed bones to the back of the skull with more glue. Finish with a leather lanyard and duck band.

364 TUNE A DUCK CALL

Just about any duck call can be tuned to produce sounds that are higher or lower in pitch or have more or less rasp or squeal than what you get with the factory-tuned setup. It's neither terribly difficult nor terribly easy, which means that it's perfect for any duck hunter with shade-tree mechanic tendencies. Here's how.

SINGLE REED First, check to make sure that the call's wedge hasn't slipped or, if it's made of cork, dried out. If it won't seat firmly in the call, get a replacement from the call manufacturer. To give the call a higher pitch, use scissors to trim off a tiny sliver at a time, and reassemble the call and test it after each trimming. To add raspiness, rough up the toneboard with 220-grit sandpaper. Or dog-ear the front corners of the reed at a 60-degree angle with a tiny diagonal cut.

DOUBLE REED Pull the barrel off and take a quick photo of the insert so you'll have a record of the reeds' placement in relation to the wedge and toneboard. To tune, move the wedge back (to lower pitch) or forward (to raise pitch), without altering the reed arrangement. Test the call after each tweak. If the call still isn't to your liking, trim very lightly with scissors. Again, test after each adjustment. To add rasp, carefully offset the top reed slightly back from the lower reed. As little as $\frac{1}{32}$ inch may do it, so go easy.

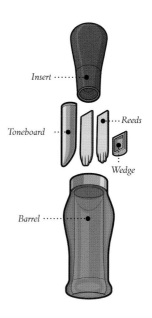

Insert

Toneboard

Reeds

Wedge

Barrel

365 BRUSH UP A DUCK CANOE

A correctly camouflaged canoe will put you so close to river ducks you'll have to give them a few seconds to open up the distance before pulling the trigger. An incorrectly brushed-up boat will get you just close enough to realize you should have done a better job with the canoe.

THE HULL TRUTH The long, smooth hull of a canoe will glint with sunlight and spook every duck on the creek long before you're close enough to shoot. Even a camo-painted canoe can use some help. Use one or two long pieces of camouflage netting to knock back the hull's shine. Drape the netting over the rails so that the bottom edge is barely above the water's surface. Start at the bow and extend the netting at least as far back as the stern seat.

FLOATING ISLAND Cut twice as much brush as you think you'll need. Use half of it to create a fan-shaped hide in the bow. Bend some limbs so they drape over the gunwales in order to break up your boat's outlines. Stand some brush up as far back as the center thwart, and drape a few branches out over the gunwales to shield the paddler's movements. Jam more cut brush behind the stern seat.

366 COLD-PROOF YOUR SHOTGUN

Some of the best duck hunting takes place in some of the worst conditions for your shotgun: bitter, bone-numbing, oil-thickening cold. Semiautomatic shotguns in particular are at risk for freezing up in temperatures that drop into the teens or even lower. The first aid that some hunters turn to—additional lubrication of the action—is actually the worst possible solution you could use. Lubricants can thicken, especially when mixed with powder residue and grime, and gum up the action. Here's what to do to make sure your scattergun performs in the next "polar vortex."

STRIP THE OIL Disassemble the barrel, receiver, and action. Spray metal parts with Break-Free CLP. Wipe all excess oil away, and wait a few minutes. Now give the parts another good wipe. Use cotton swabs to soak up any excess pooling in nooks and crannies. You want to remove any and all oil. In the field, a squirt of lighter fluid can serve as an emergency de-gunker.

DUST BATH Use powdered graphite to dust primary action parts such as bolt rails and ejection latches.

OUTSIDE STORAGE Many problems occur when a warm gun is brought into cold, outside air. Moisture condenses on metal gun parts, then freezes in the field. The night before a hunt, store your gun safely outside.

367 PUT MORE SPRING IN YOUR SEMIAUTO SHOTGUN

Duck hunters who frequently go wading in beaver swamps, timber holes, and deep impoundments should take a harder look at those springs in recoil-operated semiautomatic shotguns. Gunstocks often take a swim, and a plastic stock is not impervious to the elements. Water can seep in at the recoil pad and at the sling swivels, and once it's in, it can rust recoil springs that compress inside the stock.

Here's how to make your shotgun beaver-pond worthy. Access the spring tube and get it cleaned up. Replace the factory spring with a new one or, even better still, one made of stainless steel. While reassembling the shotgun, waterproof the hollow synthetic stock by laying down a bead of AquaSeal silicone sealant around the recoil pad seam and the holes for the sling swivel.

368 MAKE EXPLODING FLASH TARGETS FOR AN OLYMPIC-STYLE SHOOT

Those big clouds of clay pigeon dust you see on shooting shows aren't there because the shooters center every shot. Those puff balls are "flash targets"—modified clay birds that carry an extra payload of colored dust. You can pay a gazillion dollars for commercially available flash targets, which are hard to find. Or you can make your own with common clay pigeons, carpenter's chalk dust, newspaper, and glue. Get a buddy or two together for an assembly line and crank them out fast and cheap.

STEP 1 Gather the essentials. Lots of common items will provide the cloud of colored dust, including flour and baking soda. Probably the best is carpenter's chalk—it's cheap and readily available, and comes in bright colors. You'll need spare cardboard like a shoebox, or perhaps construction paper. And some kind of glue—white glue, carpenter's glue, or barge cement will all work.

STEP 2 Cut cardboard or paper circles slightly larger in diameter than the raised rim that runs around the cupped dome on top of the clay bird.

STEP 3 Fill the dome with a few spoonfuls of colored powder. Run a bead of glue around the raised rim. Cap with the paper circle and press with fingertips. Set a half dozen on a flat surface and top with a heavy book to seal the bond.

369 SHOOT THE TRICKY OUT-OF-NOWHERE STEALTH BIRD

Ducks and doves have a nasty habit of acting like wild animals, such as appearing where you least expect them. That means overhead and coming straight from behind, presenting a very tough shot. Here's how to make it.

As you rise from your seat, point the muzzle at a spot halfway between the horizon and the bird (a) as it is flying away from you. Pull the gun swiftly up toward the bird. Keeping your head up and your eyes on the bird, bring the muzzle straight toward its beak. As the muzzle approaches the bird on the upswing, circle the muzzle around and behind the bird (b). As the barrel reaches the top of this circle, bury your cheek into the stock as you prepare to swing down and past the bird.

Pull down and through the bird, accelerating the swing as you blot out the target (c). You'll lose sight of it momentarily but fire as soon as you see a slice of sky between the bead and bird.

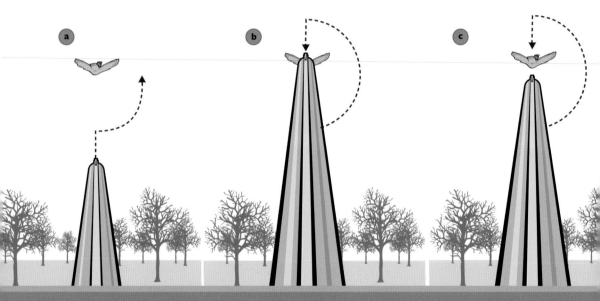

370 SIGHT IN A SCOPE ON A BOLT ACTION RIFLE

A bore collimator makes easy work of a complicated situation. But it isn't a requirement for whipping a bolt action into hunting condition. Here's a three-step process to sighting in a scope.

STEP 1 Set up a target 25 yards from your shooting position, at roughly the same height as your barrel. Remove the bolt and place the rifle firmly on sandbags or bags of kitty litter. Sight through the barrel and center the target in the bore. Then, adjust the crosshairs as needed to center the target, being careful not to move the rifle. Replace the bolt and fire one shot. Your point of impact should be less than 6 inches from the bull's-eye.

STEP 2 Readjust the rifle so that the crosshairs are centered on the target. Look through the scope and adjust the crosshairs to line up with the shot fired in Step 1; again, do it without moving the rifle. Now fire another shot. The point of impact should be within an inch or two of the target center.

STEP 3 Move the target out to 100 yards. Shoot a three-shot group, disregarding obvious fliers. Start with the elevation adjustment and move the point of impact to the desired location. (For most popular deer-size loads, a point of impact 2½ to 3 inches high at 100 yards allows for little to no holdover at hunting ranges. Check a ballistics chart for details.) Fire another three-shot group. If elevation is correct, adjust the scope for windage. Let the rifle barrel cool between groups.

371 CUSTOMIZE BINOCULARS

Even the best (read "extravagantly expensive") binoculars on the market will give you a fuzzy view of the world until you correctly set the diopter ring. This adjustment, typically found on the right eyepiece or the center-focus knob, fine-tunes the binocular settings to compensate for any visual differences between your eyes. Set properly, a diopter will not only max out the performance of a high-end binoculars, but it will even boost the sharpness of budget glass.

Set focus for the left eye barrel.   Set diopter for the right eye.

STEP 1 Set the diopter ring to the center of the adjustment scale. This is most likely marked with a zero; on some models it might be indicated with a hash mark or some other symbol. Cover the right lens barrel with a lens cap or duct tape.

STEP 2 Pick an object in the middle distance zone, about 50 yards away. Keeping both eyes open, move the focus ring (a) until the image is at its sharpest. Although you are focusing only with the left eye, keep both eyes open and relaxed. Do not squint.

STEP 3 Switch the lens cap or duct tape to the other lens barrel. Look at the same object and turn the diopter ring (see inset) to bring the object into sharp focus (b). Make sure the focus knob doesn't change. Keep both eyes open; do not squint.

STEP 4 Remove the lens cap or duct tape and look through both lens barrels. The image should remain sharp. Make a note of the diopter-ring setting, or place a small dot of fingernail polish on the correct adjustment. If your visual acuity changes during the year, you may need to reset the diopter.

372 PACK A WOODSTOVE FOR A SLOW, LONG BURN

You won't need to leave your cozy bunk to feed the stove if you load it right. Twenty minutes before sack time, rake all of the coals toward the stove's air inlets and stack large pieces of firewood tightly behind the coals. (Hardwood is best.) Open the ducts wide for 10 to 30 minutes—a large stove will require a longer burn time. Once the wood closest to the coals has burned to a thick layer of charcoal, cut back the airflow as much as 25 percent. Starved of oxygen, the burn will slow down and work its way through the stack overnight.

373 HEAR WHAT YOUR RIFLE IS TELLING YOU

Were this the best of all possible worlds, we would fire three rifle shots at a target, peer downrange, and see three holes clustered within the area of a dime at precisely the right place. But this is not the best of all possible worlds, in that it has a place for chiggers, bad cholesterol, rabies, and abdominal fat. And in this vale of sorrow, we often look at our targets and see horror, chaos, and disorder.

In any event, we know that something is wrong, but what? Rather than burst into tears, you should regard this as a heart-to-heart talk with your rifle, which, if you can speak its language, will tell you what ails it.

DIAGNOSTIC TOOL Shooting from the benchrest will tell you just what your gun is thinking.

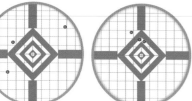   

COMPLETE BREAKDOWN PROBLEM Your shots are all over the place, and you can't get a group to save your life. There could be several causes. First is a ruptured scope. The way to test this is to put a different scope on your gun and see if it groups better. Second is loose bedding screws on the rifle. Check to see if they're tight. Third is loose ring or base screws. Sometimes, one particular bullet weight will give results this bad. If this is the case, it's usually because the barrel's rifling twist is wrong for that bullet weight.

CONSISTENT FLIER PROBLEM Your ammo is almost, but not quite, right for your gun. Usually this shows up as two holes close together and the third one off to the side by an inch or two. At 100 yards, this is not a problem, but at farther distances, it will begin to cause some trouble. It's caused by bullets traveling just above or below the optimum speed for that barrel, causing it to vibrate inconsistently. Handloaders can cure it by raising or lowering the powder charge. Non-handloaders will have to try different ammunition.

INCONSISTENT FLIER PROBLEM Most of the time you get good groups, but sometimes you have one shot go astray, and then sometimes all three go where they're not supposed to. Most likely you're flinching, and if you don't think that it's possible to flinch from a benchrest, think again. You can buy or experiment with a sled-type shooting rest, which can virtually eliminate felt recoil, or try putting a soft gun case or sandbag between your shoulder and the butt. Or, if all else fails, get a less punishing rifle.

RISING GROUP PROBLEM Your groups are usually O.K., but they seem to keep moving up on the target, sometimes up and to the left or right, sometimes straight up. This is caused by an overheated barrel. When a tube gets too hot, it warps slightly, sending bullets errantly, and in addition, the heat waves rising from it give you a distorted view of the target, sort of like shooting through a swimming pool. The cure is easy: Let your barrel cool down. Start each group with a cold barrel and never let it get beyond lukewarm.

STRINGING PROBLEM In this situation, your groups string vertically or horizontally. First check the barrel bedding. Most barrels today are free-floating; there should be no contact from 1 1/2 inches forward of the receiver right out to the end. If there is, take the gun in for a rebedding job. The horizontal grouping can be caused by wind at the target that you don't feel at the bench. The vertical groups can be caused by the fore-end jumping on too hard a surface.

374 MAKE A BUCK SCRAPE

During the early phases of the rut, making a mock scrape is a great way to get the attention of the big bucks in your area.

WHERE Your ideal spot is a trail or edge near a doe feeding area, upwind of your stand site. Look for a place where a small branch or sapling extends over the trail at about head height.

HOW Don rubber boots and gloves. With a stick, hoe, or trowel, rake bare a 2-foot circle. Work a gel-based buck urine into the soil—the gel scents tend to last longer than the liquid scents—and drip a drop or two on an overhanging branch.

375 CLEAN A PLUCKED DUCK IN 60 SECONDS

This method results in a fully dressed duck that retains its feathered head so it meets legal requirements for transport. Prepared this way, three mallards or six teal fit into a 1-gallon zip-seal bag.

STEP 1 Pluck.

STEP 2 With the blade of a hatchet, break the wing bones close to the body. Remove the wings with shears. Cut the feet off through the joint of the leg bones, taking care not to break the bones. This will leave a rounded bone at the end of the leg instead of a jagged tip. Remove the tail by snipping through the joint between the base of the pelvis and the tail.

STEP 3 Pick up the duck in one hand, with its head down and its back facing up. Run your shears along each side of the backbone and then snip the ribs down the back. If you do it this way, the backbone will stay attached to the body. Next, turn the shears perpendicular to the duck's spine and cut the backbone, windpipe, and esophagus at the neck.

STEP 4 Hold the duck over a bucket, feet down. Insert the shears under the backbone at the neck, open the blades an inch, and run the shears straight down the body. The backbone and all the organs will separate and fall into the bucket.

STEP 5 Fold the head back into the body cavity, and you're done.

376 MAKE YOUR OWN WIND CHECKER

Several manufacturers produce effective, convenient, unscented wind-checking products. So does Mother Nature. The advantage of milkweed seed filaments is that you can see them for 50 yards—farther with binoculars—and get a real-world reading on what your scent is doing out there where the deer are.

STEP 1 Drill a ⅜-inch hole in the bottom of a film canister.

STEP 2 Remove the seeds from the plumes of half a dozen milkweed pods.

STEP 3 Stuff as many milkweed plumes as possible into the canister. Replace the cap.

STEP 4 Affix one strip of Velcro to the film canister, and the other strip to wherever you want to store it—gun strap, quiver, and so on.

STEP 5 Pluck a few plumes from the film canister and let them fly.

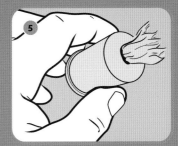

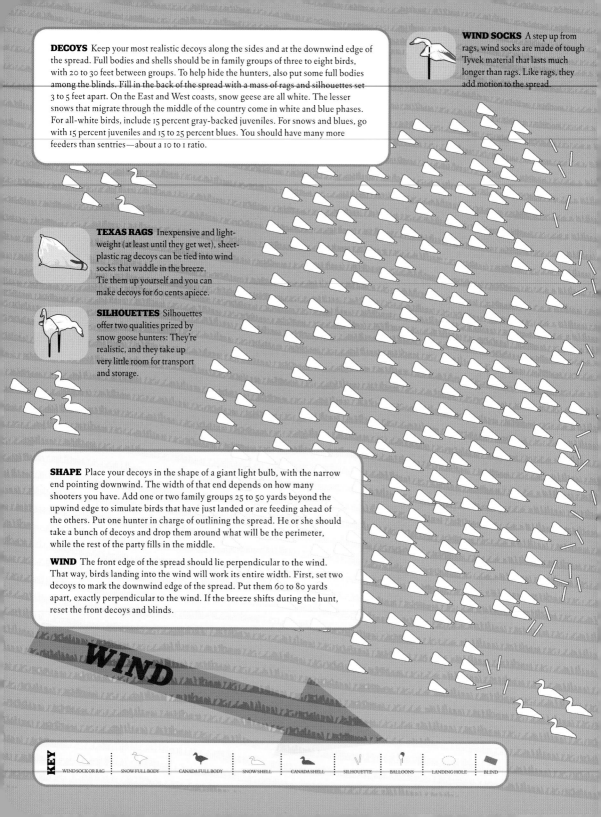

DECOYS Keep your most realistic decoys along the sides and at the downwind edge of the spread. Full bodies and shells should be in family groups of three to eight birds, with 20 to 30 feet between groups. To help hide the hunters, also put some full bodies among the blinds. Fill in the back of the spread with a mass of rags and silhouettes set 3 to 5 feet apart. On the East and West coasts, snow geese are all white. The lesser snows that migrate through the middle of the country come in white and blue phases. For all-white birds, include 15 percent gray-backed juveniles. For snows and blues, go with 15 percent juveniles and 15 to 25 percent blues. You should have many more feeders than sentries—about a 10 to 1 ratio.

WIND SOCKS A step up from rags, wind socks are made of tough Tyvek material that lasts much longer than rags. Like rags, they add motion to the spread.

TEXAS RAGS Inexpensive and light-weight (at least until they get wet), sheet-plastic rag decoys can be tied into wind socks that waddle in the breeze. Tie them up yourself and you can make decoys for 60 cents apiece.

SILHOUETTES Silhouettes offer two qualities prized by snow goose hunters: They're realistic, and they take up very little room for transport and storage.

SHAPE Place your decoys in the shape of a giant light bulb, with the narrow end pointing downwind. The width of that end depends on how many shooters you have. Add one or two family groups 25 to 50 yards beyond the upwind edge to simulate birds that have just landed or are feeding ahead of the others. Put one hunter in charge of outlining the spread. He or she should take a bunch of decoys and drop them around what will be the perimeter, while the rest of the party fills in the middle.

WIND The front edge of the spread should lie perpendicular to the wind. That way, birds landing into the wind will work its entire width. First, set two decoys to mark the downwind edge of the spread. Put them 60 to 80 yards apart, exactly perpendicular to the wind. If the breeze shifts during the hunt, reset the front decoys and blinds.

WIND

KEY WIND SOCK OR RAG · SNOW FULL BODY · CANADA FULL BODY · SNOW SHELL · CANADA SHELL · SILHOUETTE · BALLOONS · LANDING HOLE · BLIND

MOTION Feeding snow geese are always moving, hopping over one another to get to uneaten grain first. Jig flags up and down from the blinds to simulate their movements. Fly black-and-white helium balloons, about half a dozen of each, 4 feet off the ground, weighted with decoy anchors or tied to stubble.

SHELLS Shells look like geese, they're stackable, and you set them out simply by throwing them on the ground.

FULL BODIES The ultimate in realism, full bodies take up lots of trailer space but help close the deal when the birds are hanging 70 yards outside the spread, deciding whether to stay or go.

Why bother with the giant decoy spreads required to hunt snow geese? Because when you get it right, the reward is a tornado of geese 10 yards over your head—thousands of them yipping and barking so loud you can't hear yourself shout.

Start by finding the field where the birds want to be. Follow them from the roost ponds to feeding fields in the afternoon. If you can, wait until the geese have left the field for the evening and then mark the exact spot where they were feeding with an orange traffic cone. Come back well before dawn and come ready to work. You'll need a minimum of 400 to 500 decoys, but 800 to 1,000 are better. If you follow this blueprint, it's not that hard to build a killer spread.

OTHER BIRDS Canadas and specklebellies often feed in the same field as snows. Set a few dozen Canada or speck shells and full bodies downwind of the spread. You can put out duck decoys too, but white spreads will suck in flocks of mallards and pintails whether they see other ducks or not.

BLINDS Set the blinds about three steps apart, in a line 15 yards from the downwind edge of the spread. If flocks consistently come close, inspect the decoys, and then slide off to one side or the other, move the blinds 50 yards downwind of the spread and shoot the geese as they're looking. Wearing white coveralls and becoming one with the decoys is the classic way to hide. You can also use a goose chair, which is a combination decoy and field chair. Laydown field blinds blend in best and are the most comfortable way to hunt.

LANDING ZONES Leave gaps of 10 to 15 yards in front of and behind the blinds where the birds can land. Snows and ducks will aim for the holes.

378 DROP A SINGLE BIRD OUT OF A FLOCK

STEP 1 Keep your gun off your shoulder and parallel to the ground. Point the muzzle toward the flock but don't mount the gun until you're ready to swing and fire.

STEP 2 Single out one bird from the flock and don't take your eyes off of it. Try to choose the highest bird or the trailing bird. Swinging on this target first will ensure good shooting form for the next bird as your gun naturally overtakes the flock.

STEP 3 Drill your eyes at your chosen bird and push the gun muzzle toward it. Fire on the swing and keep shooting until it drops. Only then should you go for the double, and your gun is already in position for the next swing through the flock.

379 CLAIM THE BEST BUNK

Maybe you aren't the savviest hunter in the crowd, but putting your mitts on the comfiest bunk in the barn can score you points, as well. Here's how to always land the best bed available.

Half an hour before your ETA at deer camp, start whining about having to pee. Don't lay it on too thick quite yet. Unselfishly turn aside all offers for a quick rest stop: "Naw, guys, I can make it." (Wince slightly.) "Let's just get there. I know we're all in a rush."

When you're ten minutes out, start squirming. Say, "Man, I'm glad we're this close. I think something's about to rupture back here!"

As soon as the tires stop spinning, you're on the run. Don't forget to grab a small personal item on your way out of the truck. Don't hoist a large duffel bag—for cryin' out loud, your bladder's stretched beyond reason! Stake your claim to the prized mattress on your way to the privy. A slight limp on the way clinches the deal.

380 SOUND LIKE A TURKEY

The biggest mistake novice turkey hunters make is calling too much. In the real world, the gobbler calls to a hen and expects her to come to him. You're trying to reverse the equation by getting the gobbler to come to you. You don't have to be perfect, and that's why the less you call the better. If the woods are quiet—no chattering squirrels or warbling songbirds—call once or twice and then hush up. Prolonged calling in this scenario is unnatural and will spook a big tom.

There are four basic calls you need to learn, but they're actually relatively easy to master. Of course, your gobbler will be the judge of that.

OWL HOOT The first call of the morning (or the last of the evening) helps to locate a roosting tom. It's simply hoot-hoot-hoot, done six to eight syllables at a time. If a roosting gobbler responds, you know how close or how far away your target is.

YELP The hen's basic call is a simple series of single notes—often five or six at a time—strung together. Use this call to let a gobbler know a hen is in his area. If you get a booming response, don't repeat. Let him come to you.

CLUCK If you think the gobbler is on the way and you feel a need to assure him that all is well, use this in place of the yelp. It's a short, sharp call put together in three-note clusters.

CUTT A call of last resort, this one is an attraction-getting series of loud clucks with an erratic tempo. This call carries a long way and might turn the head of a distant gobbler.

381 MAKE THE PERFECT YELP

To yelp on a slate call, grasp the base in your fingers and thumb. Hold the call off the palm to create a distortion-free sound chamber. Hold the striker like a pen, and be careful that no part of your hand touches the slate. Draw small circles and ovals on the slate surface, like writing in cursive, but in a single stamp-size spot. Work on creating a high tone and a low tone. Put them together, and you've got a yelp.

382

CALL A TURKEY
WITH A PEACOCK

Owl and crow calls are the go-to locators for
shock-calling roosting toms, but pressured
gobblers can clam up after being hammered
with who-cooks-for-you hoots day after day.
Switch to a pileated woodpecker, a coyote,
or a peacock call to trick closemouthed
gobblers into giving up their position.

383 TUNE UP A BOX CALL

The box call contains several of the elements of a fine musical instrument, and like Charlie Daniels warned Johnny to "rosin up your bow" for his fiddle duel with the Devil, a box call benefits from a little preseason TLC. Here's the 5-minute drill.

STEP 1 Clean it. First, put down the sandpaper. You want to clean the wood sidewall rails, not reshape them, and sandpaper will do both. Lightly rub the rails with a Scotch-Brite pad or other scouring pad designed for non-stick pots.

STEP 2 Rechalk the bottom of the paddle with a bit of carpenter's chalk or a chalk made specifically for turkey calls. Blackboard chalk contains wax, and that will deaden the call. Some callers shy away from chalk of any kind and go with Daniels' advice and use pine rosin instead.

STEP 3 Work the call a few times, then look closely at the underside of the paddle. Are there shiny spots? That means grime or grease still soil the sidewalls. Back to step one.

STEP 4 The tension screw on a box call lid has been set precisely by the call maker, but over time, the screw can turn and affect the call's sound. To adjust, first mark the exact position of the screw with a black marker. Tighten first, since it is more common for screws to loosen than to tighten. Give the screw the slightest turn, and test for call tone before making any other adjustments.

384 BLOW A WINGBONE YELPER

The beauty of a wingbone call is the organic feel to its sound, which can fool toms sick and tired of the calls hunters today carry around in their magnetic vest pockets.

PUCKER UP Insert the call's small end between your lips—either in the middle, or slightly off to one side—and form a very tight seal. The call should just barely extend into your mouth.

GRAB HOLD Grip the larger end of the call between the base of your thumb and forefinger. Create a flared bell with this hand, and cover with the cupped fingers and palm of your other hand. Open and close the hand positions for a variety of sounds.

PLANT A SMACKER To create short clucks, suck air in as if you were making kissing sounds. For yelps, extend the kissing inhalations and suck in air, then drop the lower jaw to create the two-note break of a hen yelp. Practice makes perfect. Tell your spouse you are getting ready for your anniversary night.

385 USE AN OLD TIRE TO TEACH A NEW DOG TRICKS

The "place" command is a great tool to introduce to any dog, and it is especially good for retrievers. Waterfowl hunters often need their dogs to stay and work from a distance, be it 10 feet or 20 yards away. And retrievers should be comfortable sitting and staying on any less-than-comfortable structures, such as downed logs in beaver swamps or small platforms in marshes.

Use an old tire as a backyard "place" training tool. It provides a slightly elevated platform that helps a dog understand that this is its "place." Cut a scrap piece of plywood or even an old foam archery target to fit the top of the tire and secure in place with paracord. Ugly and effective.

ONE PLACE With the dog on leash and a treat in your non-leash hand, lead the dog to the "place" stand. Using the hand with the treat, point with your finger to the stand, say "place," and use the treat to guide the dog up to the stand. Give the treat the instant the dog sits. Repeat, repeat, repeat.

TWO PLACES Once the dog knows "place," set up a training route with multiple stations for the "place" command. Use another tire, a few cinder blocks, and other items that provide a well-defined place to sit. Once your pooch is solid on the command, add stations without any elevation, such as carpet squares.

TOUGH PLACES Add "place" stations that have a degree of difficulty or instability to your training route. Log rounds, overturned canoes, and upside-down coolers work well. While on walks, give the "place" command at park benches, retaining walls, and other similar structures.

386 TRAIN A DOG TO SCENT TRAIL

Early-season hunts often take place in the heavy cover of beaver ponds and thick timber. A good cripple dog is a major asset. To fine-tune your dog's nose, cut a piece of PVC pipe about 5 feet in length. (The diameter doesn't matter—use whatever you've got cluttering up your basement.) Run an 8-foot-long section of paracord or other cordage through the pipe, and tie a slip loop to one end. Attach the loop to a bird wing or training bumper treated with duck scent. Hold the pipe out from your body, and drag the wing or bumper along a scent trail through your yard. The pipe prevents your own foot scent from contaminating the trail.

387 MAKE A CANINE FIRST AID KIT

Think it's a dog's life? Try pushing aside briers with your own face. Packing a small, light first aid kit for your sporting dog can save a morning's hunt, or even your dog's life. All these items will fit inside a 1-gallon heavy-duty zip-seal bag.

BETADINE SOLUTION	4 ounces	Clean and irrigate cuts.
TRIPLE ANTIBIOTIC OINTMENT	1-ounce tube	Treat minor burns and cuts after cleansing.
HYDROGEN PEROXIDE	4 ounces	Clean wounds. Induce vomiting.
STERILE EYE WASH	1 ounce	Aids in removing foreign objects.
STYPTIC PENCIL	1 pencil	Stop bleeding in toepad and muzzle lacerations
SUPERGLUE	1 small tube	Close minor wounds in brier-torn ears and toepad.
GAUZE PADS	Ten 3-inch-square pads, two 2-inch-wide rolls	Stem bleeding, clean and dress wounds.
DUCT TAPE	5 feet	Emergency bandage. Use to hold gauze in place.
STERILE TAPE	1-inch-wide roll	Use to hold bandages in place.
TWEEZERS	1 pair	Remove splinters, pluck seeds from ears and nose.
BENADRYL	25-mg tablets	Treat insect stings, snakebite.
PLASTIC ZIP-SEAL BAGS	4 small bags	Emergency booties for injured feet; secure with duct tape.
NEWSPAPER	1 sports section, folded	Emergency splint for broken bones.

388

TEACH A DOG TO DIVE FOR DUCKS

Wounded ducks will frequently dive when a retriever approaches. Teach yours to match wits with these escape artists. Run an anchor line or paracord through the eye of a mushroom anchor, then tie one end to a training bumper. Use three times as much cord as the distance you can throw the anchor. Walk up to the edge of a pond, toss out your bumper with its anchor, and hold firmly onto the end of the line. Send the dog on a retrieve.

As he approaches the bumper, pull on the line so you pull the bumper under the water. You can bob the bumper up and down to encourage the dog. When he grabs it successfully, allow him plenty of slack for a drag-free retrieve.

389 HUNT SQUIRRELS LIKE A GROWN-UP

Everything you need to feel younger, eat better, and sleep through the night without having to use the bathroom is stuck in the far corner of your gun cabinet, gunked up with the last squirt of 3-in-One oil with which you bid farewell to your .22 rifle.

Well, almost everything. To turn squirrel hunting from child's play into a true rifleman's pursuit, you need to address two of the limitations of squirreling like a kid. First, get your rump off the ground so you don't end up squirming with back spasms a half-hour after you've hunkered down against a hickory. Lightweight, portable cushions and hunting seats might not make you feel like a kid again, but they'll keep you hunting longer and harder and prevent you from walking back to the truck

bent over like Old Mother Hubbard. Next, pick up an adjustable shooting stick. It'll add serious range to your rimfire shooting, which makes sniping squirrels an even bigger—and more grown-up—blast.

Now, use all your big-boy deer-hunting smarts to hone in on the perfect ambush. The open woods are where children hunt. You want an edge where open woods butt up against younger growth full of tasty fox grapes and berries, thickets where a couple pounds of protein can move around without worrying about every red-tailed hawk in the county. From there squirrels will fan out into the oak and hickory woods, secure in the knowledge that all those fuzz-faced kids with their iron-sighted .22s are either down in the big woods or working on their Guitar Hero chops back home. If they're really paying attention, they might even hear the click of your trigger safety sliding into the red zone.

390 STUMP SLUMP FOR GOBBLERS

Sitting against a tree seems a simple enough task. But if you do it wrong—and there are plenty of wrong ways—you might blow your shot at a gobbler. If you sit up, high and conspicuous, you may never get a chance to shoot. If you can't brace your arms on your knees, you'll have a difficult time holding the bead steady on the turkey or keeping the gun ready for long periods of time. If you have to move too much to prepare to shoot, the turkey will spook before you ever pull the trigger.

The hunter illustrated here isn't just slouched against a tree—he's hunkered down low to be inconspicuous to an approaching turkey. He's comfortable enough to stay in that position without moving. And he's braced to make a quick and accurate shot at a gobbler approaching from anywhere in front of him with minimum movement.

A great advantage of this "stump slump" is that you can balance the gun's fore-end on your knee and tuck the butt lightly under your shoulder, keeping the gun stable as you work a call or eat a granola bar. If a turkey comes in unexpectedly, all you have to do is reach slowly for the gun and lower your cheek onto the stock. Once you've assumed that position, your gun is solidly rested so you can wait for the perfect shot—and make it.

BACK Lean against the tree. The trunk protects your back, and it's your camouflage, too, because it hides your silhouette. Get comfortable; you may be there awhile. But don't slouch down so far and put so much weight on the trunk that you have to struggle and lurch upright in order to make a minor adjustment in aim.

LEFT HAND The back of your left hand lies flat on your knee. You can use it to make small adjustments in elevation and windage.

RIGHT ELBOW Brace your right elbow against the inside of your right leg. Having your shooting-side elbow supported helps steady your hold.

RIGHT LEG Splay your right knee out and down. It will provide a remarkably steady rest for your right elbow.

MUZZLE The muzzle faces just past your left foot. This is the natural point of aim, where no muscular effort is required to point the gun. Since it is much easier for a right-handed shooter to twist to the left than to the right, set up with your natural point of aim to the right of where you expect to see the turkey.

LEFT LEG Place your left foot flat so your lower leg is more or less perpendicular to the ground. That allows your gun to be supported by bone, not muscle.

FEET If the bird comes in too far to the right or left, wait until it goes behind a tree, then lean forward slightly to center your weight on your seat, not your back, and use short, choppy sideways "steps" to scoot yourself around to face in the right direction.

391 DRILL FOR THE SCAMPERING SQUIRREL

Given a solid rest and enough time to find a clear shot, most hunters can topple a squirrel from the treetops. The ones that get away are the ones that aren't in the treetops at all. They're the squirrels that show up close and scurry along a fallen log at 30 feet.

These squirrels never stop long enough to offer you a stationary shot. They can accelerate and decelerate like a pinball, and somehow they still have the ability to see you raise your rifle, which transforms them into a speeding, vanishing gray blur. The trick here is to shoot before that happens—meaning you have to hit that small, erratically moving target at relatively close range.

How to drill for this? Channel the spirit of a bocce ball champ, and bounce and roll a spherical squirrel-size target along the ground. You'll need a bucket of old tennis balls and a buddy to toss them, and make sure there's an appropriate background in order to absorb the bullets.

The thrower stands a yard or two behind and at varying distances perpendicular to the shooter.

STEP 1 Start out by tossing balls about 25 yards down the line. Each of the balls will cross in front of the shooter in near profile, just like that movement of an unalarmed but actively foraging squirrel.

STEP 2 Make each shot more difficult by having your thrower stand closer to the gun. With the balls coming from beside the shooter, the shot simulates those all-too-frequent times when you're busted by a feeding squirrel and he's hightailing it to the nearest tree. Your goal: three out of five hits on a bouncing tennis-ball squirrel.

CHALLENGE YOURSELF Once you're acing the tennis balls, switch to golf balls.

392 CALL SQUIRRELS WITH STUFF IN YOUR JUNK DRAWER

In his historic 1984 research paper on the language of gray squirrels, Dr. Robert Lishak identified four different alarm vocalizations. Avid squirrel hunters might be a bit surprised at such a low number. Personally, I know that squirrels have cussed me out using at least 83 separate potty-mouth squirrel-words. Point is, the limb dancer is a loquacious fellow, which can be his undoing. You can buy a squirrel call, but here are three ways to use common household objects to strike up a conversation with a tasty squirrel—just before you shut him up for good.

TOY SQUEAKER	BOLT AND WASHER	SPARE CHANGE
Cut open squeaky dog and baby toys and you'll find a small plastic bulb. Its high-pitched squeak can imitate the distress call of a young squirrel in the clutches of a fox or hawk, and that racket draws other squirrels that are concerned or just plain curious. There are a few different sizes of squeakers, so experiment to find the pitch that works.	Cutter calls involve a ridged rod and a striker and replicate the sound of a squirrel's teeth on tough nut hulls. For the rod, try threaded plastic or metal bolts or even the brass bolts that hold toilet seats in place. For a striker, use metal or plastic washers of varying thickness. In the woods, toss a few light rocks into the leaves, which sounds like nut fragments falling.	Something about the clink-clank of a couple of coins can turn a squirrel inside-out with curiosity. Rubbing the ridged edges of quarters together makes a sound not unlike a squirrel cutting nuts (poker chips are even louder). Or hold a quarter and penny between thumb and forefinger and rasp them together in short, quick movements.
Works best early in the season, when young squirrels are still plentiful.	Try this technique after you've been busted. Sit quietly for 10 minutes, then lure the squirrel back into the open.	This is a short-range game, which makes the one-handed quarter-and-penny call a deadly finisher.

393 BE THE TRIPOD

A wily old South Carolina squirrel hunter named Mac English perfected this rather unorthodox prone position. It is deadly, as your upper arm and entire upper body are in solid contact with the ground, bolstered by a bent leg that serves as an outrigger.

STEP 1 With your rifle in your left hand, lie on your right side. (Do the opposite if you're a lefty.) Keep your right thigh in a straight plane with your torso, and bend the right knee back at a 90-degree angle.

STEP 2 Cross left leg over right, placing your left foot across the right knee on or close to the ground. Move the rifle into position against your shoulder, keeping your upper right arm flat against the ground.

STEP 3 Hold the fore-end with your left hand, and position this hand against your left knee. You can make adjustments by shifting the left knee, keeping contact between the left leg and the right knee joint.

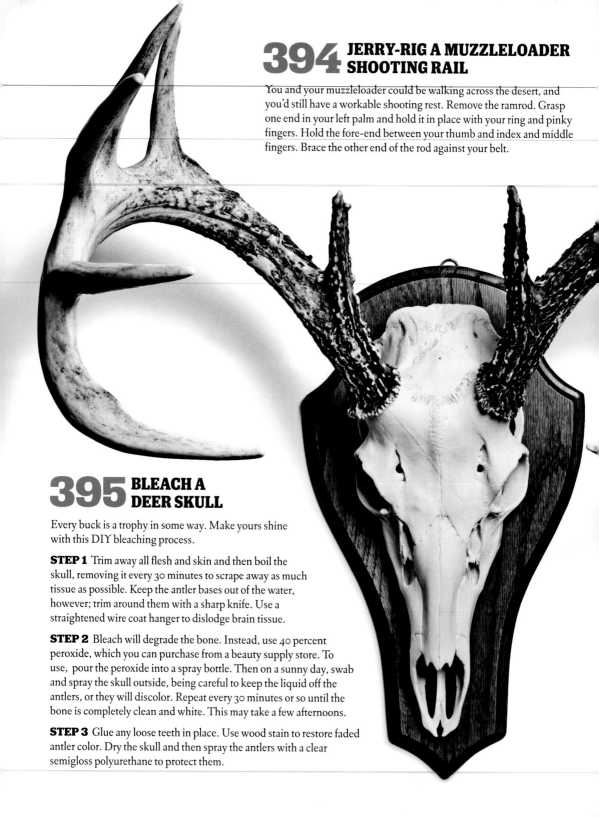

394 JERRY-RIG A MUZZLELOADER SHOOTING RAIL

You and your muzzleloader could be walking across the desert, and you'd still have a workable shooting rest. Remove the ramrod. Grasp one end in your left palm and hold it in place with your ring and pinky fingers. Hold the fore-end between your thumb and index and middle fingers. Brace the other end of the rod against your belt.

395 BLEACH A DEER SKULL

Every buck is a trophy in some way. Make yours shine with this DIY bleaching process.

STEP 1 Trim away all flesh and skin and then boil the skull, removing it every 30 minutes to scrape away as much tissue as possible. Keep the antler bases out of the water, however; trim around them with a sharp knife. Use a straightened wire coat hanger to dislodge brain tissue.

STEP 2 Bleach will degrade the bone. Instead, use 40 percent peroxide, which you can purchase from a beauty supply store. To use, pour the peroxide into a spray bottle. Then on a sunny day, swab and spray the skull outside, being careful to keep the liquid off the antlers, or they will discolor. Repeat every 30 minutes or so until the bone is completely clean and white. This may take a few afternoons.

STEP 3 Glue any loose teeth in place. Use wood stain to restore faded antler color. Dry the skull and then spray the antlers with a clear semigloss polyurethane to protect them.

396 CLEAN A SQUIRREL

Pound for pound (okay, ounce for ounce), squirrels are among the most difficult game animals to clean. Their skin is tougher than duct tape, and squirrel hair sticks to squirrel flesh with the tenacity of five-minute epoxy. Fortunately, you can create a simple device that makes stripping them a cinch. Here's how.

MAKE THE STRIPPER

STEP 1 First draw two lines across a 5x3 ¾-inch piece of ¹/₁₆-inch aluminum plate, sectioning it into thirds.

STEP 2 Cut three slots from the long edge of an outer third (see below for slot sizes). Smooth the edges with sandpaper.

STEP 3 Drill two holes through the middle of the other outer third. Then bend the two outer thirds up at a 90-degree angle, so that they form a U-shaped channel.

STEP 4 Using the holes that you drilled, nail the squirrel skinner firmly to a tree or post at shoulder height.

SKIN THE SQUIRREL

STEP 1 Hook the squirrel's rear legs in the two narrow slots, its back facing you.

STEP 2 Bend the tail over the back and make a cut between the anus and the base of the tail, through the skin and tailbone. Extend this cut about an inch down the squirrel's back, filleting a ¹/₂-inch-wide strip of skin away from the muscle, but leaving it attached at the bottom.

STEP 3 Make two cuts, each starting at the opposite sides of the base of this strip and extending laterally halfway around the squirrel, stopping just in front of the hind legs.

STEP 4 Now grasp the tail and loosened hide and pull firmly down. Except for the skin covering the back legs and part of the belly, the hide should shuck off inside out.

STEP 5 Flip the squirrel around, and slide its neck and two front paws into the slots. Grasp the edges of the remaining hide and strip the "pants" off the squirrel.

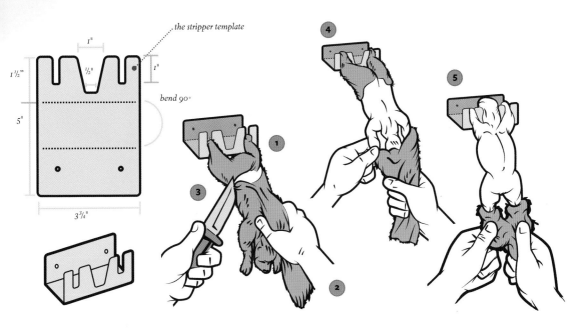

the stripper template

bend 90°

1" 1" ½" 1½" 5" 3¾"

397 MAKE A FROG GIG

These are the nights to channel your inner Huck Finn. Frog gigging feeds the stomach and the soul, because there's something downright spiritual about a lily-fringed frog pond on a new-moon night. You can use a retro cane pole—or you can get fancy with this telescoping gig fashioned from a 16-foot collapsible bream pole. It's perfect for any small-boat frogman, plus the golf-course gigger who needs a pole that will fit in a car. Once armed, get to it. Gigging a gigged-out pond is like batting cleanup in a game of spin the bottle.

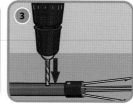
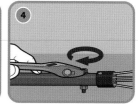

SBT Outdoors gig head

STEP 1 Remove the butt cap from the bream pole, then slide out the rod-tip end of the nested sections. Replace the cap.

STEP 2 Saw off the front end of the pole at the point where it snugly fits inside the gig head. The gig head sold by SBT Outdoors is the best I've seen and has replaceable tines sharp as a surgeon's scalpel.

STEP 3 Drill a 1/8-inch hole through the gig shaft and pole. Remove the gig head and coat the inside with epoxy.

STEP 4 Affix the gig head to the pole using a 3/4-inch-long 6-32 stainless-steel bolt, a washer, and a locking nut. Let the glue set, and you're done.

398 PREPARE YOUR FROGS

To clean your frogs, remove the legs above the hips. A perfect cut helps keep the legs attached. Pull the skin down to the ankle and cut off the feet. Dredge legs through a milk-and-egg bath, then batter. Fry in hot peanut oil.

399

MARK YOUR POT CALL

There's always an area on the surface of any pot-style turkey call that will produce the best sound. To mark it, rotate the call so that the sweet spot lies between the thumb and index finger of the hand that holds the pot. Then use a knife to score the sides where those fingers lay. Now, you can easily orient the call to make the best tone without ever looking at it.

400

MAKE YOUR OWN LAYOUT BLIND

Will that brand-new $450 layout blind with spring-assisted doors and integrated camouflage work better than these ones? Probably. Will it work $450 worth better? Ask the geese.

a **CHEAP** Go comfy with a camp chair that folds all the way flat. Wrap the exposed metal on the frame with camouflage duct tape, walk into the field with a handful of long black cable ties, and brush it up. Do your best not to doze off.

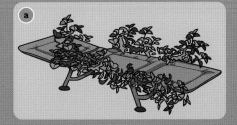

b **CHEAPER** Buy a plastic snow toboggan in a dull color, or spray-paint it. Use it to haul your gear and decoys across the field, then toss your hunting pack into the top for a pillow, and cover it all up with some camouflage material and vegetation cut from the field.

c **CHEAPEST** Find an old beach or lawn chair. Cover exposed metal with camouflage duct tape and weave green paracord line through the webbings for additional tie-ins for natural vegetation. Line it with an insulated camping pad or a camouflaged space blanket, brush it up, line down, and bring home pâté!

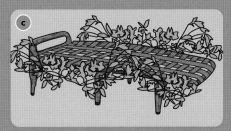

401 TURN A UTILITY TABLE INTO A BUTCHER SHOP

Butchering a deer can be a chore that will make a mess of your basement and send you limping up the steps with a backache. This DIY butchering table will make your meat cutting a more pleasant experience. It's cheap, easy to store and clean, large enough for two people to work at together, and raised to a spine-pleasing height. Before butchering, clean the table with a 50-50 mix of bleach and water. Rinse it with distilled water.

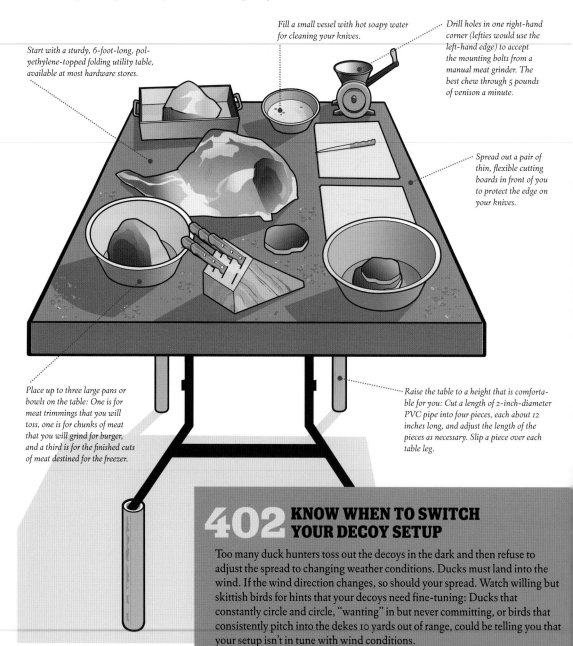

Fill a small vessel with hot soapy water for cleaning your knives.

Drill holes in one right-hand corner (lefties would use the left-hand edge) to accept the mounting bolts from a manual meat grinder. The best chew through 5 pounds of venison a minute.

Start with a sturdy, 6-foot-long, polyethylene-topped folding utility table, available at most hardware stores.

Spread out a pair of thin, flexible cutting boards in front of you to protect the edge on your knives.

Place up to three large pans or bowls on the table: One is for meat trimmings that you will toss, one is for chunks of meat that you will grind for burger, and a third is for the finished cuts of meat destined for the freezer.

Raise the table to a height that is comfortable for you: Cut a length of 2-inch-diameter PVC pipe into four pieces, each about 12 inches long, and adjust the length of the pieces as necessary. Slip a piece over each table leg.

402 KNOW WHEN TO SWITCH YOUR DECOY SETUP

Too many duck hunters toss out the decoys in the dark and then refuse to adjust the spread to changing weather conditions. Ducks must land into the wind. If the wind direction changes, so should your spread. Watch willing but skittish birds for hints that your decoys need fine-tuning: Ducks that constantly circle and circle, "wanting" in but never committing, or birds that consistently pitch into the dekes 10 yards out of range, could be telling you that your setup isn't in tune with wind conditions.

403 SHOOT DOWNHILL AND UPHILL

Let's settle this old argument right here, and we won't need cosine angles. This is hunting, not geometry. Gravity only affects a bullet or arrow along its horizontal distance, not the linear distance taken by the projectile. To calculate your hold, simply figure out the distance between you and the target on a horizontal line. If you're 20 feet high in a tree and the deer is 3 yards from the base of the tree, then hold for 3 yards. If the ram is 200 feet above you, on a ledge 300 yards away on a horizontal line, hold for 300 yards and pull the trigger.

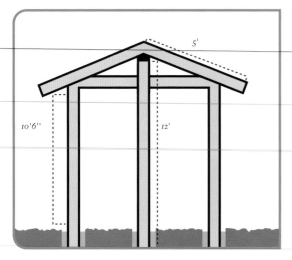

404 BUILD A ROOFED MEAT POLE

Most meat poles get the game off the ground but they don't protect it from rain or snow. This gable-roofed version does, and with style. The overall dimensions of the structure can vary, depending on the size of your club (and the construction skills of your hunters).

STEP 1 Mark the ground for four corner posts and two ridge posts constructed of 5x5 treated timbers. Sink the posts into 30-inch holes and anchor them with cement.

STEP 2 Attach a 5x5 ridge joist on top of the center posts. Allow for an 18-inch overhang on each end.

STEP 3 Nail in 2x4 or 2x6 rafters, allowing for an 18-inch overhang. Nail in roof sheathing of plywood or 1x6 boards. Cover with shingles or roofing tin.

STEP 4 Hang a 3-inch-diameter galvanized steel pole from the two ridge posts, about a foot below the ridge joist. Affix large eye screws or eyebolts to the ridge pole at 3-foot intervals. Attach a block and tackle to these when you're raising the deer up.

405 BLAZE SECRET TRAILS TO YOUR STAND

Marking a trail to a favorite stand site or hidden blind is a dark art of the savvy hunter. Here's the secret formula.

CAMOUFLAGE THE TRAILHEAD Mark the entrance to the trail with a rock or other natural feature that is visible at night. Enter the trailhead from different angles to avoid wearing an obvious path in the ground.

BE TACK SHARP Flat thumbtacks reflect light at angles close to perpendicular, so they'll only show up if you're on the right trail. Cylindrical or cube-shaped tacks reflect light from all angles. Don't use them.

LEAVE CODED MESSAGES Use as few tacks as you can and devise a code only you and your hunting buddies can decipher. Three tacks in a triangle: Turn left. Single tack head high: Proceed straight.

406

REMEMBER FOUR KNIFE "NEVERS"

1 Never store a knife in a leather sheath. It can cause rusting or discoloration.

2 Never use water to clean a horn handle. Horn absorbs moisture and can splinter.

3 Never use hot water to clean a wood handle. If the wood is cracked or dried, rub it with olive oil.

4 Never touch the blade or metal parts after oiling. This can leave behind salt and acids, which can cause oxidation.

407

ASSEMBLE A RIFLE REPAIR KIT

The most important 2 pounds you can carry on any (actually, every) hunt is a zippered nylon bag that measures 8x4x1 inches. It's a rifle repair kit, and it can save not only your bacon but the pork of other people who aren't so smart.

The cleaning rod is not for cleaning bores but for knocking stuck cases out of chambers. Any short and strong takedown rod will do. (A small-diameter rod works in all bore sizes.) Here are two other hints: Always carry a spare scope with a long tube that will fit a wide variety of mounts, and if you do work on a gun, do it over a bunk or a sleeping bag so when you drop small parts you can find them again.

THE KIT SHOULD CONTAIN **(a)** a Lyman interchangeable-bit screwdriver, **(b)** a gunsmith bedding tool, **(c)** a Leupold multitool with Torx- and hex-head screwdrivers, **(d)** a set of small Allen wrenches (for working on triggers), **(e)** a collection of patches, and **(f)** a multisection .270-caliber steel cleaning rod.

408

JUDGE A TROPHY BUCK BY ITS EARS

The best way to tell the length of a whitetail's antler tines is by comparing them to the length of its ears, which typically measure about 8 inches. If the first or longest tine appears longer than the ear, and the second point is only a little shorter than the ear, you have all the information you need to make your decision. Shoot.

409

HOLD A SHOTGUN TENDERLY

Some shooters clutch their guns almost tightly enough to leave dents in the wood. Relax your grip, and you might start breaking more clay birds—or downing more birds with feathers.

It's impossible to swing a shotgun smoothly if you strangle it. Try this: Put a death grip on an unloaded gun and mount it on an imaginary duck or dove. You'll feel the tension all the way up through your shoulders. Now hold the gun lightly in your hands and see how much more easily it flows to the target.

How tightly should you hold a gun? Ever-quotable instructor Gil Ash says: "Just tight enough to squeeze a little toothpaste from a full tube." You may want to hold your gun even more lightly, tightening your grip only at the instant you make the shot so you can control the gun under recoil.

410 DOUBLE YOUR RANGE WITH A BIPOD

Reaching out for long-range coyotes, varmints, and even open-country big game will require a rock-solid rest, and nothing does the trick like using a rifle-mounted bipod from the prone shooting position. There's a little more to mastering this two-footed rest than simply flopping on the ground with the bipod deployed, so here's the drill for the long-range game.

GO LOW The longer the legs, the more they will flex, and the shorter the legs, the more stable the platform. Adjust the bipod so the rifle is as close to the ground as possible without forcing you into an uncomfortable position.

NOT ROCK SOLID You'd never shoot a rifle rested on a rock, because recoil will jump the stock, sending your bullet high. It is the same idea with a bipod. Place the bipod feet on a surface with some give. Dig down to reach softer subsoil under a hard crust. At the very least, spread a jacket over an unforgiving surface and place the bipod on the material.

THE GOOD FLEX Once in position behind the bipod, seat the stock against your shoulder and push it slightly forward. This will "load" the bipod, seating the feet more firmly into the ground and reducing how much the legs will flex with the rifle's recoil.

REAR SUPPORT With the gun's forestock resting on the bipod, your left hand (for a right-handed shooter) needs something to do. Double down on bracing by using your fist to steady the toe of the stock. Reach under your right armpit, grab the rifle's rear swivel sling and make a fist. Make slight elevation changes in point of impact by squeezing or relaxing your fist.

411 USE BINOCULARS AS A SPOTTING SCOPE

Backcountry elk hunters and high-country sheep and goat hunters look to shave ounces from their loads, so converting binoculars for use as a spotting scope holds down weight and limited pack space. A couple of aftermarket accessories make the conversion work. The results aren't as clear and bright as a dedicated spotting scope, but not having to carry both binoculars and a spotting scope is a definite bonus for wilderness hunters.

MOUNT STEADY Tripod adapters allow binoculars to be mounted to the ¼-inch screw bolt of a tripod. Many manufacturers offer adapters specific to their models.

TWICE AS NICE Optical doublers double the magnification of binoculars, turning an 8X binocular into a 16X spotting scope, or a 10X binocular into a 20X elk-finder. The doubler typically fits over one eyepiece. Doublers are light enough you can toss one in your pack and, in a pinch, use it without a tripod. Just brace the device against a tree.

412

MAKE A PVC RIFLE REST

Carry a folding saw and this modified PVC T-joint, and you'll never be without your own shooting stick for long-range squirrel shots. Glue a 4-inch piece of 1 ½-inch PVC pipe into the branch of the T-joint (1), and pad it with black foam or camouflage tape (2). In the field, cut a 1-inch-thick sapling about 4 feet long. Slip the T-joint over the stick (3) so the padded branch juts off to the side—voilà, a mini shooting rail. To aim, grasp the stick and pipe at the proper level, cradle the rifle in the rest, and bring home the good stuff.

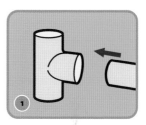

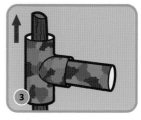

413 HUNT ON SNOWSHOES

Floating over deep snow in pursuit of snowshoe hares, coyotes, and deer is a classic method of hunting, and easier than you think. A revolution in snowshoe design has spawned a wide variety of high-tech aluminum snowshoes, but the ancient wooden snowshoe still gets the nod for many hunters.

CHOOSE THE RIGHT SHOE A very big advantage to wooden snowshoes: They are sneaky-quiet in the brush. Smack into a rock or sapling with wooden snowshoes and you'll hear a dull thud. Do the same with some aluminum snowshoes and the loud metallic thwack will spook every animal within a quarter mile. The modified or elongated bearpaw style offers plenty of flotation, a slight lift to the tip for maneuvering through brush, and a stable enough

platform that you can use to step on top of downed trees in tough cover.

TURN AROUND The toughest snowshoe maneuver is turning around, and it's particularly challenging for hunters who don't have the advantage of poles. It's similar to pulling a 180 on skis: keep one planted, lift the other foot high over the snow, and put it down at a right angle to the other. Bring the other foot around, and repeat for the full 180.

TAKE A SEAT A bearpaw snowshoe makes a handy seat with a built-in comfy backrest, perfect for watching forest openings and open glades. Stick one snowshoe vertically into the snow for a backrest, and use the other as the seat. Kick out a comfortable footrest and sit down.

414 KEEP HUNTING CLOTHES CLEAN IN CAMP

Most hunting camps will have most of what you'll need to jerry-rig a washing machine in the field. Just provide baking soda or your own scent-free washing detergent and you are ready to rid your duds of cigar smoke, sweat, and spilled bean dip.

Grab a 5-gallon bucket and the camp plunger.

Disinfect and deodorize that plunger by filling the bucket with boiling water. Add a bit of baking soda or detergent and work the plunger up and down to clean. Now replace the water with clean water and more baking soda or detergent, toss in your clothes, and churn your way to clean. Rinse with fresh water.

415 RE-PROOF WAXED COTTON

First-generation waxed cotton was just sailcloth smeared with fish oil, so don't go whining about the relatively low maintenance requirements of modern waxed-cotton duds. Heavily used clothing needs re-proofing once a year or so, and it's easy. It's best to do this during summer, when warm temperatures keep the wax soft and workable.

CLEAN IT Clean the jacket (A) with cold water and a soft cloth or sponge. No soap, ever. Let the jacket dry.

WAX IT Place a tin of wax dressing in hot water and allow the wax to warm into a semiliquid state. Warm the jacket, either by placing it in a sunny spot or by stuffing it into a couple of pillowcases and tossing it in the dryer (B).

FINISH IT Roll a soft cotton cloth into a tight roll (C); use rubber bands to hold it in shape (D). Use this to work the wax into the jacket exterior (E). Concentrate on a small area at a time, and pay close attention to seams, worn spots, and creases. Go for even coverage, and wipe excess with another clean cloth. Use a blow-dryer to finish the wax (F).

NEW-SCHOOL TWIST You can use re-proofing wax on other 100-percent cotton apparel, so give your favorite hunting cap an old-school spa treatment. While waxed cotton won't breathe quite as well as nontreated cotton, your broken-in lid will turn away showers and wear a retro patina.

416 SILENCE YOUR ZIPPER

Zipper pulls made of metal or heavy plastic can clink and clank just enough to spook game. Give them the silent treatment with a little electrical heat-shrink tubing. Just slip it over the zipper pull and hit with a lighter. The tubing shrinks when heated and provides a sound-dampening cover. Or cut the pulls off and replace with paracord or loops of old fly line.

417 KEEP CALLS CLEAN

Plug your duck, goose, owl, predator, and crow calls with a wine cork. Now you can stuff them into your filthy pockets without fear of dirt sticking in the reeds.

"Difficulties are just things to overcome, after all."

—Ernest Shackleton

Survival of the Most Prepared

He fell 70 feet, skipping off the rock cliff twice on the way down, and the first thing I did when I got to my brother was to gently lift his head so he wouldn't drown in a pool of his own blood. I compressed the gashes in his forehead and rib cage to stem the bleeding as he coughed bits of lung in my face. We immobilized his back as best we could and sent a friend racing for help. That simple, straightforward, right-out-of-the-books first aid probably saved my brother's life.

These days, it's all too easy to think that survival skills are a lost and useless art. The reality is that modern life puts the unprepared in precarious situations. More and more of us are going farther and farther into the wilds. When we get there, we rely too heavily on things that go blank when the batteries die. And just when we really need to know how to signal with smoke or build a fire in the rain, the skills necessary to dig our way out of the hole have all but eroded away.

Few of us appreciate how quickly life afield can turn south. We plan and pack for rough weather, high water, flat tires, ripped tents, broken rods, and all the other crap that can wreck a blissful fishing or hunting trip. But when it comes to planning for situations where life or limb lie literally in the balance, we stuff a weak flashlight and a wad of old Band-Aids into a pack pocket and head out the door.

I may not know how to set a compound femur fracture—although I do think I could perform an emergency field tracheotomy—but this much I do know: There's space in every tackle pack for a wilderness first aid kit. They don't make a duffel bag that can't swallow one more fist-sized lump— an emergency survival blanket, another bundle

of firestarter. This is the time to take the time to read up, bone up, and be prepared. Fishing and hiking and camping and hunting aren't any more dangerous than a high school football game. But guess what's on every sideline of those Friday night lights? An ambulance with the engine running.

I can tell you just how bad it can get out there. It's up to us. You and me.

418

PACK A 1-DAY SURVIVAL KIT

Here are suggestions for an Altoids survival kit. Choose as many as you think you'll need and can fit. Wind the paracord outside the can to keep it securely closed.

SHELTER AND FIRE
- Butane lighter wrapped with duct tape (Duct tape is an excellent fire accelerant.)
- Spark-Lite wheel flint
- Tinder-Quik fire tabs
- Wire saw

WATER AND FOOD
- Potable Aqua iodine water purification tablets
- Nonlubricated condom for carrying water
- Fishhooks, sinkers, 2 dry flies, 2 wet flies
- 10 feet 24-gauge wire for snares

SIGNALING AND NAVIGATION
- Button compass
- Signal mirror (Use the top of the Altoids can for a signal mirror. Punch a hole in the middle as a sighting hole.)

MEDICAL
- Antibiotic ointment
- Butterfly closures

MULTIPURPOSE
- Single-edged razor blade
- 10 feet of monofilament fishing line
- Small pencil
- Waterproof paper, 2 small sheets

419 PACK A 3-DAY SURVIVAL KIT

Place all items inside a 1-gallon zippered plastic bag, then place in a small waterproof stuff sack or fanny pack.

SHELTER AND FIRE
- Space blanket
- Butane lighter wrapped with loops of rubber inner tube (Inner tube makes a great fire accelerant.)
- Spark-Lite wheel flint
- Tinder-Quik fire tabs
- Waterproof matches
- 1 garbage bag, rolled up tightly
- Wire saw

WATER AND FOOD
- Potable Aqua iodine water purification tablets
- Nonlubricated condom for carrying water
- GSI Outdoors foldable cup
- Fish hooks, sinkers, 2 dry flies, 2 wet flies
- 10 feet 24-gauge wire for snares
- Instant coffee
- Vacuum-packed beef jerky

SIGNALING AND NAVIGATION
- Compass
- Headlamp
- 2 glow sticks
- StarFlash signal mirror
- Signal whistle

MEDICAL
- Antibacterial wipes
- Antibacterial ointment
- Butterfly closures
- Gauze and tape
- Ibuprofen
- Benadryl
- Artificial tears for irrigating eyes

MULTIPURPOSE
- 50 feet of paracord (Mil-spec 550 cord has seven smaller lines inside the nylon sheath.)
- Aluminum foil for reflector oven
- Needle and thread
- Safety pins
- Spare knife
- Small pencil
- 5 sheets waterproof paper
- 10 feet of monofilament fishing line
- Superglue
- Surgical tubing (Use to suck water from shallow seeps, as a tourniquet, or to blow spark to flame.)
- Red crayon (Mark trees as you move, and use it as a firestarter.)
- Duct tape and wooden tongue depressor (1-inch strips of blaze orange duct tape serve as firestarter or route markers. Shave tinder from the tongue depressor.)

420

PACK A 1-WEEK, MULTIPERSON SURVIVAL KIT

Place all items in a waterproof stuff sack. Each group of items (Shelter and Fire, Water and Food, etc.) could also fit into a separate stuff sack.

SHELTER AND FIRE
- All-weather blanket
- Butane lighter wrapped with loops of rubber inner tube (Inner tube makes a great fire accelerant.)
- Spark-Lite wheel flint
- Tinder-Quik fire tabs
- Waterproof matches
- Wire saw

WATER AND FOOD
- Water treatment filter bottle (With these, you can drink straight from the stream.)
- Potable Aqua iodine water purification tablets
- Nonlubricated condom for carrying water
- GSI Outdoors foldable cup
- Fish hooks, sinkers, 2 dry flies, 2 wet flies
- 10 feet 24-gauge wire for snares
- Instant coffee
- Vacuum packed chicken and salmon.
- Pasta

SIGNALING AND NAVIGATION
- Full-sized compass
- Personal Locater Beacon
- 2 Flashlights: headlamp and small handheld
- Handheld flare
- StarFlash signal mirror
- Signal whistle

MEDICAL
- Antibacterial wipes
- Antibacterial ointment
- Butterfly closures
- Gauze & tape
- Ibuprofen
- Benadryl
- Imodium

- Artificial tears for irrigating eyes
- DenTec Dental First Aid Kit (Repacked into single zippered baggie. Includes a dental pain medication, cracked tooth and filling repair kit, and special tooth saver container for dislodged teeth.)
- SAM splint (Moldable aluminum alloy sheets between closed-cell foam provide support for a variety of bones and joints.)
- Azithromycin (A Z-Pak from your doctor will treat a number of backcountry ills: strep throat, sinus infections, bronchitis, ear infections, and some skin infections.)

MULTIPURPOSE
- Bush knife
- 100 feet of paracord
- Surgical tubing. Use it as a straw to suck water from shallow seeps, as a tourniquet, or to blow a spark to flame.
- One complete set: synthetic insulated top and bottoms, and socks, vacuum bagged
- Travel toilet paper
- Small pencil
- Waterproof notepad
- Small photo of loved ones (According to survival experts, thinking of family and friends keeps survival instincts strong.)

421

BEAT THE BUGS

A challenge in many survival situations is dealing with hordes of mosquitoes, black flies, and other biting, stinging pests. Here's what to use for a natural smokescreen.

CATTAIL While all parts of the plant are edible, burning the dried flower spikes will turn away mosquitoes.

SAGE The aromatic twigs and leaves burn quickly, so collect a large pile.

POOP Aboriginal peoples the world over burn buffalo, cow, and horse poop as an insect repellent—if the bugs get bad, so can you.

422 BEAT BLISTERS WITH DUCT TAPE

STEP 1 Drain the blister with a sterilized needle or knife Insert the tip into the base of the blister, then press the fluid. Keep the flap of skin intact.

STEP 2 Cut a hole slightly larger than the blister in some pliable cloth. Put a second layer on top and seal this "doughnut bandage" to your foot with duct tape. No duct tape? Then there's little hope for you to begin with.

FIELD & STREAM-APPROVED KNOT

---

423 TIE A HUNTER'S BEND

Unlike most knots, the hunter's bend is relatively new, invented only in the 20th century.

It's perfect for joining two ropes, of either equal or dissimilar diameters, which makes it perfect for survival situations when odd scraps of cordage might be all you have at hand. And it's a great knot to use with slick synthetic ropes.

1 Lay the two lines side by side, with tag ends in opposite directions.

2 Loop the lines, making sure neither rope twists on top of the other.

Keep lines from twisting.

3 Bring the front working end around behind the loops and up through the center.

Pull.

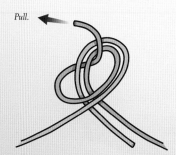

4 Push the rear working end through the middle of both loops.

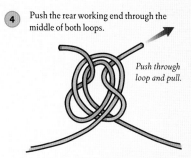

Push through loop and pull.

5 Seat the knot by holding the standing parts firmly and pulling both working ends. Pull the standing parts in opposite directions.

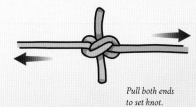

Pull both ends to set knot.

424 UPGRADE YOUR SURVIVAL KIT

Every personal survival kit should contain the fundamentals—waterproof matches, whistle, compass, knife, water-purifying tablets, a small flashlight. Think you have all your bases covered? See if you have room for a few of these low-volume lifesavers.

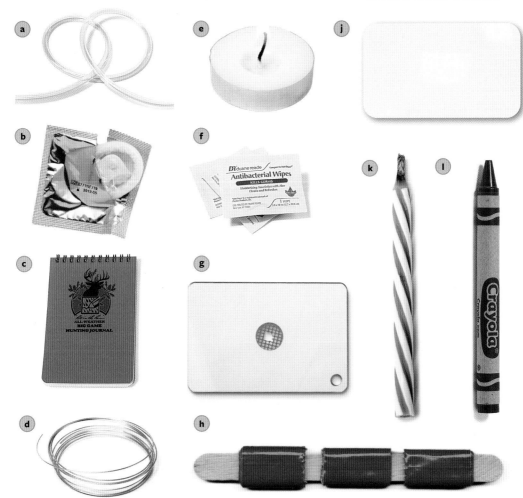

(A) SURGICAL TUBING Use it as a straw to suck water from shallow seeps, as a tourniquet, or as a means to blow a spark to flame.
(B) UNLUBRICATED CONDOM The best emergency canteen there is. **(C) WATERPROOF PAPER** Leave a note for rescuers—even in a howling blizzard. **(D) WIRE** If you can't think of 10 ways to use this, you're not an outdoorsman to begin with. **(E) TEA LIGHT CANDLE** The longer-burning flame will light wet wood. **(F) ANTIBACTERIAL WIPES** Stave off infection with a single-use packet. **(G) SIGNAL MIRROR** On a clear day, a strong flash can be seen from 10 miles away. **(h) BLAZE ORANGE DUCT TAPE WOUND AROUND A TONGUE DEPRESSOR** Tear off 1-inch strips of tape to use as fire starters or route markers. Shave wood with your knife to use as tinder. **(I) SMALL PHOTO OF LOVED ONES** Thinking of family and friends helps keep survival instincts strong. **(J) FRESNEL LENS** The size of a credit card, this clear lens will start a fire using sunlight. **(K) TRICK BIRTHDAY CANDLES** The wind can't blow them out. **(L) RED CRAYON** Mark trees as you move. You can also use the crayon as a fire starter.

425 MAKE A SWISS SEAT

You can make an emergency climbing harness in the field with a carabiner and just 12 to 14 feet of rope. Use it to rappel down a cliff or as a backup for when you get to your treestand but realize you left your harness at home.

STEP 1 Find the middle point of the rope, make a loop there, and place this loop at the hipbone of your off-hand side with the closed section of loop pointing up (a). Bring one end of the rope around your back, above the hipbone, and all the way around to your front. You'll have one longer and one shorter length of rope.

STEP 2 Cross one length of the rope over the other twice. Let the ends of the rope drape between your legs (b).

STEP 3 Pull the ropes through your legs and around each buttock, angling towards the side (c). Pull the end of each rope under the waist rope, then back under the buttock section, and tie a half hitch around the rope angling across each buttock at the waist rope (d).

STEP 4 Bring the free ends of rope together at the hipbone on your weak hand side. Tie them together with a square knot, and lock each running end with a half hitch (e). Clip a carabiner into both the twisted rope section and the upper waist rope (f).

426 RIG THE Z-DRAG

Hardcore white-water paddlers use the Z-Drag to free kayaks and canoes that are pinned to boulders in heavy current, but this simple mechanical advantage system is also useful for dragging or hoisting anything heavy (stuck ATVs, dead game off a cliff, a tree atop your buddy's legs) short distances. With a minimum of gear, the Z-Drag gives you a 3-to-1 hauling advantage, so you can be thrice the man when the chips are down.

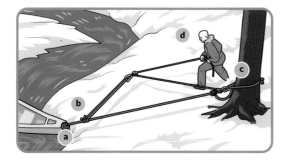

YOU'LL NEED
about 75 feet of hauling rope • two 12-feet-long sections of 5-mm rope tied into loops • about 10 feet of strong webbing or rope for an anchor loop • 2 carabiners • 2 petzl ultra legere pulleys, clipped to each 'biner

STEP 1 Tie the hauling rope to the stranded item (a). Using one of the loops of 5mm rope, tie a Prusik knot to the hauling rope close to the stranded item and clip a carabiner to the loop (b).

STEP 2 Tie an anchor loop around a strong anchor point, such as a tree trunk or a vehicle and clip a carabiner to the loop (c). Run the hauling line on the pulleys as shown. Use the other 5mm-rope loop to tie in a second Prusik knot to the hauling rope between the stranded item and through the anchor loop, close to this second carabiner. This will serve as an emergency braking device.

STEP 3 Stand next to the anchor point and pull on the working end of the hauling rope (d). There is no primary braking device on a Z-Drag, so hold the haul rope tight once you've pulled. As you take in line, have a partner slide the first Prusik loop down the hauling rope and toward the stranded item. If you're on your own, tie the pull rope off to a tree once you've retrieved the stranded object.

427

MAKE WATERPROOF MATCHES

These easy-to-make firestarters provide an all-in-one solution to starting a blaze: ignition, accelerant, and fuel in a single handy, cheap package. To use, scrape the wax off the tip and strike against a rock. Each match will burn for five minutes or better.

YOU'LL NEED
strike-anywhere matches • paraffin wax • cotton yarn or wicking • straight pins • aluminum foil

STEP 1 Tie an overhand knot in the yarn at the base of the match head, and wrap the match shaft. Tuck the tag end of the yarn under the last wrap and pull snug. Cut excess yarn.

STEP 2 Melt paraffin wax in a DIY double boiler. Select an old pot that will nest in a larger pot. (A clean coffee can works in a pinch.) Fill the larger pot about half full with water and place on medium heat on the stove. Place the wax in the smaller pot and place this double boiler in the larger pot. Pay close attention. Paraffin wax has a low flash point and can burst into flame when overheated. When fully melted, move the setup off the heat.

STEP 3 Insert a straight pin into the nonstriking end of a match, and dip the entire match in the wax for a few seconds. Set on the foil to harden. Dip every match several times to build up a waterproof coating that also serves as fuel. After the last dip, remove the pin and tamp down the moist wax to seal the pinhole.

428 DESCEND A CLIFF WITH A SINGLE ROPE

If you have to rappel down a cliff with a single rope, you won't get a second chance to do it right. Take notes.

CHOOSE AN ANCHOR POINT This can be a sturdy tree or rock outcrop near the edge of the precipice. Make sure the anchor point won't pinch the rope as you pull it down from below. Pass the rope around the anchor so that the two ends are even and meet the landing point with a few feet of extra rope.

WRAP YOUR BODY With your back to the cliff, straddle the double strand of rope. Pass it around your right hip and then across your chest and over your left shoulder. Grasp the ropes at your lower back with your right hand, and bring them around to your right hip. With your left hand, grasp the ropes in front at chest height.

DESCEND Keeping close to perpendicular to the cliff, walk down the precipice. Relax your grips periodically to slide down the rope. To arrest a swift descent, grip tightly with your right hand while pulling the rope to the front of your waist. At the bottom, retrieve the rope by pulling one end.

429 BREAK BIGGER BRANCHES

No axe, no saw, and here comes the bitter cold. In such a situation, knowing what to do can mean the difference between a cozy bivvy and a frigid one. The trick is to break unwieldy limbs of dead and downed trees into usable 18-inch sections When you need heartier fuel than what you can render by breaking a few branches across your knee, turn to these useful methods.

FIRE GIRDLE You can use your campfire to help you by digging a small trench radiating outward from the fire, then scraping hot coals into the trench to fill it. Place larger branches across the coals and rotate them. Once they are partially burned through, they will be easy to break.

TREE-CROTCH LEVER Find a sturdy tree crotch about waist high. Insert a dead tree branch into the crotch and push or pull the ends until the wood breaks. This is the quickest way to render dead branches up to 20 feet long into campfire-size chunks.

KNIFE NOTCH Cut a V-notch into one side of a branch, lean it against a tree trunk or place one end on top of a rock, and kick the branch at the notch.

TWO-MAN PUSH-PULL Two men can break a long branch into pieces by centering the branch on a sturdy tree and pushing or pulling against opposite ends.

430 SPARK FIRE WITH A KNIFE

Use a high-carbon steel blade or scrounge up an axe head or steel file; stainless steel blades won't work. Find a hunk of hard stone. Besides flint, quartz, quartzite, and chert work well. The trick is to stay away from round rocks; you need one with a ridge sharp enough to peel minuscule slivers of metal from the steel. When they catch fire from friction, that's what causes the spark. Add highly flammable tinder. Start sparking.

STEP 1 Hold the stone with the sharp ridge on a horizontal plane extending from your hand. Depending on where the sparks land, hold a piece of char cloth, tinder fungus, dry grass bundle, or Vaseline-soaked cotton ball under your thumb and on top of the rock, or set the fire-starting material on the ground.

STEP 2 If you're using a fixed-blade knife or axe head, wrap the sharp edge with a piece of leather or cloth. With the back of the blade, strike the stone with a glancing, vertical blow. If the tinder is on the ground, aim the sparks down toward it.

STEP 3 Gently blow any embers or coals into a flame.

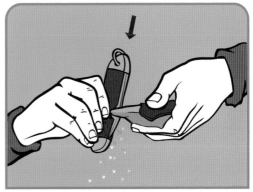

flint and knife blade

flint and file

flint and axe head

431 STAY ALIVE WITH TOILET PAPER

Get stuck in your car in a blizzard? You can create an emergency heater out of toilet paper, a coffee can, and rubbing alcohol.

First, crack the windows on each side of the car to let in some fresh air.

Loosen the cardboard tube from a toilet paper roll by kneading the roll in your hands, then remove the cardboard tube. Place the toilet paper in an empty coffee can, a one-quart paint can, or a similarly sized clean metal can.

Pour rubbing alcohol into the can, soaking the toilet paper. Carefully light the top of the paper. It should produce a hot, clean flame.

When the edges of the toilet paper turn brown, blow out the flame. Let the can cool, add some more rubbing alcohol, and relight.

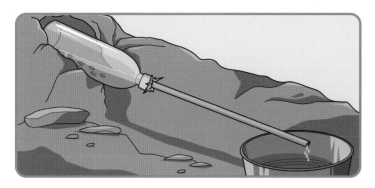

432 MAKE A SURVIVAL FAUCET

In a survival situation, every drop of found water is critical. The problem is that many springs and seeps put out a tiny trickle of water that is difficult to collect. Here's how to turn a weak spring into a survival faucet.

STEP 1 Dig a small basin where the water is seeping from the ground or dribbling over a rock.

STEP 2 Punch holes into the bottom of a spare water bottle or other lidded container. Wrap the container with a clean cloth and secure with cord. Cut a hole in the cap just large enough to insert some kind of tubing. A hollow reed will work, as will an aluminum tent pole. Stuff some clean vegetation around the tubing to seal up the hole. Place the water bottle firmly into the depression with the cap and tubing facing downhill. Anchor it with a log or stone to press the bottle into the bottom of the basin.

STEP 3 Run the tubing downhill into a collecting bucket. Treat or filter before drinking.

433 SHAVE THE DAY

Pencil shavings make great tinder. Just toss a pocket-size pencil sharpener and a stub of a good ol' No. 2 into your pack and you'll never be without a handy source for fire-building. Or simply shave thin curls with a knife.

434 REUSE A SHOTSHELL

To keep matches dry and handy, fill a spent 16-gauge shell with matches and top it with a spent 12-gauge shell. Wrap the seam between the shells with a few layers of duct tape to waterproof the case and provide a handy source of fire accelerant.

435 SCROUNGE UP SURVIVAL WIRE

You might know that 550 paracord is made with a sheath, inside which are 7 to 9 strong inner cords that are perfectly sized for things like snare loops, fishing lines, and small-diameter lashings. Here are other sources of wire and cordage to seek out in a survival situation.

GOT A POWER CORD? Remove the twisted copper strands.

GOT HEADPHONES? Separate each wire.

GOT A SPIRAL-BOUND NOTEPAD? Pull out the wire and straighten for nooses.

GOT A BALLPOINT PEN? Remove the spring and straighten.

ARE YOU WEARING A BRA? If it's an underwire bra, remove the wire.

GOT A BUSTED RADIO? There's wire inside.

ARE YOU WEARING SHOES? You have snare loops on each foot.

DID YOU PACK DENTAL FLOSS? It can be used as light lashing or fishing line.

When the zombie apocalypse reigns in the streets—or you stumble into a remote cabin after having been lost in the woods for a week—being able to open a can of food without any utensils will put you at the front of the survival line. All you need on hand is your food can, a flat rock or piece of concrete, and enough remaining muscle strength to rub the can just the right way.

Most canned foods are made with a rimmed top that is crimped closed with an extra layer of metal. It might be hard to see, but it's there, and once you remove that thin layer of metal from the rim, the top will pop off.

You'll need to find a hard, flat surface such as slate or other flat rock, or a piece of concrete or a smooth brick. Be sure that surface remains steady, turn the can upside down, and grind the top rim vigorously back and forth (a). You might see liquid dribbling out; that indicates progress.

At this point you can turn the can right side up and pry the lid off by sticking a knife blade into the open seam (b), or keep on grinding it until you see that you've removed metal from all the way around the rim. Turn the can over and squeeze the sides of the can to pop the top free (c). Be very careful—all that grinding has created sharp metal edges.

437 COOK FISH ON A LOG

The modern variant of planked fish involves a store-bought cedar board and a stainless steel backyard grill. It wasn't always so. In a survival situation you can cook planked fish without any utensils at all. Trout and panfish are small and thin enough to cook quickly, and fat enough to stay moist in the heat of an open flame. And you don't even need a carefully squared plank.

First, split an 8- to 12-inch log round in half. (Stay away from the wood of pine and other conifers.) No way to split wood? No sweat. Just use a round log. Whittle a half-dozen 2-inch wooden pegs with one sharp end. Clean the surface of the log and lay out the fish, either whole or skin side down. With the point of a knife, poke through the fish to mark the log where the pegs should be, remove the fish, then use the tip of a knife to drill a starter hole for the pegs. Replace the fish and then tap the pegs into place.

Build a teepee fire so the flames rise at least to the level of the fish, and scoot the fish in place. If needed, chock the log with a rock or stick.

438 MAKE A DUCT TAPE BOWL

Tear off two pieces of duct tape in equal lengths, about 18 inches long. Sit down on the ground with a bent knee. Form a cross with the tape, with the intersection of the cross on top of your knee, sticky side down, and press the tape against your leg. Make a bowl shape by wrapping your pants leg with more tape until you have it sized just right. Carefully remove the tape bowl, and add more duct tape to the interior to waterproof the bowl.

439

BANDAGE WITH DUCT TAPE

A butterfly bandage is used to pull together the edges of a wound for quicker, cleaner healing. Here's how to make one on the fly.

Clean the wound thoroughly and dry the skin.

Cut a strip of duct tape 1 to 1 1/2 inches long by one-quarter to 1/2 inch wide. Using sharp scissors or a knife, make small cuts to create two tabs in the middle of the bandage (a).

Fold one tab in so the two sticky sides are together (b). Fold the other tab over the first (c) to create a nonadhesive strip in the that will not stick to the cut.

Stick one end of the butterfly bandage to one side of the cut, pinch the cut together, pull the bandage across the cut, and stick the other end in place. For larger wounds, additional butterfly bandages can be used like sutures.

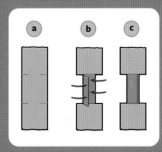

440 BUILD A FIRE IN THE RAIN

There are those who can and those who think they can. Here's how to be one of those who really can.

STEP 1 Allow three times as much time for fire building as you'd need in dry conditions. If you're hiking, gather dry tinder as you go along the trail.

STEP 2 Look down when looking for tinder. Dry tinder may be under rocks, ledges, and logs, and in tree hollows. The underside of leaning deadfalls can be dry in a downpour; chop out chunks of good wood. Conifer stumps hold flammable resins.

STEP 3 Look up. Search for dry kindling and fuel off the wet ground. Fallen branches that are suspended in smaller trees will likely be rot-free. Locate a dense conifer and harvest the low, dead twigs and branches that die off as the tree grows. Shred the bark with your fingers.

STEP 4 Make what you can't find. Use a knife or hatchet blade to scrape away wet wood surfaces.

As the fire sustains itself (a), construct a crosshatched "log cabin" of wet wood around it (b) with a double-layered roof (c). The top layer of wood will deflect rain while the lower level dries.

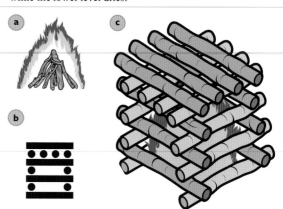

441 AIM A MAKESHIFT SIGNAL MIRROR

The best commercial signal mirrors are made with aiming devices. But there are ways to aim a jerry-rigged signal mirror—aluminum foil wrapped neatly around a playing card, or the shiny interior surface of an aluminum can—that can also attract attention.

FOR A MOVING TARGET

STEP 1 Hold the mirror in one hand and extend the other in front, fingers spread to form a V between your fingers and thumb.

STEP 2 Move your hand until the target rests in the V.

STEP 3 Angle the mirror so the reflected sunlight flashes through the V and directly onto the target.

FOR A STATIONARY TARGET

STEP 1 Drive an aiming stake chest-high into the ground, or choose a similar object such as a broken sapling or rock.

STEP 2 Stand so the target, the top of the aiming stake, and the signal mirror are in a straight line.

STEP 3 Move the mirror so the reflected sunlight flashes from the top of the aiming stake to the target.

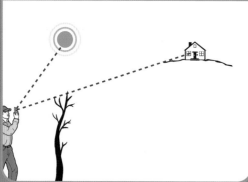

442

SPEAR FISH IN A FUNNEL TRAP

Make the walls of the funnel trap with piled-up stones or tightly spaced sticks driven solidly into the river or lakebed. Once fish are in the trap, close the entrance, roil the water, and either spear them or net them with a seine made by tying a shirt or other cloth between two stout poles.

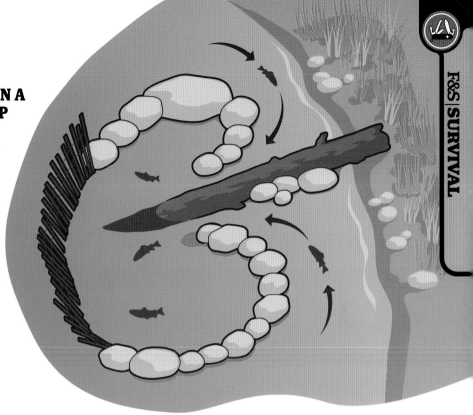

443 MAKE A TINDER BUNDLE

Fire making does not end with the birth of a red-hot coal, nor does a glowing char cloth ensure that you're going to get a flame. You must transfer the coal or char cloth to a bundle of fine tinder before blowing it into flame. Good sources include dried grasses; lichens (including old man's beard); shavings from the inner bark of aspen, poplar, and cottonwood trees (which burn even when wet); and windblown seed or fluff. The tinder bundle should be roughly the size of a softball and loosely formed to allow air circulation.

To blow the bundle into a flame, make a small pocket in the center. Tuck the glowing coal or char cloth into the pocket and then loosely fold the edges around it. Next, pick up the bundle and gently blow on it. Once it has burst into flame, place it under a tepee formation of small twigs and add larger pieces until you establish a strong fire.

444 REMOVE A FISH HOOK

Getting hooked is a rite of passage for anglers. It's going to happen eventually. The worst case I ever saw involved my buddy who was asleep on his boat. In the middle of the night he rolled over onto a jointed Rapala plug, and stuck two of the hooks into the back of his thigh—to the bends—and he was wrapped up in a blanket to boot. By the time he stumbled into my tent the flesh around the hooks was swollen and leathery. That was ugly. Still, if you've got a Woolly Bugger in your thumb, a crankbait hook in the leg, or a spinnerbait in your arm, there's no need to quit fishing. Here's how to remove a hook sans screaming and get back in the action.

STEP 1 Snip the hook or lure free of the main fishing line to get rid of any tension. If possible, detach a treble hook from its lure and clip off any of the hook points not stuck

in your person. Next, cut a 15-inch strand of line from your reel and tie the ends together to create a loop.

STEP 2 Double the loop of fishing line, then pass it under the bend in the hook close to your skin. The line should be resting against the hook bend. Push down on the eye of the hook. This raises the point—better aligning it with the hole it made when entering.

STEP 3 Now, take a deep breath, and in a single, quick, sharp tug, yank the line straight back. (This step is often best executed by a fishing partner.) As with a Band-Aid, the faster you pull, the less it hurts, often popping right out without causing pain. If the wound is still bleeding, apply pressure until it stops. Put on antiseptic ointment and a bandage before you get back to fishing.

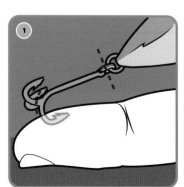

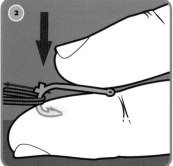

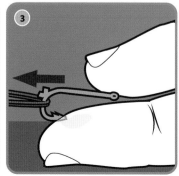

445 CATCH FISH WITH A TRIGGER SNARE

Trigger snares are among the most basic and effective tools for obtaining survival food, and just about everyone has seen photos or illustrations of these snares set along game trails and logs where small animals frequent. But the same primitive technology can be used to catch fish. Here's how.

STEP 1 Find a sapling located approximately 4 to 6 feet from the bank of a body of water. Look for places where fish congregate—deep holes on the outside of stream bends, near blowdowns where trees have fallen into the water, and other structures.

STEP 2 Carve the trigger. You'll need a simple one made of a base peg and a hook. Cut a notch into both. Tension from the bent sapling will keep the trigger "cocked" until a fish takes the bait, pulling the hook free of the peg and snapping the bent sapling upright.

STEP 3 Tie a cord from the top of the sapling to the top of the trigger hook. Tie a hook to one end of the fishing line and bait it. Tie the other end to the bottom of the

trigger hook, where it fits into the notch, making sure you have enough line to reach into the water. Now, bend the sapling over, pointing straight towards the water. Pull the trigger hook straight down to the ground—that's where you pound the trigger base into the ground. Set the snare trigger by fitting the notches together.

STEP 4 Carefully place the baited hook in the water. Be gentle so that you don't spring the trap.

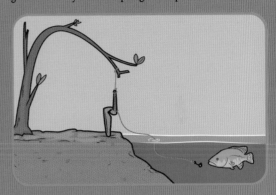

446
CONSTRUCT A FISH WEIR

Every year, biologists with the Alaska Department of Fish and Game count rainbow trout, Dolly Varden, and salmon, by using fish weirs in migration streams. In a days-long survival situation you can build such a fish trap to help fill your belly.

In a shallow stream, build a weir with a low stone wall that extends out into the stream. The migratory fish will swim into the trap. Once enough fish are in the trap, close off the entrance. Water flowing through the weir will keep fish alive for several days.

447
STOP BLEEDING

Instead of using a tourniquet if you injure a limb, apply direct pressure to the wound with a cloth or even your hand. Wrap a some kind of bandage all the way around your limb. If the bleeding keeps up, put more dressings on top of the old ones, and elevate the limb if possible. Wait until the bleeding stops, then attempt to hike back to your car.

448 READ A BEAR'S MIND

A defensive bear (a) will appear stressed and unsure of how to act, pacing about and popping its jaws. Talk to it in a very calm voice. Don't throw anything. When it is not moving toward you, move away from it slowly and carefully. A stumble now could provoke a charge. If the bear continues to approach you, stop. Stand your ground and continue talking calmly. If the bear charges, use your spray or gun; wait until the last possible moment before hitting the dirt.

A predatory bear (b) isn't intent on rendering you harmless but rather on rendering you digestible. If a bear is aware of your presence and approaches in a nondefensive, unconcerned manner, get very serious. Speak to it in a loud, firm voice. Try to get out of the bear's direction of travel but do not run. If the animal follows, stop again and make a stand. Shout at the bear and stare at it. Make yourself appear larger—step up on a rock or move uphill. Prepare for a charge.

449 BOIL WATER FOR SAFE DRINKING

Without chemicals or a filtering or purifying device, the only option for disinfecting water is to bring it to a boil. But how long to simmer plain ol' H_2O? Heat will kill bacteria, viruses, and parasites before the water reaches 212 degrees F, so once the liquid is roiling—and has cooled down a bit—it's safe to drink.

But there's more to the process than simply setting a pot on a fire or stove. First, bring a small amount of water to a rapid boil, swirl it around the pot to clean the sides, and pour it out. Refill the pot and bring the fresh batch to a roiling boil. Pour a quarter-cup on the ground to help sterilize the rim of the container and then fill water bottles as needed. And be sure you don't pour disinfected water back into the water bottle you used to dip the dirty stuff from the creek in the first place.

Boiling water removes much of its oxygen and gives it a flat taste, so add a drink flavoring agent or pour the water back and forth between two clean containers to aerate it as it cools.

450 CARRY 50 FEET OF ROPE ON YOUR FEET

Real parachute cord is rated to 550 pounds. It's made of a tough outer sheath rated to 200 pounds, which protects seven interior strands, each rated to 50 pounds. Take apart a single 3-foot length of paracord, and you'll have almost 25 feet of cordage. Use it to rig shelters and snares, lash knife blades to spears, fix broken tent poles—you name it. If you replace both laces with paracord as soon as you buy a new pair of boots, you'll never be without a stash. Just make sure you buy the 550-pound-test cord.

451 HURL A BACK-COUNTRY DEATHSTAR

Boomerang, schmoomerang. When you need to kill a rabbit, grouse, or squirrel with a stick, throw a backcountry deathstar. Cut two pieces of straight, wrist-thick hardwood about 2 to 3 feet long. Carve a notch in the middle of each stick and lash them tightly together with notches together. Sharpen each of the four points. Throw it sidearm for a whirling, slashing disk of death—or, in a survival situation, life.

452 MAKE A TRAP OR DIE TRYING

Compared to the hours of energy expended while foraging or hunting in a survival situation, traps take little time to set, and, unlike firearms or fishing rods, they work for you while you sleep. But to trap animals with enough regularity to feed yourself, you need to heed these three principles as you set up.

1. LOCATION Rabbits, muskrats, groundhogs, and other animals make distinct trails that they use over and over. These trails are the best places to set traps, but they can be difficult to see in bright sunlight. Search for them early or late in the day when the shadows that define them are growing longer.

2. DIRECTION Where possible, narrow an existing trail—by brushing vegetation or driving a couple of small sticks into the ground—to direct the animal into the trap, or place a horizontal stick at the top of the snare so that the animal must duck slightly, ensuring that its head will go right into the noose.

3. SIZE Scale your trap correctly for what you're trying to catch. As a rule, the noose should be one and a half times the diameter of the head of the animal you wish to capture and made of material that will break should you inadvertently snare, say, a cougar's foot.

The most important tool you can carry if you're planning on catching your dinner is a spool of snare wire (26 gauge will be about right for all-purpose small-game snares; use 28 gauge for squirrels, 24 or heavier for beaver-size animals). Soft single-strand wire is superior to nylon monofilament because it holds its shape and game can't chew through it. You can also make snares from braided fishing superlines or 550 parachute cord, depending on the kind of trap you're making.

SQUIRREL SNARE
Make a small loop by wrapping the snare wire around a pencil-diameter stick twice and then turning the stick to twist the wire strands together. Pass the long wire end through the loop to form the snare (a). To build a squirrel snare, attach a series of small wire snares around a long stick propped against a tree (b). You can catch several squirrels at a time with this setup.

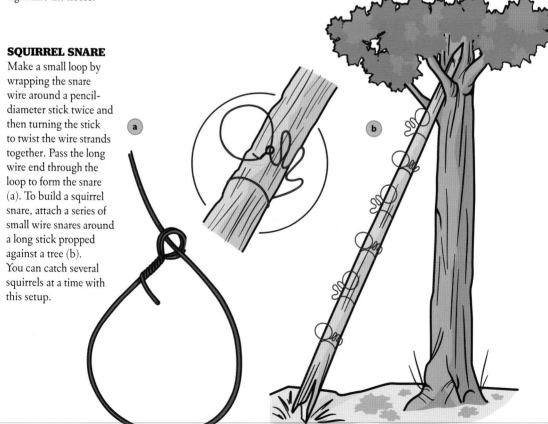

TWITCH-UP SNARE

Tie a small overhand loop knot in your parachute cord. Then fold the loop back on itself to form Mickey Mouse ears and weave the tag end through the ears (a). To build the twitch-up snare, use more cord to tie a spring pole or the branch of a small tree in tension (b). Set up a trigger mechanism like the one shown (c). When the animal's head goes through the loop, the trigger is released, and it snatches the animal into the air, out of reach of other predators.

FIELD & STREAM CRAZY-GOOD GRUB

453 CHOKE DOWN BUGS

A fistful of bugs for dinner might seem a little crazy. And good? Not so much. But when the chips are down, this is the original MRE (meal, ready to eat), packed with enough nutritional punch to help get you through the night. The average grasshopper sports 20.6 grams of protein and 5 milligrams of iron—that's twice the iron and just 3 grams of protein less than a similar spoonful of lean ground beef. The FDA allows one rodent feces per sampling of popcorn. Wouldn't you rather eat a hopper?

START WITH THE LEGS Remove the grasshopper's legs to help control the bug and keep it from hanging up in your gullet. Some grasshopper gourmets remove the head by grasping the thorax and slowly pulling off the head. This pulls out much of the entrails, and the rest can be scraped away with a stick.

COOK BEFORE EATING Cooking is critical to kill internal parasites. Skewer insects on a thin stick and hold the stick over a fire, or roast the grasshoppers on a rock set close to the flame. A grasshopper is just like any other small piece of meat. In fact, once you get over the bug phobia, that's exactly what it is.

454 RATE AN INSECT STING

What's worse: the bite of a bullet ant or the hemolytic horrors of a bald-faced hornet sting? Ten fire ants on your big toe or one giant tarantula hawk with its rear-end sunk deep into your thigh? While assigning a pain factor to a "holy-$#&@!-that-hurts-like-#%*&!" insect sting won't mean that the agony goes away, it's still fun to try to figure out just where your torment fits on the Schmidt Pain Index of insect stings.

Yes, there actually is such a thing. Developed by Justin O. Schmidt, an entomologist at the Southwest Biological Institute in Tucson, Arizona, this index is used to rate the various degrees of perceived pain visited upon a person by the large number of stinging hordes that have stung Schmidt and his colleagues over the years.

Schmidt's index rates those stings on a scale of 0 to 4; I've provided the real-world context.

PAIN FACTOR INDEX	
0	Imperceptible. You don't even know you got stung.
1	One sweat bee or a single fire ant. Aggravating. Swat-worthy. Continue your normal activity.
2	The honeybee's signature sting. Involuntary jerking of limb. Howl of pain. Application of wet tobacco.
3	We're talking harvester ant. Pain that endures for 4 to 8 hours. Associated with snarling obscenities, much hopping up and down. There could be tears. Your fishing trip is over.
4	Only 3 critters are known to be capable of delivering such a life-changing wallop: the tarantula hawk, warrior wasp, and bullet ant. Of the three, only the tarantula hawk (pictured right) is found in North America. Schmidt described Level 4 pain as "a running hair dryer has just been dropped in your bubble bath."

455 PREPARE FOR ANAPHYLAXIS

While you really shouldn't ignore the possibilities of a fatal encounter with a wolf pack, enraged polar bear, or—if you are in the Florida Everglades—feral Burmese pythons, the far more serious threat to outdoorspeople comes in the form of winged venomous arthropods. Severe allergic reactions to insect stings and other complications from allergens can lead to anaphylaxis, which includes a sudden drop in blood pressure and difficulty breathing. In extreme instances, the reaction can kill within half an hour. This is not to be taken lightly. Anyone can have a life-threatening allergic reaction to an insect sting, even if they've never had a problem with stings before. Avid backcountry travelers should know how to treat the condition.

BE PREPARED When traveling with new companions, ask if anyone has issues with insect stings or other allergic reactions. If so, find out if they carry an epinephrine auto-injector, such as an EpiPen. If you like to travel widely in the backcountry, it's a good idea to carry one with you.

ACT QUICKLY Be alert to the first signs of a bad allergic reaction: skin reactions such as itching (especially around wrists, the insides of elbows, and on the face), hives, pale skin, or swelling of the lips, throat, or anywhere on the face. Be aware of any constriction of the airways or any trouble breathing, a weak pulse, or vomiting or nausea. At the very first sign of any of these indicators, take action. Do not wait to see if symptoms worsen.

GET HELP Head to emergency medical facilities, whether a hospital or doctor's office. If in the backcountry, begin an evacuation plan: Contact emergency personnel about the potential need for rescue, and plan on where the rescue will take place. My son's life was once saved because we split the family into two teams: My wife remained with my son while my daughter and I immediately raced towards the nearest backcountry ranger station.

PERFORM FIRST AID Administer an over-the-counter diphenhydramine such as Benadryl. While this won't be sufficient on its own to ultimately stave off a severe case of anaphylaxis, it is a first step. The liquid form is the fastest. Prepare to perform CPR and rescue breathing. Prepare to administer epinephrine via auto-injector.

GIVE EMERGENCY TREATMENT If the victim begins to experience trouble breathing, use the epinephrine auto-injector. Do whatever you can to get the person to medical personnel. Time is absolutely critical here. If the situation warrants, perform CPR and rescue breathing. Administer additional epinephrine if available.

BOTTOM LINE There are only limited actions you can take when faced with this situation. You must act early and decisively. If there are no emergency medications available, you should factor this in when you're deciding to reach out to emergency officials.

456 CALL FOR RESCUE WITH A NUT

If you're lost or hurt with no signaling device, head for the nearest oak tree. Find a fresh acorn and remove the cap. (The larger the acorn and cap, the lower the pitch of the corresponding whistle.) Form fists with your hands and pinch the cap between your thumbs and index fingers with its open side facing you. Create a Y with your thumbs by rotating wrists outwards. Now, rest the first joints of your thumbs against your lower lip and blow hard. Adjust the angle of the cap until you sound like a referee's whistle.

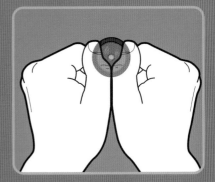

457 SURVIVE IN FAST WATER

Maybe you fell out of your fishing boat, or maybe you slipped while wading the river. Either way, you're suddenly sucked downstream into a long, violent rapid. What do you do?

STEP 1 The safest way to ride a rapid is on your back, with your head pointed upstream, your feet pointing downstream, legs flexed, and toes just above the water's surface. Lift your head to watch ahead. Use your feet to bounce off rocks and logs.

STEP 2 Choking on water will unleash a panic reaction in even the most experienced swimmer. The surest way to avoid a sudden, massive gulp of water is to inhale in the troughs (low points) and exhale or hold your breath at the crests (tops) of the waves.

STEP 3 You will naturally look downstream to avoid obstacles, such as logjams, but don't forget to also scan the shoreline for calmer water, such as an eddy on the downstream side of a rock or river bend.

STEP 4 As the current carries you toward quieter water, paddle with your arms and kick with your legs to steer yourself toward shore. When you get close, roll onto your stomach and swim upstream at a 45-degree angle, which will ferry you to the bank.

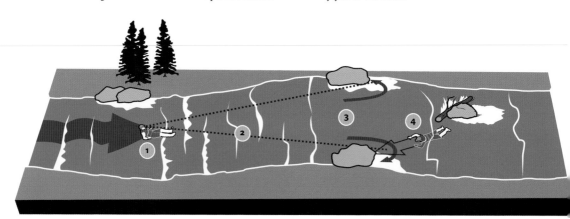

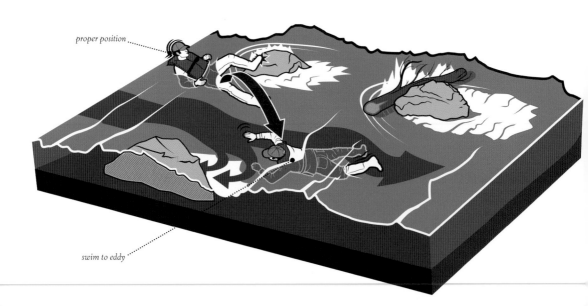

proper position

swim to eddy

458 SURVIVE A LIGHTNING STRIKE

There are lots of snappy sayings to help you remember lightning safety: When the thunder roars, get indoors! If you can see it, flee it! But what do you do when you're caught outdoors with almost nowhere to hide? Try this.

NEAR YOUR VEHICLE OR AN ENCLOSED STRUCTURE Get inside something—your car, a house, a barn. Open structures such as picnic shelters provide little to no protection.

OUT CAMPING Avoid open fields and ridgetops if camping during seasons when thunderstorms are prevalent. Stay away from tall, isolated trees, fence lines, and metal. Move into a lower stand of trees if possible; a tent provides no protection.

IN OPEN COUNTRY Avoid the high ground and points of contact with dissimilar objects, such as water and land, boulders and land, or single trees and land. Head for ditches, gullies, or low ground, and clumps of trees and shrubs of uniform height. Spread out: Group members should be at least 15 feet apart.

ON THE WATER Head inside a boat cabin, which offers a safer environment. Stay off the radio unless it is an emergency. Drop anchor and get as low in the boat as possible. If you're in a canoe on open water, get as low in the canoe as possible and as far as possible from any metal object. If shore only offers rocky crags and tall isolated trees, stay in the boat.

AT THE LAST MOMENT When your hair is standing on end, it's almost too late. Many experts believe that the "Lightning Crunch" provides little to no protection for direct or close strikes, but at this point, some action is better than nothing. Put your feet together and balance on the balls of your feet. Squat low, tuck your head, close your eyes, and cover your ears.

459 CUT SAPLINGS FOR SHELTER

If you find yourself in need of a shelter, you can gather the wood to construct one by felling a tree. If you can bend a green sapling, you can cut it, but it helps if you bend the trunk back and forth several times to weaken the wood fibers before bringing your knife to bear on it. To cut a sapling, hold it bent with one hand and then press down on the outside of the curve with your knife blade angled slightly (a). Rock the blade as you cut, while maintaining steady downward pressure (b). Support the trunk as you work to keep it from splintering, which would make it difficult for you to finish the cut.

Bend the sapling to make the cut easier.

Use straight downward force.

460 DRINK SNOW

Snacking on snow is fine until you're in a survival situation, when stuffing your face full of snow will consume critical energy reserves. To convert water from a frozen to a liquid state, choose ice over snow if possible, for it often contains fewer foreign objects that can carry pathogens, and ice will convert to more water than an equal volume of snow. Here are three ways to fill your water bottle from the hard stuff.

WATER MACHINE To melt snow or ice, snip a pea-size hole in the bottom corner of a T-shirt, pillowcase, or other makeshift fabric bag. Pack the bag with snow and hang it near a fire. Place a container under the hole to catch water melted by radiant heat. To keep the fabric from burning, refill the bag as the snow or ice melts.

FLAME ON Avoid scorching the pot—which will give the water a burned taste—by heating a small amount of "starter water" before adding snow or ice. Place the pot over a low flame or just a few coals and agitate frequently.

BODY HEAT You may have no other option than to use body heat to melt the snow. If so, put small quantities of snow or ice in a waterproof container and then place the container between layers of clothing next to your body—but not against your skin. A soft plastic bag works better than a hard-shell canteen. Shake the container often to speed up the process.

461 START A FIRE WITH BINOCULARS

It's not easy, but it's not impossible. And if it has come down to this, you're probably running out of options, so there's no harm in giving it a shot.

STEP 1 Disassemble the binoculars and remove one convex objective lens. Gather tinder, a stick to hold the tinder, some kindling, and a Y-shaped twig to hold the lens in place.

STEP 2 Arrange the tinder on the end of the small stick and put this on the ground. Having the tinder slightly elevated will increase airflow and flammability, and having it on the stick will allow you to move it to the area where the sun's rays are most concentrated.

STEP 3 Drive the Y-shaped stick into the ground and settle the lens inside its fork—carving some grooves will help. Focus the smallest point of intensified sunlight onto the tinder. It is critical that this focused beam not wobble. Once the tinder smolders, blow gently, and have larger twigs ready to light.

462 SURVIVE ON ACORNS

Stick with acorns from the white oak family (white oak, chestnut oak, bur oak), which have less tannin than red oak nuts. Cull any nuts with a tiny hole in the husk—this is made by an acorn weevil. Remove the cap and shell the rest with a knife or pliers from a multitool.

THE EASY WAY TO EAT ACORNS

To leach out the tannins, tie the nuts in a T-shirt. Submerge it in a running stream for several hours. Taste occasionally to test for bitterness. Or boil the nuts, changing the water frequently until it runs fairly clear. Then roast near a fire. Eat as is or grind into flour.

THE HARD WAY TO EAT ACORNS

Grind or pound shelled acorns, then mix with enough water to create a paste. Place a clean cloth in a wire sieve, scoop the acorn mush on top, and run fresh cold water over the mixture, squeezing water through the mush and out through the sieve. Taste occasionally, until the bitterness is removed. Use as a coarse meal like grits, or pound it into finer flour.

463 SURVIVE A FALL OVERBOARD

More than 200 sportsmen drown or succumb to hypothermia in boating accidents each year; most deaths occur when the boat capsizes or the sportsman falls overboard. Statistically, no other hunting or fishing activity has a higher fatality rate. Here's how to protect yourself.

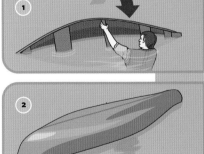

THE CAPISTRANO FLIP

Because cold water conducts heat from the body much more rapidly than air, it's vitally important that you get out of the water. Canoes and narrow-beam boats can often be righted by a maneuver called the Capistrano flip. Turn your boat completely over (1) and then duck into the pocket of air trapped beneath it (2). Hold the gunwales at the center of the boat. If there are two of you, face each other a couple of feet apart. Lift one edge slightly out of the water. Then scissor-kick, push to break the boat free of the surface, and flip it upright over that lifted edge (3).

464 STAY ON TOP OF THIN ICE

Crossing a frozen lake or pond, whether you're ice fishing or you're lost and trying to navigate back to camp, is one of the most dangerous outdoor activities. It's especially perilous in spring, when the ice pack is deteriorating and thickness alone is not an accurate gauge of safety. Here's how to travel safely.

Slushiness is a sign of a weakening pack; so is finding snow cover or water on top of ice. Depressions in the snow indicate a spring.

Stay away from inlet and outlet streams. Under-the-ice current can reduce ice strength by 20 percent or more.

Use your walking stick or ice chisel to test ice conditions.

Cattails and other vegetation, as well as rocks and logs, conduct heat, weakening the ice.

Tow your equipment sled on a long rope. You can push it toward a victim who has fallen through.

Carry cutoff broom handles tipped with sharp nails and attached with 2 feet of cord. Dig them alternately into the ice to haul yourself out.

Beware of black, gray, or milky ice. It lacks the strength of clear blue or green ice.

If you break through, face the ice you've already crossed. It will be stronger than ice in the direction of your fall. Crawl until you reach safe ice.

A 50-foot cord wrapped around an empty plastic jug makes a handy flotation device. Stand on sturdy ice and toss the jug to the victim.

Thin cracks may let you see whether the ice is thick or not.

Eroded shore ice is a sign of a thinning ice pack. Beware.

Ice sloping from a bank may trap air underneath, reducing its strength.

Pressure ridges are caused by fluctuating temperatures. Avoid them.

Open water is a red flag, pointing to a marginal ice pack nearer the shore.

465 NAVIGATE BY THE NIGHT SKY

The lost have turned their eyes upward for direction since long before man slew his first mammoth. Here is how the moon and stars can help you find your way home.

NORTH BY NORTH STAR

Polaris is the only star in the northern hemisphere that doesn't travel. It always points within 2 degrees of true north, making orientation simple. Locate the pointer stars on the bucket of the Big Dipper in Ursa Major. Observe the spacing between the two stars and then follow their direction five equal spaces to Polaris. You can also fix the position of Polaris, which is not a particularly bright star, using Cassiopeia.

DIRECTIONS BY MOONLIGHT

By noting when the moon rises, it's simple to tell east from west. When the moon rises before midnight, the illuminated side faces west. If it rises after midnight, the illuminated side faces east.

LET THE HUNTER BE YOUR GUIDE

During hunting season in the northern hemisphere, Orion can be found patrolling the southern horizon. This one is easy to spot because Orion rises due east and sets due west and the three horizontal stars that form his belt line up on an east-west line.

SIGHT ON A STAR

You can roughly calculate direction by noting the path of a star's travel (with the exception of Polaris, all stars rise in the east and set in the west). Face a star and drive a stick into the ground. Next back up 10 feet and drive in a second stick so that the two sticks line up pointing toward the star. If the star seems to fall after a few minutes, you are facing west; if it rises, you are facing east; if it curves to the right, you are facing south; if it curves to the left, you are facing north. Can't find a stick? Use the open sights on your rifle or the crosshairs of the scope to sight on the star and then track its movement by its deviation from the sights.

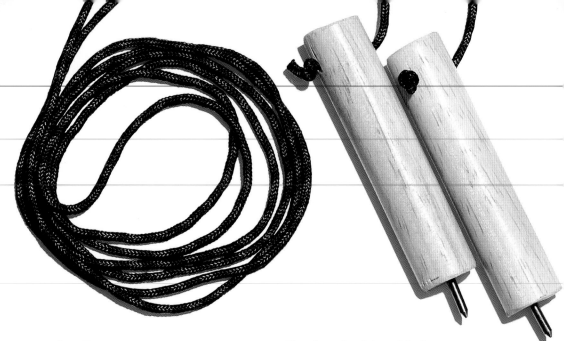

466 SURVIVE A FALL THROUGH THE ICE

Say "hard water" in northern regions, and folks know you're not complaining about rinsing soap out of your hair. In these cold climes, hard water is ice—as in ice fishing. And up here, you'd better know how to climb out when the water is not as hard as you thought. Here's a handy self-rescue device that has saved many a life.

HOW IT'S DONE Cut two 5-inch sections from a broomstick or 1-inch wooden dowel. On each of the pieces, drill a hole into one end that's slightly smaller than the diameter of whatever nails you have handy, and another hole crosswise at the other end. Drive a nail into each end hole. Cut off the nailhead, leaving 1 inch of protruding nail. Sharpen with a file to a semi-sharp point. Thread a 6-foot length (or a length that's equal to your arm span) of parachute cord through the crosswise holes and tie off with stopper knots.

Thread one dowel through both coat sleeves. When you slip the coat on, keep the dowels just below your cuffs. If you do go through the ice, grab the dowels and drive the nails into the ice to drag yourself out.

467 MAKE EMERGENCY MUKLUKS

Keep toes and feet intact with makeshift mukluks. Find some insulating material—a piece of fleece, sleeping pad, or boat carpet—and do the following for each foot.

STEP 1 Cut it into a circle about 24 inches across.

STEP 2 Fold the circle of insulation into quarters.

STEP 3 Move one layer of the insulation aside and insert your foot into the folded material. There should be a single layer at the heel.

STEP 4 Alternate the remaining layers around your foot. Slip an outer shell—part of a tarp or even a pants leg cut from spare clothing—over the insulation.

STEP 5 Crisscross a piece of cord around the outer layer, or use duct tape to secure firmly.

468 CALL FOR HELP IN ANY LANGUAGE

The international signal for distress is a sequence of short and long signals, designed for telegraph operators—three short, three long, three short. Adopted at the Berlin Radiotelegraphic Conference in 1906, the SOS sequence was based solely on its ease of transmitting. It does not mean "save our ship" or anything else you've heard. But you can transmit the code with just about any device imaginable: whistle blasts, car horns, gunshots, light flashes, even pots and pans.

469 SURVIVE THE ROUGHEST NIGHT WITH A KNIFE

You can use a strong knife to turn a single conifer tree into an overnight bivvy. First, fell a 9-foot balsam or other evergreen and remove all the branches close to the trunk.

MAKE A BOUGH BED Cut the tips of the evergreen branches to 1 foot in length. Use wooden stakes to chock a 3-foot-long, 4-inch-diameter log (cut from the tree trunk) where you want the head of your bed to be. Shingle the boughs at a 45-degree angle pointing away from the foot of the bed. Compress tightly as you work your way down. Anchor with a second 3-foot-long log from the trunk chocked with wooden stakes.

GLEAN TINDER The low, dead branches and sucker twigs of conifers make excellent tinder. Carve a fuzz stick from the thickest branch. Gather wood shavings from the others by scraping with the knife held at a 90-degree angle to the twigs.

GIN POLE A FISH To cook a fish with no utensils, snip away all twigs from the longest branch. Sharpen the fat end and drive it into the ground at about a 45-degree angle. Chock it with a rock or Y-shaped stick. Run cord through a fish's mouth and gill like a stringer, tie it to the branch, and let it dangle and cook beside the fire.

470 TEST A KNIFE WITH A NEWSPAPER

Your daily newspaper is packed full of plenty of critical information—including three tests that will tell you just how sharp you've gotten your knife.

ⓐ LET IT BITE Hold a single page of newsprint up at a 45-degree angle at shoulder height. Rest your knife blade on the edge of the paper at a shallow angle, and slice. A sharp blade will immediately bite into the newspaper and begin a clean cut. A dull blade will skip along the edge, or tear into the paper.

ⓑ WATCH IT GLIDE As the knife blade bites into the paper, it should easily glide with no significant sticking points. Run the entire length of your blade through the paper. If the blade cuts cleanly then hangs up, that may indicate a tiny nick or burr at that spot on the edge of the blade. Listen to the glide as it cuts: The higher the pitch, the sharper the blade.

ⓒ MAKE A FILET The sharpest knives will literally filet newsprint. Tear off a notebook-sized piece from the newspaper. Hold the knife horizontally, one hand around the handle, the other thumb on the blade spine as a guide. The palms of your hands will hold the paper firmly on a table or desk top. Try to slice a tiny half-pea-sized piece of newsprint without cutting all the way through the paper, like removing the skin from a fish. Success? That is one sharp knife, alright.

471 ESCAPE FROM WILDFIRE

If it seems like wildfires are becoming more common, it's because they are. A warming climate and drought across much of the American West makes wildfire a growing threat to wilderness travelers.

When fire conditions are high, remain vigilant. Situational awareness is your first line of defense. At the first sign of smoke, start making a plan. Even if the fire is distant, know that the powerful updrafts of a blaze can send embers for long distances and ignite a secondary blaze nearby.

PLOT AN ESCAPE ROUTE Look for a route that heads downhill, but avoid canyons, deep gullies, and draws. Heated air can rush up these natural chutes.

Stay away from resinous trees such as fir. When heated, expanding tree sap can cause trees to explode.

Try to make it to a wet area—a swamp, stream or marsh. Jump in if flames get close.

IF FLAMES CLOSE IN Shed your pack and as much synthetic clothing (nylon, Gore-Tex, etc.) as possible; it will melt quicker than most natural materials will catch fire. Find the lowest spot you can, ideally in a clearing or field as far from trees as possible. Kick away as much flammable material as you can to create a 20-foot-diameter circle. Dig a shallow trench and keep the soil nearby. If the flames come, lie face down and scoop dirt over your body. Bury your face in a bandana or piece of cloth. If the heat gets unbearable, that's precisely the point at which you must will yourself to stay down.

472

MAKE A
WICKED SLINGSHOT

Slingshot aficionados turn out sturdy handmade models capable of firing heavy slugs at 225 feet per second—fast enough to take down game from squirrels to wild turkeys to ducks on the wing. Here's the drill on crafting the world's most awesome slingshot.

FRAME IT Dogwood, hickory, and oak make the best frames. You don't have to find the perfect Y-shaped fork. The typical right-hander will hold the slingshot in the left hand, so look for a fork where the main branch crooks to the left at 30 degrees or so, but a fork goes off to the right at a 45-degree angle. Cut the frame and let it dry for three weeks.

POWER UP A number of companies sell ready-made replacement bands with pouches attached for slingshots. The trick lies in a strong connection: An inch and a half from the top of each slingshot "arm," drill a hole that's slightly smaller in diameter than the band. Bevel the end of the band with scissors and thread it through the hole—a pair of hemostat clamps will make this easier. Snip off the bevel. Next, take a dried stick slightly larger in diameter than the inside diameter of the tubing and carve two half-inch-long stoppers to a point. Plug each end of the tubing with a stopper.

473 MAINTAIN A KNIFE CLIP

To keep a pocket clip from loosening and falling off, treat the clip screws with a threadlocker such as Blue Loctite. To remove the pocket clip, place the knife in a small box so you won't lose the tiny clip screws as they are being removed. Choose the right screwdriver. Most quality knife clips are attached with Torx screws. Find the right size, then try one size larger. The Torx screw head indentations can get gunked up with soil, thus making a smaller size driver head appear to be the correct one. Take out the screws and clean them. Then, put a tiny drop of threadlocker on each screw and replace them. The compound will set the screws with a tight grip.

474

START A FIRE
WITH A FLARE

An emergency road flare will burn in just about any conditions, and will stay lit long enough to dry out some small pieces of soaked wood. Pack a few in your vehicle, your boat, and cabin survival kits.

475 PITCH A SURVIVAL CAMP

As a lost hunter or fisherman, your job is to make the search and rescue (SAR) team's job easier by staying put. But as you wait to be found, there are other things you should do to stay comfortable—and alive.

MIXED SIGNALS

1 Build a fire in an open area, such as a ridgetop. Stack green boughs beside it so you'll be ready to make a smoke signal to alert search aircraft.

2 Pack extra orange mesh hunting vests. Hang them from small trees or spread them on the snow, where they can be seen from a great distance.

3 Drag logs to construct an SOS sign with the sides of each letter at least 10 feet long.

4 Practice aiming your signal mirror so you can direct the flash when SAR aircraft appear. If you don't have a mirror, you can use a pot, a space blanket, or even a credit card.

When the SAR aircraft approaches, raise both hands to indicate that you need help. If you need medical care, lie down on your back with your arms stretched above your head.

THE ULTIMATE SHELTER

5 Pack a headlamp instead of a flashlight. It leaves your hands free to start the fire.

6 Gather a big pile of firewood to burn all night. Your supply should include wrist-diameter sticks, plus some 5-foot-long logs.

7 Night air flows downhill. Pitch your camp in a lee with the opening of your shelter parallel to the wind direction. That way, the shelter doesn't fill with smoke.

8 Pack a square cut from a closed-cell sleeping pad. It insulates you from cold ground. If you don't have a pad, sit on your pack.

9 Blow three whistle blasts at regular intervals to alert any nearby search teams.

10 Stay hydrated. A small titanium pot weighs less than an ounce and can be used to boil snow for safe drinking water.

11 If you don't have a tarp, one of the quickest shelters to build is a lean-to that uses a tree branch for the ridgepole. Break or saw branches for the framework and then lace smaller branches through the frame to make the shelter rigid.

12 Thatch the shelter with branches or pine boughs. Arrange them with tips pointing down to direct runoff. Tilt branches against the thatching to keep it in place.

13 Bank the lower sides of the lean-to with snow for insulation.

14 Once you build a fire, it's unnecessary to wrap up in your space blanket. Instead, tuck its edges into the shelter so the silver film forms a reflecting wall. It will provide warmth and cheery light.

15 Insulate your body from the ground and snow. Snap branch ends to make a bough bed at least 8 inches thick.

16 Place a retaining log across the shelter opening. It makes a comfortable seat and blocks the heat of the fire from melting the snow under the bough bed.

17 Use logs to build a wall in back of the fire, directing the fire's warmth toward your shelter.

18 Wet clothes quicken hypothermia. Hang your clothes by the fire to dry.

WIND

BUILDING YOUR FIRE

If your hands are too cold to shave fuzz sticks or scrape bark for tinder, try getting your fire started with the following: tiny twigs (a), pine tips with rusted needles (b), and cut strips of a gamebag or your underwear (c), since cotton burns fiercely.

476 START A FIRE

BURNING SENSATIONS Always have a couple of these D.I.Y. options on hand.

DUCT TAPE A fist-size ball of loosely wadded duct tape is easy to light and will burn long enough to dry out tinder and kindling.

INNER TUBE Three-inch strips or squares of bicycle inner tube burn with a rank, smoky flame hot enough to dry small kindling. No bike? Try the rubber squares in a wader-patch kit (don't forget the flammable patch glue) or a slice from a boot insole.

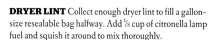

EGG CARTON AND SAWDUST Stuff each opening in a cardboard egg carton about half full of sawdust (collect this from your local school wood shop) and then add melted paraffin wax. Mix, let cool, and break apart.

DRYER LINT Collect enough dryer lint to fill a gallon-size resealable bag halfway. Add ⅛ cup of citronella lamp fuel and squish it around to mix thoroughly.

EMERGENCY FLARE Cut a 2- to 4-inch section from an emergency road flare and seal the end with wax. It's easily lit even with wet gloves on.

COTTON BALLS AND PETROLEUM JELLY It's a Boy Scout standby because it works. Stuff petroleum jelly–soaked cotton balls into a film canister or waterproof pill bottle and you have several minutes of open flame at the ready.

NATURAL WONDERS Learn to identify and gather natural tinder in your neck of the woods.

SPANISH MOSS Not a moist moss, at all, but an epiphytic, or "air plant," Spanish moss is a great tinder. But don't carry it around; it's notorious for harboring chiggers.

CEDAR BARK Common cedar bark should be worked over with a rock to smash the fibers. Pull the strands apart with your fingers, and roll the material back and forth between your hands.

BIRCH BARK The flammable oils in the papery bark of birches make this a time-tested fire catcher. Strip ribbons of bark from downed trees; it works just as well as bark from live ones.

SAGEBRUSH BARK Pound strips of bark with a rock and then shred them between your palms and fashion a tinder basket.

CATTAIL FLUFF The cottony interior of a cattail spike can be fluffed into a spark-catching blaze. Have more tinder nearby, because cattail fluff burns out quickly.

TINDER FUNGUS In northern areas, look for bulbous blotches of blackish wood on live birch trees. The inside of the fungus, which is reddish-brown, easily catches a spark. Crumble it for a quick start to a fire or use chunks of it to keep a coal alive.

PUNK WOOD Rotten, dry wood will flame up with just a few sparks. Use a knife blade held at 90 degrees to file off punk dust, and have larger pieces handy to transfer the sparks to larger punk wood that will burn with a coal.

477 CARVE A FUZZ STICK FOR A FAST FIRESTARTER

A fire-starting fuzz stick, or feather stick, is a super tool for starting a blaze and hard to beat for teasing flame from wet wood. It's not as simple as scoring a few flakes into a twig, however. With just a little practice, you can carve a fuzz stick in 90 seconds or less, and putting a mass of thin, spark-catching curls on a stick of wood is nearly as impressive as the flames it will produce. Here's the drill.

STEP 1 Split soft wood such as pine, spruce, or aspen into a foot-long length, 1 to 11/2 inches on each side. Choose a knot-free stick that has a long, straight grain. Flat-ground blades work better than hollow-ground, but experiment to find a knife that you can control with steady pressure.

STEP 2 Wedge the stick between your chest and a tree trunk, or hold it firmly against a chopping block at a 45-degree angle. Lock your wrist and use slow, steady pressure to push the knife edge—starting at the middle of the stick—down the corner to shave a thin, curly strip. Bring the knife back up to the starting point, rotate the stick very slightly, and begin another. Avoid sawing back and forth, but experiment with the orientation of the knife tip to create curls that trend toward one side or the other. Point the tip down and curls will come off to the right. Point the tip up and the curls will shave off to the left.

STEP 3 Longer, thicker curls are needed to ignite larger kindling, but to boost the fuzz stick's spark-catching ability, finish off with short, super-fine curls. Done with one corner? You're not done yet. Rotate the stick, and work up another.

478

MAKE FIRE WICK AT HOME

Fire wick—a wax-impregnated cotton string used to start fires—will burn for several minutes, and it's a snap to make at home. Use a thick laundry string, commercially available candle wicking, or other 100-percent cotton cordage. Melt paraffin wax in a double boiler, slowly, never allowing it to smoke. Dip cotton string into the wax slowly, using pliers to hold one end (a). Remove by dragging the string over the edge of the pot (b) in order to wring excess wax from the wicking. Hang the wicking by a nail (c), let it cool, then snip into 2- to 3-inch pieces. Store in small zip-sealed plastic bags or water-proof match cases.

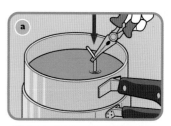

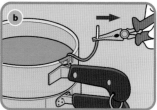

479 IMPROVISE SNOWSHOES

Got paracord? Got a knife? Then you have all you need to lash together a set of emergency snowshoes. Here's how.

STEP 1 Cut a couple of flexible branches, each at least 3 feet in length. Then, cut a couple of small pieces about 6 inches each, and a couple of about 10 inches.

STEP 2 Bend each long branch into a teardrop shape, and lash it together at the narrow end.

STEP 3 Lace paracord in a zigzag pattern the entire length of each shoe.

STEP 4 Test the snowshoe's size.

STEP 5 Add some bracing crosspieces where your toe and heel will fall.

STEP 6 Lash your boots to the snowshoes.

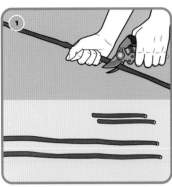

480 STAY FOUND FOR LESS THAN 10 BUCKS

Pin a simple bubble compass to the front of your coat and you'll circumvent half of the problems that lead to getting lost. Look for one that has luminous readouts and liquid dampening. The rotating sphere remains upright, so you can glance at the compass for a quick bearing read whether you're on the trail or hanging one-handed from a cliff.

481 MAKE A BLOWGUN

Drop your squirrel rifle in the river? It's time to channel your inner aboriginal and hunt squirrels with a blowgun and darts fletched with thistle.

STEP 1 Cut a piece of river cane 6 to 8 feet long. If necessary, straighten it by heating the bent parts over a fire and bending until straight. Leave it to dry in the sun for a week.

STEP 2 To remove the solid joints, heat the end of a straight steel rod until it's red-hot and burn out the joints inside your cane. Repeat until the cane is hollow. Smooth the bore by wrapping the steel rod with sandpaper and sanding the interior joints smooth. The smoother the bore, the faster the dart will fly.

STEP 3 To make a dart, whittle a hardwood shaft to about 12 inches long and 3/16 inch in diameter. Then, whittle a sharp point on one end.

STEP 4 Tie a 2-foot string to the dart's blunt end. Hold a bundle of bull thistle or cotton against the blunt end, hold the end of the string taut in your mouth, and roll the dart shaft so that the thistle or cotton is held tight to the shaft but is still fluffy enough to form a fletching larger than the inside diameter of the blowgun. Tie off the string.

482 USE SUPERGLUE TO CLOSE A WOUND

So-called "superglues" were used in the Vietnam War to close wounds and stem bleeding. Dermabond, a medical formulation, is a slightly different composition that minimizes skin irritation, but as many an outdoorsman will attest, plain ol' superglue will hold a cut together better than a strip bandage, and instances of irritation are rare. If you're stuck in the backcountry with no other way to close a wound, this will get you through until you can get to a doctor. Always use an unopened tube of glue. Clean the cut and pinch it shut. Dab a drop or two of superglue directly on the incision and then spread it along the length of the cut with something clean. The bandage is watertight and will seal out infecting agents.

483 RESET A DISLOCATED SHOULDER

You wrench your arm out of its socket while taking a nasty fall, or your buddy screams in pain while hoisting a deer into the truck. If you're far from a hospital, try this method for resetting a dislocated shoulder in the backcountry.

STEP 1 Create a weight of approximately 7 to 10 pounds with a rock or stuff sack full of sand or pebbles.

STEP 2 Have the victim lie face down on a rock, large log, or upside-down boat and get as comfortable as possible. Drape the affected arm over the makeshift gurney's edge so it hangs free at a 90-degree angle. Tie the weight to the wrist of the affected shoulder, being careful not to cut off blood circulation. As the weight pulls on the arm, muscles will relax and the shoulder will relocate. This could take 30 minutes.

484 MAKE A FIRE BED

It's cold enough to freeze whiskey, and you're stuck in the woods sans a sleeping bag? Make like a pot roast and construct a life-saving fire bed. Scrape out a gravelike trench in the dirt about 1 foot wide and 8 inches deep. Line it with very dry, egg-size to fist-size stones, if available. (Wet rocks from a stream or lake can explode when heated.)

Next, burn a hot fire into coals and spread a layer in the trench. Cover with at least 4 inches of dirt and tamp down with your boot. Wait one hour. If the ground warms in less than an hour, add more dirt. Now spread out a ground sheet of canvas, plastic, or spare clothing. Check the area twice for loose coals that could ignite your makeshift mattress. Ease onto your fire bed and snooze away.

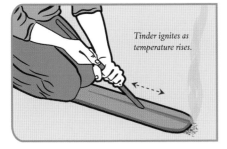

Tinder ignites as temperature rises.

485 MAKE A FIRE PLOUGH

This produces its own tinder by pushing out particles of wood ahead of the friction. Cut a groove in the softwood fireboard, then plough or rub the tip of a slightly harder shaft up and down the groove. The friction will push out dusty particles of the fireboard, which will ignite as the temperature increases.

486 SKIN AND COOK A SNAKE

Mr. No Shoulders might give you the willies, but a hot meal of snake meat might also give you enough energy to make it back to civilization. This should be a last resort, as some of these creatures are protected.

STEP 1 Cut off the snake's head. Insert the knife tip into the anal vent and run the blade all the way up the belly.

STEP 2 Free a section of the skin. Grasp the snake in one hand, the freed skin section in the other, and pull apart.

STEP 3 Remove all of the entrails, which lie along the base of the spine.

STEP 4 Chop into bite-size pieces. Fry or boil.

487 NAVIGATE BY DELIBERATE OFFSET

Say you climb a big hill to glass prime elk country. Now you have to bushwhack back, and even though it's no big deal to find the trail, moving in a straight line will be difficult. So, which way do you turn on the lakeshore or trail to find your original location?

Figure it out by using deliberate offset: Add or subtract about 10 degrees to your required compass bearing. Each degree of offset will move your arrival about 20 yards to the right or left for every 1,000 yards traveled. Hoof it back to the trail, and you'll know that you're off to one side. No guesswork. Make the turn.

488 BUILD A FIRE ON SNOW

Go through the ice, over the bow, or into a blizzard and you'll need a fire—fast and before your fleece and fingers freeze. Let's assume you're not a complete moron: You have a workable lighter. Here's how to spark an inferno no matter how much snow is on the ground.

STEP 1 Start busting brush. You'll need a two-layer fire platform of green, wrist-thick (or larger) branches to raft your blaze above deep snow cover. Lay down a row of 3-foot-long branches and then another perpendicular row on top. Stay away from overhanging boughs; rising heat will melt snow trapped in foliage.

STEP 2 Lay out the fuel and don't scrimp on this step.

Collect and organize plenty of dry tinder and kindling and twice as many large branches as you think you'll need. Super-dry tinder is critical. Birch bark, pine needles, wood shavings, pitch splinters, cattail fluff, and the dead, dry twigs from the sheltered lower branches of conifers are standards. Place tinder between your hands and rub vigorously to shred the material. You'll need a nest as least as large as a Ping-Pong ball. Pouring rain and snow? Think creatively: dollar bills, pocket lint, fuzzy wool, and a snipped piece of shirt fabric will work.

STEP 3 Plan the fire so it dries out wet wood as it burns. Place a large branch or dry rock across the back of the fire and arrange wet wood across the fire a few inches above the flame. Don't crisscross; laying the wood parallel will aid the drying process.

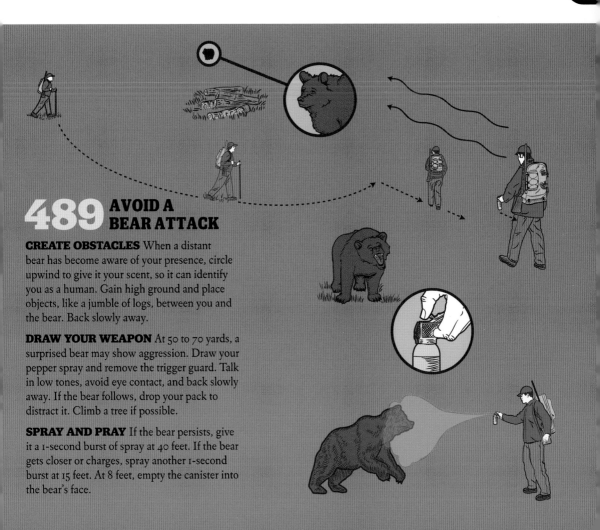

489 AVOID A BEAR ATTACK

CREATE OBSTACLES When a distant bear has become aware of your presence, circle upwind to give it your scent, so it can identify you as a human. Gain high ground and place objects, like a jumble of logs, between you and the bear. Back slowly away.

DRAW YOUR WEAPON At 50 to 70 yards, a surprised bear may show aggression. Draw your pepper spray and remove the trigger guard. Talk in low tones, avoid eye contact, and back slowly away. If the bear follows, drop your pack to distract it. Climb a tree if possible.

SPRAY AND PRAY If the bear persists, give it a 1-second burst of spray at 40 feet. If the bear gets closer or charges, spray another 1-second burst at 15 feet. At 8 feet, empty the canister into the bear's face.

490 BUILD A ONE-MATCH FIRE WHEN YOUR LIFE DEPENDS ON IT

If things are so bad that you're down to one match, then it's no time for you to be taking chances. The secret to last-chance fire building is attention to detail long before the match comes out of your pocket.

STEP 1 Begin with tinder. Collect three times as much as you think you'll need; don't stop looking until you have a double handful. Shred it well; what you're going for is a fiberlike consistency.

Conifer pitch, pine needles, cedar bark, birch bark, and dry bulrushes all make excellent natural tinder. Lots of other common items make good fire-starting material, too. Turn your pockets inside out to look for lint or candy bar wrappers. Duct tape burns like crazy; maybe there's a strip stuck to your gun case. Wader patch glue and plastic arrow fletching will work, too. The more variety you have, the longer the burn.

STEP 2 Gather twice as much kindling as you think you're going to need, and separate it into piles of like-size pieces. If you have to stop what you're doing and fumble for a pencil-size piece of pine at the wrong moment, your fire will go up in smoke. Your piles should consist pieces the diameter of a red wiggler, of a .22 cartridge, and of a 20-gauge shell. Use a knife to fuzz up the outer edges of a few sticks for a quicker catch.

STEP 3 Start small. Use two-thirds of your tinder to begin with and save the other third in case you need a second try with the dying embers of your first shot. Arrangement is important: You want to be able to get your match head near the bottom of the pile, and you also want to ensure that the slightest breeze pushes emerging flames toward your materials. Blow gently and feed only the fast-burning flames.

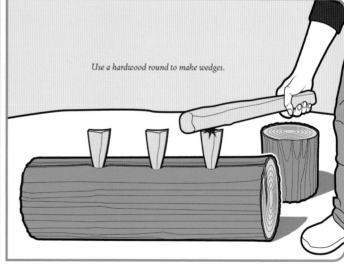

Use a hardwood round to make wedges.

491 SPLIT A LOG WITH A KNIFE

A knife is no replacement for an axe when it comes to rendering firewood. Still, you can use a hunting knife to expose the dry interior of a damp log by pounding the back of the blade with a wood baton.

Make several shingles this way, splitting thin, U-shaped wooden slices from the side of a round of firewood. Angle the edges of the shingles to make wedges and then insert the wedges into an existing lengthwise crack in a log. (If there isn't one, create one with your blade.) Hammer the wedges with a wood baton to split the log end-to-end and expose more surface for burning.

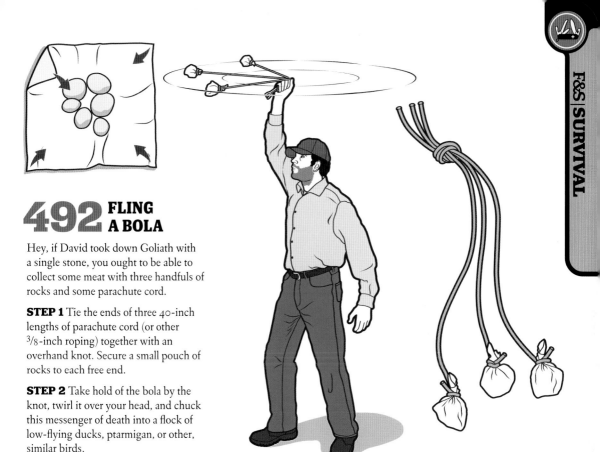

492 FLING A BOLA

Hey, if David took down Goliath with a single stone, you ought to be able to collect some meat with three handfuls of rocks and some parachute cord.

STEP 1 Tie the ends of three 40-inch lengths of parachute cord (or other $^3/_8$-inch roping) together with an overhand knot. Secure a small pouch of rocks to each free end.

STEP 2 Take hold of the bola by the knot, twirl it over your head, and chuck this messenger of death into a flock of low-flying ducks, ptarmigan, or other, similar birds.

493 EAT ROADKILL

If you make it to a road, rescue is likely just around the corner. If not, however, even the least-traveled highways can serve as a buffet for the feral forager. To separate plate-worthy roadkill from vulture food, follow these guidelines:

BODY CHECK Look for critters that have been clipped and tossed to the side of the road. If you have to use a flat shovel to retrieve your prize, well. . . .

SMELL TEST Any hunter knows what fresh dead meat smells like. Give the carcass a good sniff.

CLOUDY EYES Pass it up; it's been dead awhile.

FLEA CHECK If you find maggots, keep it out of your shopping cart. Fleas and ticks, however, are a good indicator of a fresh kill.

494 TRACK BACK WITH A GPS UNIT

Most people treat a GPS like a digital toaster with a 100-page instruction manual—they use it only for the most basic tasks it's capable of. The track-log and track-back functions of most popular GPS units, however, are just the ticket for outdoorsmen who want to figure out how to return to a truck or cabin from a distant tree stand or duck blind. Here's how it works.

STEP 1 Turn on the GPS unit, leave it on, and leave it out where it can get a clear signal.

STEP 2 Activate the unit's track-log function. (Look for a menu choice called "Tracks" or "Trails.") Don't customize the settings, such as choosing how often the unit plots a waypoint. These will already be preset to monitor your rate of movement and lay down electronic crumbs at just the right time.

STEP 3 At your final destination, stop the track log and store and name the track before powering off. You can now easily follow that track back the way you came with your unit's return feature, or even download it to GPS mapping software.

495 MAKE A BOW DRILL

Of all the friction fire-starting methods, the bow drill is the most efficient at maintaining the speed and pressure needed to produce a coal and the easiest to master. The combination of the right fireboard and spindle is the key to success, so experiment with different dry softwoods until you find a set that produces. Remember that the drill must be as hard as or slightly harder than the fireboard.

STEP 1 Cut a notch at the edge of a round impression bored into the fireboard, as you would for a hand drill. Loosely affix the string to a stick bow, which can be any stout wood.

STEP 2 Place the end of a wood drill about the diameter of your thumb into the round impression. Bear down on the drill with a socket (a wood block or stone with a hollow ground into it), catch the drill in a loop of the bowstring, and then vigorously saw back and forth until the friction of the spinning drill produces a coal.

STEP 3 Drop the glowing coal into a bird's nest of fine tinder, lift the nest in your cupped hands, and lightly blow until it catches fire.

496 BE A BACKCOUNTRY DENTIST

Lose a filling in the backcountry and you might wish you were dead. Make a dental first-aid kit with dental floss, dental wax, cotton pellets, a temporary filling material such as Tempanol, oil of cloves, and a tiny pair of tweezers. To replace a filling, put a few drops of oil of cloves (be careful; it can burn) on a cotton pellet. Use tweezers to place the medicated cotton in the hole, then tamp down with a blade from a multitool. Cover it with the temporary filling material.

497 SURVIVE A FRIGID DUNKING

An adult has a 50-50 chance of surviving for 50 minutes in 50-degree F water. In some parts of the United States and Canada, that's summertime water temperature. Go overboard in frigid water, and your first challenge is to live long enough to worry about hypothermia.

COLD SHOCK Hit cold water quickly and your body takes an involuntary few gasps of breath followed by up to three minutes of hyperventilation. You can literally drown while floating, before you have the chance to freeze to death. Keep your face out of the water. Turn away from waves and spray. If you're not wearing a personal flotation device (PFD), float on your back until you catch your breath. Don't panic. Cold shock passes after a minute or two. Only then can you plot your next steps.

HYPOTHERMIA The more of your body that you can manage to get out of the water, the better. Crawl up on anything that floats. Also, the more you flail around, the more your body will actually cool off. Unless you plan to swim to safety, stay still.

HELP Assume the heat-escape-lessening posture, also known as HELP. Hold your arms across your chest, with your upper arms pressed firmly against your sides; and your legs pulled up as far toward your chest as you can. This buffers the core areas of your chest, armpits, and groin. Remember that you can also lose a lot of body heat through your head, so try and find your hat if at all possible. The ultimate decision is whether to float or swim. Your ability to swim is severely hampered in cold water. Swimming increases the rate of heat loss up to 50 percent. It should be considered a last resort for rescue.

EVALUATE A BUBBLY COMPASS

The liquid that's found inside most compass housings is a specialized mineral oil. Its two main purposes are to dampen excessive needle movement and prevent static electricity from throwing off the bearing. Bubbles can form in two ways: At high altitude or in extremely cold temperatures, the liquid can contract, leaving a bubble. Or liquid can leak out of the seal or a tiny crack in the housing. Compass air bubbles are very common and won't affect the compass unless they are so large—say, a quarter-inch in diameter—that the movement of the direction arrow is impeded. If your compass develops a small bubble, place it in direct sun. The heated liquid in the housing will then expand to its original volume. If the bubble continues to grow, it's likely that there's a tiny leak in the housing. If this is the case, you should simply replace the compass.

499 TREAT A SNAKE BITE

Snake bites require prompt attention, so don't hesitate to begin moving towards medical facilities ASAP.

STEP 1 Remove jewelry and clothing such as boots and socks immediately. Once the bitten area swells, they can constrict tissues and hold venom in place.

STEP 2 Clean the wound lightly. Do not flush with water and do not apply ice.

STEP 3 Affix a wide, flat constriction band a few inches above the bite. Two fingers should slide easily under the band.

STEP 4 If a pump suction device is available, use it with the first 5 minutes after the bite.

STEP 5 Immobilize the bitten area with a loose splint and keep it lower than heart level.

STEP 6 Get to help. If the victim can be carried, do so. If the victim must walk out, first sit calmy for 20 to 30 minutes as the venom localizes at the bite site. Stay calm and walk out. Try to avoid unnecessary exertion.

500 SAVE YOUR BACKTRAIL ON A GPS

One of the most useful features on a modern GPS is the ability to save the track or trail you have traveled. This will allow you to easily return to your starting point, or to duplicate the route of travel at a future date. Track logs are, basically, electronic bread crumbs that the GPS drops at various intervals of time and location. They are fabulous tools, provided you know how to operate the function on your GPS unit.

Look for a menu heading that reads "track log," "track recording," or something similar. Turn the function on. Now the GPS will record a track point at predetermined intervals. The default settings are likely something along the lines of one point for every 25 meters traveled or whenever there's a significant change in your speed or direction. For most of the applications this works well, but there may be times when you want to drop more or fewer bread crumbs. If your route needs a finer scale—say you are trying to stay in a narrow creek channel on a flooded lake—then you should set your GPS unit to record more frequent track points.

Another setting to consider is "record" mode. Choose "wrap" to keep the display on and the track log will keep continually operating, even if it fills up and needs to overwrite your starting data. Choose "fill" if you do not want the starting data to be overwritten. The unit should sound an alarm to let you know when it's reaching its storage capacity.

Once set, let the track log function keep you on track. When you arrive at your destination, don't forget to save the track if you want to keep it for future use.

501 CREATE A WHIRLING PROPELLER OF SIGNAL LIGHT

A small flashlight or chemical light stick is a pretty good signaling device, but you can supersize the effect with a small length of paracord. Simply tie an 18-inch length of cord to the light, and whirl it in a circle. Now you will have created a pulsing light source some 40 inches in diameter. Do the same during the daylight with aluminum foil or other shiny objects.

INDEX

FIELD & STREAM

In every issue of *Field & Stream* you'll find a lot of stuff: beautiful photography and artwork, adventure stories, wild game recipes, humor, commentary, reviews, and more. That mix is what makes the magazine so great, what's helped it remain relevant since 1895. But at the heart of every issue are the skills. The tips that explain how to land a big trout, the tactics that help you shoot the deer of your life, the lessons that teach you how to survive a cold night outside—those are the stories that readers have come to expect from *Field & Stream*.

You'll find a ton of those skills in *The Total Outdoorsman Manual*, but there's not a book big enough to hold them all in one volume. Besides, whether you're new to hunting and fishing or an old pro, there's always more to learn. You can continue to expect *Field & Stream* to teach you those essential skills in every issue. Plus, there's all that other stuff in the magazine, too, which is pretty great. To order a subscription, visit www.fieldandstream.com/subscription.

FIELDANDSTREAM.COM

When *Field & Stream* readers aren't hunting or fishing, they kill hours (and hours) on www.fieldandstream.com. And once you visit the site, you'll understand why. First, if you enjoy the skills in this book, there's plenty more online—both within our extensive archives of stories from the writers featured here, as well as our network of 50,000-plus experts who can answer all of your questions about the outdoors.

At Fieldandstream.com, you'll get to explore the world's largest online destination for hunters and anglers. Our blogs, written by the leading experts in the outdoors, cover every facet of hunting and fishing and provide constant content that instructs, enlightens, and always entertains. Our collection of adventure videos contains footage that's almost as thrilling to watch as it is to experience for real. And our photo galleries include the best wildlife and outdoor photography you'll find anywhere.

Perhaps best of all is the community you'll find at Fieldandstream.com. It's where you can argue with other readers about the best whitetail cartridge or the perfect venison chili recipe. It's where you can share photos of the fish you catch and the game you shoot. It's where you can enter contests to win guns, gear, and other great prizes. And it's a place where you can spend a lot of time. Which is OK. Just make sure to reserve some hours for the outdoors, too.

CONTRIBUTORS

The content in this book was written by T. Edward Nickens, with assistance from the following experts:

Anthony Licata, Editorial Director of *Field & Stream*

Phil Bourjaily, *Field & Stream*'s shotguns editor.

Joe Cermele, *Field & Stream*'s fishing editor.

Kirk Deeter, editor-at-large for *Field & Stream* and co-writer of the "Fly Talk" blog on fieldandstream.com.

Keith McCafferty, survival and outdoor writer for *Field & Stream*.

John Merwin, *Field & Stream*'s long-time fishing editor.

David E. Petzal, *Field & Stream*'s rifles editor.

Additional contributors: Bill Heavey, Peter B. Mathiesen, Tom Tiberio, and Slayton L. White

ACKNOWLEDGMENTS

From the Author, T. Edward Nickens

I would like to thank all of the talented people who made this book possible, including the *Field & Stream* staff editors who guided this project with great care and insight. *Field & Stream* field editors Phil Bourjaily, Keith McCafferty, John Merwin, and David E. Petzal, and editor-at-large Kirk Deeter, provided unmatched expertise. Just good enough is never good enough for them. I wish I could name all the guides, outfitters, and hunting, fishing, and camping companions I've enjoyed over the years. Every trip has been a graduate course in outdoor skills, and much of the knowledge within the covers of this book I've learned at the feet of others. And last, thanks to my longtime field partner, Scott Wood, who has pulled me out of many a bad spot, and whose skillful, detailed approach to hunting and fishing is an inspiration.

CREDITS

Photography courtesy of *Rick Adair:* 98, 141 (scissors), 306; *Charles Alsheimer:* Hunting Intro (deer); *Barry and Cathy Beck:* 179, 223; *Scott Bestul:* 290; *Denver Bryan/ Images on the Wildside:* 137, 162, 196 (fisherman), 199, 230, 247, 310, 311, 359, 366, 382, 399, 413; *Boca Bearings:* 127; *The Bohning Company:* 239; *Bill Buckley:* Survival Intro (fisherman catching fish), 90, 108, 357, 358 (turkey), 378, 444; *Buck Pak Lite:* 417; *Mike Butler/Big Game International:* 150 (7); *Cabelas:* 150 (1, 4, 9), 288 (GPS); *Cascade Designs:* 54; *Coleman:* 221; *P. Crawford:* 141 (pliers); *Drybags.com:* 420; *Wally Eberhart:* 195; *Eric Engbretson:* 115, 181, 192; *John Eriksson/Images on the Wildside:* 329; *Cliff Gardiner & John Keller:* 37, 40 (wire saw), 152, 156, 198, 204, 371, 407, 424 (a, c, d, f, k, l), 443, 450, 451, 476 (cedar bark, tinder fungus), 477, 480, 481; *Gemmy Brand:* 218 (palm tree); *goFASTandLIGHT:* 24 (26); *Brian Grossenbacher:* 89, 110, 157; *Andrew Hetherington:* 391; *High Plains Showdown:* 424 (b, e); *Todd Huffman:* 150 (6, 13); *Brent Humphreys:* 373; *Hunter's Specialties:* 327 (5); *iStockphoto:* 70, 252, 379, 418, 486, 497; *Alexander Ivanov:* 62, 118, 145 (soft plastic, stickbait, spinnerbait, crank bait, surface lure), 424 (g, j), 476 (duct tape, egg carton and sawdust, cotton balls and petroleum jelly, flare, tube, dryer lint, Spanish moss, birch bark, sagebrush bark, punk wood, cattail fluff); *Spencer Jones:* 40 (t-shirt, portable stove), 123, 238 (cartridges); *Damon Jones/GoPro:* 287; *Donald M. Jones:* 269, 281, 286; *Rich Kirchner:* 316; *Anthony Licata:* 301; *Holly Lindem:* 282, 319; *Lodge Manufacturing:* 24 (4, 5, 21), 26; *William Mack:* 24 (6, 20, 24), 132, 150 (5), 232, 362, 436; *Neal Mishler:* 351; *Montana Decoy:* 249; *Pippa Morris:* 53, 185 (gold ribbed hare's ear, black ant, popping bug, cricket, mini-tube spinner), 217; *Ted Morrison:* 145 (panfish), 164, 182; *Jay Nichols:* 172; *Jack Nickens:* 298; *T. Edward Nickens:* Camping Intro (cabin), 13, 188, 206, 209, 261, 262, 336, 343, 347, 372, 395, 424 (i); *Lujke Nillson:* 196 (lure), 197; *Opinel USA:* 24 (9, 10); *Optics:* 411; *Over Board:* 419; *Lee Patel:* 27; *Primos Hunting:* 294 (call); *Purell:* 327 (8); *Rapala:* 150 (3, 10-12); *Travis Rathbone:* 34, 45, 112, 178, 234, 453, 466, 472; *Rat-L-Trap:* 150 (8); *Rig'em Right Waterfowl:* 344; *Dan Saelinger:* Camping Intro (lantern), Fishing Intro (tackle box), Hunting Intro (backpack), Survival Intro, 94, 124, 126, 143, 145 (walleye, pike, smallmouth, trout, striper), 183, 325, 328, 358 (box call), 469, 498; *Seigo Saito:* 397; *SBT Outdoors:* (Old Time Frog Collector Gig); *Sea to Summit:* 24 (16); *Seattle Sports Co.:* 24 (15); *Shelby:* 24 (30); *Shutterstock:* 1, 2, 3, 6, 7, 8, 11, 12, 15, 17, 24 (1-3, 7, 11-14, 17-19, 22-23, 25, 27-29), 25, 29, 30, 47, 55, 57, 59, 61, 64, 66, 69, 73, 76, 78, 82, 83, 85, 86, 88, 96, 104, 113, 128, 131, 133, 136, 168, 174, 177, 185 (cricket,

red wiggler), 218 (fisherman), 226, 229, 235, 237, 238 (animals) 240, 241, 242, 246, 248, 249, 256, 257, 263, 273, 274, 276, 278, 288 (deer), 293, 294 (coyote), 296, 300, 326, 327 (1-4, 6-7, 9-10), 337, 340, 353, 361, 380, 383, 385, 389, 397 (frog), 406, 425, 431, 438, 449, 454, 455, 458, 460-462, 471, 473, 487, 493, 499-501, backmatter; *Dusan Smetana:* 12, 106, 203, 216, 280, 285, 308, 334, 350; SmoothDrag: 125; *Snow Peak:* 24 (8); *Will Styer:* 368; *SureFire:* 410; *Sur La Table:* 24 (31); *Greg Sweeney:* 403; *Tankara USA:* 303; *Thermacell:* 24 (32); *Jarren Vink:* 363; *Woodcraft Supply LLC:* 71

Illustration courtesy of *Conor Buckley:* 28, 72, 84, 138, 139, 155, 165, 166, 182, 238, 295, 348, 396, 439, 444-446, 456; *Flying-chilli.com:* 377; *Hayden Foell:* 33, 56, 67, 68, 102, 105, 205, 289, 325, 342, 346, 351, 354, 364, 365, 384, 386, 388, 425, 463, 479; *Alan Kikuchi:* four section icons (Camping, Fishing, Hunting, Survival); *Raymond Larrett:* 19, 32, 98, 99, 106, 109, 111, 190, 201, 228, 243, 253, 318, 369, 393, 404, 409, 426, 437, 478, 484; *Daniel Marsiglio:* 20, 22, 35, 36, 39, 46, 77, 117, 120, 144, 153, 158, 169, 184, 193, 215, 222, 224, 264, 279, 314, 321, 333, 335, 360, 390, 429, 457, 459, 466, 475, 491, 492; *Will McDermott:* 37; *Chris Philpot:* 178; *Robert L. Prince:* 16, 41, 43, 48, 87, 95, 149, 154, 167, 191, 247, 309, 331, 352, 412; *Paula Rogers:* 130; *Graham Samuels:* 297; *Jameson Simpson:* 23, 208, 212, 260, 440, 448; *Jamie Spinello:* 129, 151, 175, 219, 236, 415, 441, 485, 489, 495; *Peter Sucheski:* 89, 146, 147, 324; *Mike Sudal:* 18, 97, 159, 259, 401; *Bryon Thompson:* 134, 268, 286, 309, 442, 464, 465; *Lauren Towner:* 4, 14, 49, 63, 79, 91, 114, 119, 121, 148, 160, 202, 207, 231, 255, 272, 275, 277, 284, 304, 356, 367, 400, 427, 432, 452, 470; *Paul Williams:* 44, 81, 376, 430

All text by T. Edward Nickens, with the following exceptions: *Ryan Arch* 434; *Scott Bestul:* 242; *Phil Bourjaily:* 377, 390, 409; *Jacob Campbell:* 8; *Joe Cermele:* 119, 131, 137, 146-148, 150, 158, 162, 167, 168, 196, 444; *Eddie Crane III:* 68; *Kirk Deeter:* 89, 157, 178; *Joe Doss:* 55; *Bill Heavey:* 79; *Dave Hurteau:* 240, 254; *Tom Keer:* 200; *David Kretzschmar:* 133; *Anthony Licata:* 358; *Greg Martin:* 28; *Keith McCafferty:* 20, 22, 73, 77, 265, 271, 286, 300, 314, 322, 408, 431, 442, 443, 452, 457, 459, 463-465, 475, 485, 489, 491, 495; *John Merwin:* 98, 120, 153, 160, 207, 219; *David Petzal:* 237, 238, 251, 341, 373, 407; *Michael R. Shea:* 362; *Slayton L. White:* 205, 259, 380-381; *Kathy Zaborowski Richardson:* 9

Weldon Owen would like to thank Harry Bates, Kagan McLeod, and Steve Sanford for work done to accompany the original magazine articles.

weldon**owen**

President & Publisher Roger Shaw
SVP, Sales & Marketing Amy Kaneko
Associate Publisher Mariah Bear
Associate Editor Ian Cannon
Creative Director Kelly Booth
Art Director Allister Fein
Senior Production Designer Rachel Lopez Metzger
Associate Production Director Michelle Duggan
Imaging Manager Don Hill

Weldon Owen would also like to thank Amy Bauman, Iain R. Morris, William Mack, Jennifer Durrant, Megan Hildebrand, Conor Buckley, Bryn Walls for design development, Kendra DeMoura, Michael Alexander Eros, Katharine Moore, Gail Nelson-Bonebrake, and Charles Wormhouldt for editorial assistance; Marianna Monaco for the index; and Michael Toussaint and Darryl & Terry Penry of Petaluma Gun & Reloading Supply for prop assistance.

Weldon Owen
1150 Brickyard Cove Road
Richmond, CA 94801
www.weldonowen.com

Library of Congress Cataloging in Publication data is available.

ISBN: 978-1-68188-761-6

10 9 8 7 6 5 4 3 2

2023

Printed in China

Waterbury Publications, Inc., Des Moines, IA
Creative Director Ken Carlson
Editorial Director Lisa Kingsley
Associate Design Director Doug Samuelson
Associate Editor Tricia Bergman
Production Designer Mindy Samuelson
Proofreader Lindsey Davis
Indexer Kevin Broccoli

FIELD& STREAM

EDITORIAL DIRECTOR Anthony Licata
EDITOR-IN-CHIEF Colin Kearns
GROUP CREATIVE DIRECTOR Sean Johnston
MANAGING EDITOR Jean McKenna
DEPUTY EDITORS Dave Hurteau, Slaton L. White
COPY CHIEF Donna L. Ng
FISHING EDITOR Joe Cermele
HUNTING EDITOR Will Brantley
ASSOCIATE EDITOR JR Sullivan
EDITORIAL ASSISTANT Hilary Ribons
PHOTOGRAPHY DIRECTOR John Toolan
ART DIRECTOR Brian Struble
ASSOCIATE ART DIRECTORS Russ Smith, James A. Walsh
PRODUCTION MANAGER Judith Weber
DIGITAL DIRECTOR Nate Matthews
ONLINE CONTENT EDITOR Alex Robinson
ASSOCIATE ONLINE EDITOR JR Sullivan
SPECIAL PROJECTS EDITOR Mike Toth

2 Park Avenue
New York, NY 10016
www.fieldandstream.com